#uncensored
inside the animal liberation movement

camille a. marino

#uncensored: inside the animal liberation movement
Copyright © 2018 Camille A. Marino

Published by Eleventh Hour Publishers
Cover illustration by Ana Canosa

ISBN: 978-0-692-08683-4

"May all beings everywhere be happy and free, and may the thoughts, words, and actions of my own life contribute in some way to that happiness and to that freedom for all."

Lokah Samastah Sukhino Bhavantu
(Sanskrit mantra)

Table of Contents

Part One

Acknowledgments

It would be impossible for me to adequately thank everyone who has stuck by me over the past several years, remained loyal to me and, above all, to the mission of Animal Liberation. But this book would not be possible were it not for those who gave me the strength to continue, especially at those times when I struggled and had to dig deeper and deeper to see this through.

I deeply appreciate Anne O'Berry, David Tenenbaum, Kim Socha, Barry Friedman, and Virginia Ray for taking the time and effort to read through my manuscripts, offer their constructive criticism, edits, and observations. Without them, this book would not exist.

Because I always knew that Mike Crandall would care for our four-legged children and make sure I had a home to which I could return, I was allowed the freedom to fight for the animals on my terms. For that, I will always remain grateful. Peanut and Socks, both of whom died during different incarcerations, will always be in my heart. I rescued Brutus with my own hands during a period when I was out on bond. In doing so, he rescued me. And I love him dearly. I'm glad he and his little brother, Petey, are happy and healthy and thriving living with Mike. And to my two constant companions, Max and Jazz, I thank them for their love, friendship, and loyalty.

Anne O'Berry and David Tenenbaum remain my most-trusted legal advisers. They never abandoned me, even though, because of their ongoing support, they have been repeatedly battered along the way. They started out as my legal team. They became my friends. Both worked tirelessly to help drag me out from under the wheels of legal corruption, an assortment of abuses, and personal devastation. It is only because of them that I am able to return and advance the struggle for Animal Liberation.

John D. Watson, a man who got a phone call at 8 pm one Saturday night, took on the job of defending me in a New Mexico courtroom where I had been convicted before I ever even set foot in the state. Considering that our professional contract should have covered two or three civil hearings, he wound up standing by me, eventually at his own expense, for months which turned into years as I was dragged in and out of jails. I was incredibly fortunate that this warm and compassionate man of such generous spirit answered the phone that Saturday evening in 2014.

Barry Friedman only knew I was an activist caught up in a corrupt system driven by very powerful adversaries. He was never scared off by the headlines that reported a *stalker* or *insane* woman was back in jail. He generously gave me counsel and comfort when things looked quite bleak. We sat on my sofa one day and I told him I worried occasionally that our association would damage him professionally. His response was "what good is respect and credibility if I don't use them to fight for what I believe in?" That sums up the character of a man I am fortunate to call a friend.

Until the publication of this book, Virginia Ray has gone by the pseudonym *Green Consciousness*. A veteran domestic violence advocate, her identity was initially protected in some parts of this memoir because she still lives under the specter of threats of physical harm. A pioneer in forcing legislation to protect victims of domestic abuse, Virginia was uniquely disturbed to watch those same laws being used to abuse and silence me. She once expressed regret that she was financially barred from adequately confronting her abuser in court. In some of my darkest hours, it was the echo of our discussions that gave me the strength to keep fighting and see everything through to its conclusion. In an email with the subject "no fear," she gave me permission in March of 2018 to use her true identity. With this act of sisterhood and empowerment, we both move forward today with no fear.

On another continent, Natalie Beach-Shacham, an activist I greatly admire, became a confidante and a close friend, even teaching me to cook amazing meals from Israel over Skype. A more genuine person I have never known. Living in isolation and exile from my own community, she remained my strongest lifeline to the world of activism.

While we've only communicated once or twice since my last incarceration in 2015, Gary Yourofsky's support during an extremely difficult period gave me the strength to push through. I'm not sure I ever told him that.

To the women I met behind bars who became my family and to all of the other activists who became my extended family, if I could write a paragraph each to express my appreciation, it would take another book to do so. But I hope they know that I could not have gotten through the last several years without them.

Untested loyalty is meaningless. And of those who remain in my life, their loyalties and integrity have been tested relentlessly.

With much love.

Foreword

by Dr. Kim Socha

This book would not exist if its author was not a woman. Some of the details may still be there – fighting for other species, governmental abuse of the law, movement infighting; however, the author's experiences would not be such if she did not inhabit a female body.

Camille Marino weaves many threads into *#uncensored*: autobiography, repression of dissent, cyberbullying, cults of personality, and, of course, the focus to which she always returns: Animal Liberation. You'll read about all of that in the coming pages. In this Foreword, however, I want to focus on a topic Camille brushes on from time to time: patriarchy. More specifically, I see this book as being about misogyny, an ugly word in its own right that encapsulates an uglier truth. This is a book about hating women.

Sadly, this accusation of misogyny is not against the usual opponents of Animal Liberation – the corporations, universities, and courthouses. No matter Camille's gender, I think "the system" generally would have treated her the same way. The woman-hating I refer to most clearly manifests within a community of proclaimed compassionate advocates who maligned and tormented Camille when she no longer had the stamp of approval of a "radical" academic male who, it turns out, will stop at nothing to make his hands appear clean – sounds like some vivisectors I know of.

The terms "prostitute" and "drug addict" used to defame Camille by her former comrades would never have worked so powerfully if hurled against a man, especially the former, neither would notation of her age and abilities. And to those activists who think sex workers (which Camille never was, incidentally) shouldn't sound their voices for the oppressed, you haven't a clue what "total liberation" entails.

#uncensored: inside the animal liberation movement

We know the statistics, right? The animal rights/liberation movement is made up of about 65-80% female-identified persons. In other words, there wouldn't be a movement without women, though there'd still be plenty of theorizing. Despite the strong presence of the feminine, I once had a male activist say to me that protests would be better if they weren't comprised of "screaming women." And I consider him to be fairly progressive. His view is not unique. There's something about a screaming woman that infuriates people, and Camille is an unrelenting, unrepentant screaming woman. So, the movement and its opponents call her "crazy." Makes it easier not to listen, and perhaps not to act. When Camille chained herself to a door at Wayne State University, she was pegged by some as a one-off madwoman. If a critical mass of activists had joined her, we might have had a revolution.

To be clear, I'm not painting the author as a saint. Indeed, Camille does not paint herself as such, quite the opposite, as she makes herself vulnerable through honest account of where she erred and where she took action against her better judgment. Some of the latter actions were done to please a man, to keep her mentor happy. That's part of the reason I'm writing this, because I understand that piece. It's why this book resonated with me at times, often painfully, but that is a different story, and one I don't know if I'll ever be brave enough to tell. I'm glad Camille is brave.

#uncensored is also a cautionary tale with Camille as a sort of movement Id. If one has even a modicum of empathy, it is impossible to hear stories of animals' lives in labs and not feel rage. For me, that ire often boils over into a pool of tears, but not before ferocious thoughts may run through my mind about what should happen to abusers. And if you only feel love for such individuals, work that angle. My mind doesn't react that way, neither does Camille's, and neither do most activists', I would wager. Camille took an additional step and published such thoughts online, even ones that weren't her own. This is where caution comes in.

The Internet age allows our enemies to create narratives of our lives. Sometimes I think of public information about me that, if carefully balanced with a personal agenda and believable lies, could make me seem a monster. The thought of someone then carefully picking through long forgotten emails, Facebook missives, and offhanded comments said in anger or jest – as if snippets of our lives create the sum of our being – is terrifying. However, when you are not the target of a smear campaign, it is easy, even fun, to laugh at another's misery, perhaps because you think it would never be you. *Your* style of activism is beyond reproach. Let's be clear: if you do something that genuinely threatens the animal industrial complex, you may be the state's next target.

In 2014, when I was planning an outreach event to coincide with Eleventh Hour's day of action for animals in labs, my organization received a message from a man I respect not to work with Camille because she colludes with fascists. This was a problem for me and my co-organizers, but when we asked for evidence, nothing materialized. Thus, we held our event. (Camille tackles this accusation in *#uncensored*'s Conclusion.)

In 2016, we were then contacted by someone telling us not to work with that same man because he abuses women. Again, this was a problem for us, and we asked for more information, not names or gossip, just something for us to better understand the situation. Nothing materialized, so we continue to support him and his campaign even as we have signed onto public statements to hold other predators in the movement accountable, but we only did this after careful research and consideration. See, *cautionary tale*.

As a movement, as human beings in the broadest sense, we must move beyond accepting "the truth" simply because someone tells us it is so. If more people had done that, Camille may not have been targeted by the government with fuel hand delivered by her fellow activists.

As a promoter of Animal Liberation, Camille Marino speaks for those silenced in labs and other hidden places because humans have determined those beings don't matter due to the nonhuman bodies in which they were born. This is a familiar story. Consider all of the injustice, hatred, and cruelty that human beings have and continue to endure because of the bodies they are born in: dark bodies, feminine bodies, "abnormal" bodies, etc. Camille would not have endured the beating she got from the movement if she did not navigate the world in a female body, if she did not speak with a woman's voice. And in a style of stubbornness I share with the author, no one can convince me otherwise.

However, Camille did not let circumstance break her, though she is achingly honest about how close it came to doing so. For that story alone, you should read this book. You should read it for other reasons too: to know how to act and how not to act, to know when to trust and when be to wary, to know when rage works and when it will likely fail you, and to see you are not alone in your intense anger ... nor in your intense love.

This is a recipe for revolution: anger and love. Camille exemplifies both, so read her story not to be just like her, but to learn from what she has experienced and risen above and to find your own storehouse of love and anger to take into the world and fight the brutal mosaic of oppressions.

Until all are free ...

Kim Socha *holds a Ph.D. in English and teaches writing and literature. She is an organizer with Minnesota Animal Liberation, which focuses on the fur trade, and Progress for Science, an anti-vivisection feminist collective. In addition, Kim is co-founder of RESONATE, whose mission is to share Black women's stories of overcoming oppression in white, patriarchal culture. She also volunteer teaches English to immigrants and refugees. Her publications include Animal Liberation and Atheism: Dismantling the Procrustean Bed and Women, Destruction, and the Avant-Garde: A Paradigm for Animal Liberation. She is also contributing editor of Defining Critical Animal Studies: An Intersectional Social Justice Approach for Liberation and Confronting Animal Exploitation: Grassroots Essays on Liberation and Veganism.*

PART ONE

The seed of revolution is repression.
-Woodrow Wilson

Prologue

In 1979, I was granted a restraining order against an abusive boyfriend. When I chose to leave the relationship, the brutality escalated. Courts were beginning to recognize personal protection orders as essential tools to protect women and men who were victims of domestic violence. At the age of 15, I understood what it was like to have a violent man sit outside my home, imprisoning me inside. I knew how it felt to walk to a store, turn a corner, and be assaulted. I knew how it felt to be followed, harassed, and taunted. I knew how it felt to be raped. I consider myself lucky to have had this experience so early in life. Able to identify the red flags, I would never allow that situation to repeat itself. With this learning experience far behind me, I left New York three decades later.

In 2009, I was served with a restraining order in Florida that prevented me from contacting or speaking about James David Jentsch, a college professor who experimented on animals at the University of California, Los Angeles (UCLA). Even though I had never set foot on that campus, I was also banned from UCLA. In 2010, I was served with a restraining order in Florida that prevented me from contacting or speaking about Donal O'Leary, a college professor at Wayne State University (WSU)

1

who experiments on animals. Even though I had never set foot in the state of Michigan at that point, I was also banned from the WSU campus. In response, I staged an act of civil disobedience, chaining myself to the university's library with my mouth taped shut. I was charged with two felonies. Thereafter, I was repeatedly jailed and temporarily banned from the internet. In 2012, I was served in Florida with a restraining order that prevented me from contacting Steven Best, a philosophy professor at the University of Texas, El Paso. Although we had only been friends and colleagues living 1700 miles apart, Dr. Best was issued a Domestic Violence Restraining Order in a New Mexico circuit court. He used it to criminalize my right to speak about him. My former mentor alleged a pattern of stalking college professors for which I was ultimately jailed and banned from the internet for a second time. As I write, that conviction is under appeal in the Court of Appeals of the State of New Mexico.

In 2014, I was one of 33 activists named in a lawsuit by Worldwide Primates in South Florida. This legal vehicle was designed to prevent all of us from discussing or protesting their sale of monkeys for experimentation. After nearly a year of litigation, our pro bono lawyers successfully had the lawsuit dismissed. In 2015, 7 activists from Progress for Science and Minnesota Animal Liberation were served with restraining orders (without a hearing) for their efforts to protest the work of Marilyn Carroll Santi and her husband, Peter Santi, both of whom experiment on animals. A restraining order was granted in Minnesota to the animal abusers and the protesters were forced to pay over $300 each to fight to get the orders lifted. All of the restraining orders were lifted except those against the two protest organizers: Dr. Carol Glasser and Dr. Kim Socha, both college professors. Socha and Glasser ultimately accepted a continuance for dismissal. This means that they did not have to make a plea of guilt or innocence to the charge of breaking a targeted residential picketing ordinance and, assuming no further interaction between them and Carroll/ Santi, the charges will officially be dropped from the record in 2021.

Protection orders are intended to protect an individual's physical safety. We are seeing courts use them with increasing regularity, however, to dispense with activists' First Amendment rights. Further, irrespective of the commonly-held belief that we are all presumed innocent until proven guilty, in reality, Americans are presumed guilty unless we have the financial resources to prove our innocence. Those who manipulate the law understand this. In addition to depriving us of our liberty, the legal system is used to break its victims financially, psychologically, and emotionally. The objective is to secure our silence. Chris Hedges observes, "... as many activists have discovered, the courts already are being used as a fundamental weapon of repression, and this abuse will explode in size should there be widespread unrest and dissent. Our civil liberties have been transformed into privileges..."[1]

While my story is clearly anecdotal, I am by no means unique. Many activists understand that being hauled into court has become an occupational hazard. My colleagues and I fight commercialized abuse to protect the most innocent among us, nonhuman animals. And as anyone who challenges the status quo becomes effective, they will likely find themselves fighting for their own freedom inside the legal system as well. This should concern every single person who has ever logged onto Facebook. My odyssey demonstrates how the laws that are employed to chill political dissent are being further perverted and manipulated to silence any outspoken citizen. I spent six months in jail in 2015 and am currently banned from the internet for using words like "coward" and "hypocrite" on Facebook. When courts see fit to simply throw people in jail over Facebook wars, then tyranny, indeed, has become the law of the land.

At the age of 47, I was arrested for the first time in my life. It was a political arrest. I had won my first lawsuit against the University of Florida (UF), gaining access to records documenting the taxpayer-funded experiments to which they subject monkeys. UF needed to silence me. They chose to get me out of the state. There were several arrests, a raid on my home, extraditions, persecutions, prosecutions, and incarcerations. I walked through

1   Chris Hedges, "The Mirage of Justice," Truthdig (January 17, 2016),
    http://www.truthdig.com/report/item/the_mirage_of_justice_20160117

all of it with my head held high and my integrity intact.

But it was a betrayal, a relentless campaign of internet bullying and cyberstalking, of defamation and harassment, that brought me to my knees. It sounds absurd that cyberbullying can have a greater impact on a person than incarceration. But it can. It did. We've all heard the stories about children and young adults who've committed suicide in the face of a cyber onslaught. Professor Jim Aune of Texas A&M leapt to his death in 2013 as an online sex scandal broke.[2] Personally, I spent many nights drinking and contemplating driving head first into a truck to make it all stop.

Even in my own despair, I never lost sight of my mission to liberate animals from enslavement. I had to transcend all of the chaos and damage in my own life, however, to regain my ability to fight for them. This book is the first step in paving a road toward my future and their freedom. It is my privilege to use my life and my story to illustrate exactly how repression works, because standing behind me and the devastation wreaked upon me are the unheard cries of the animals for whom I fight; the animals that live and die without anyone ever knowing they were here. I threaten billions of dollars of industrial abusers' profits by giving a voice and dimension to their victims. And history demonstrates the fantastic lengths to which they've gone to stop me.

We all have challenges to overcome and we all have obstacles thrown in our path. We all feel overwhelmed and desperate from time to time. I found a strength and peace born of never deviating from my beliefs. Despite having my universe implode and everything I once knew proven false, I found an inner peace and empowerment that I never knew was missing. I found me. And unless they break my pens and pencils and cut my vocal chords, I will never stop speaking the truth. I will never stop fighting for justice.

---

2 Alyssa Newcomb, "Texas Professor's Suicide Came After Sending Text to Alleged Sex Scammer," ABC News, March 26, 2013, http://abcnews. go.com/US/texas-professors-suicide-sending-text-alleged-sex-scammer/ story?id=18814474.

And I believe the truth will prevail.

No price is too high to pay for the privilege of owning yourself. -Friedrich Nietzsche

Skeletons in My Closet

I used to have secrets, events and experiences that make me who I am. I used to enjoy sharing my private life with those I held dear. When my world imploded a few years back, when I was betrayed in a very public forum, every word I ever shared privately with my former best friend and mentor was distorted and used in a devastating campaign of hate and slander. Through his malevolent efforts designed to destroy me, he became the catalyst in my personal liberation. As I write today, that individual no longer holds any relevance or importance in my life; yet, paradoxically, he remains both pivotal and incidental to both my evolution and to this story. Steve Best teaches online courses at the University of Texas, El Paso (UTEP); in retrospect, perhaps he was my greatest teacher. While others may continue to take my life out of context in desperate attempts to harm me, I own my truth.

I was born in Brooklyn in 1964 to an unwed mother. I grew up believing that my parents were married and that my father left because he didn't want me. It was only when my mother

5

died in 2008, when I was 44 years old, that I began to learn some of the family secrets and contextualize my life. It was a bit disconcerting. My whole family knew who I was; everyone but me. From what little I know combined with what I was told by my godfather before he died in 2012, my father was some variety of hoodlum; my brother would just call him a "bum." In the movie *Goodfellas*, I learned that Saturday nights are for wives and Friday nights are for girlfriends in the tradition of the underworld. I guess my mother was the latter. I never even considered that my father might be married and have a family of his own. I have half brothers and sisters I am told, but I know so little about my paternal roots that it would be very difficult to learn anything more. Other than this little piece of the puzzle which explained why we were poor and different from all the other families in our working-class Jewish/Italian neighborhood, I believed that our poverty and my father's abandonment were a function of my birth. My mother tried unsuccessfully to abort me by falling down on her stomach on a glass bottle of milk in the street. As the story goes, the man who owned the Chinese laundry around the corner from us on Avenue L ran out of the store to help her up. She was okay. Unfortunately for her, so was I.

My brother was 4 1/2 years old when I was born on July 5. As a child growing up, I did not understand that my brother was imprisoned in the same world as I. I only knew that he was the good child, I was the bad child; he was her pride and joy, I was a burden and should never have been born; and, inasmuch as I loved and looked up to my big brother, we were pitted against one another from the beginning. I will never discuss the abuses to which he was subjected, those that I remember, and will never intrude into his privacy. Suffice it to say that our mother was unbalanced and neither of us went out into the world unscathed.

I must have been about 3 or 4 because Louis would be at elementary school and my mother and I would be home alone. I would be dragged out of the bedroom I shared with her and I knew what was coming. The image of me being outside myself watching myself holding on the door frame molding while she carried my little body and pried my fingers free is one that stays with me. Decades later, when I would see scientists prying a monkey's fingers from his cage as they carried his little body off to harm him, a visceral discomfort would seize my being. Sometimes I would get away and run into my brother's room and hide behind his dresser waiting to be caught. There was no escape inside the dirty little apartment, only prolonging the inevitable. All I really remember is being thrown on the couch and putting my arms and legs over me to fend off the blows. Then we would walk to Public School 242 to go pick my brother up and walk home. Neither Louis nor I were allowed out of her sight nor were we allowed any freedom or friends, at least not until we were big enough to take our own liberties. On rare occasions, my mother would run to a store and leave us alone for 5 or 10 minutes. As soon as we heard the door close behind her, we would get up and chase each other around a circular gray area rug in the living room. We would take our books and put them on the floor, climb on top of them and make noise. And as soon as we heard the door open when she returned, we would quickly put the books away and take our positions on the couch in front of the television like silent little soldiers.

I have little memory of most of my childhood, although it unfolded against a soundtrack of incoherent screaming, crying, and profanities. There was a thread of paranoia that permeated everything. My mother believed our phone was tapped; she would rail about the neighbors who were looking through our trash or breaking into our apartment when we were out; and when we walked in the street, she was convinced people were watching and taking notes about our every movement. There was a great deal of hysteria about there being "communists on the roof." I'm unclear about whether this was my mother's delusion or that of our Finnish landlords who occupied the first floor. I was surrounded by crazy. That was my normal.

I dreaded my birthdays or Christmas because, inasmuch as I enjoyed being with family, I felt like a bright red beacon of obligation for anyone who would have to spend money on me. One year my mother bought me a Barbie stage with movable parts but it didn't work. We brought it back to the store and had her money refunded. Although I knew it only needed batteries, I was relived to not have to shoulder the extra weight I felt. One Sunday morning, my brother, my mother and I were on our weekly walk to my grandma's where we would eat dinner. A neighbor passed in his car and said to me "you look so pretty today." I liked the compliment. After he left, I asked my mother what the neighbor said. I wanted to hear it again. She said "he said you look pretty." And she simultaneously smacked me across the face. I remember the taste of blood in my mouth. But my ego was far more bruised. I must have been about 5. When I started school, she was always there, just waiting to scold or embarrass me while cultivating the appearance of an engaged, conscientious single parent. One day she took me by the hand to use the restroom in school. The floor was wet and when I lowered my pants, they soaked up the water. For the rest of the afternoon, she took me by the hand and showed everyone how "she wet her pants." The children laughed. The adults cringed. Finally, my friend Ilene's mother, a lady named Mrs. Rabinowitz, took her aside and said something. The taunting stopped that day. The emotional abuse very much defined me. I wished I was invisible a lot of the time.

When I was older, maybe 6 or 7, I had committed some infraction and was locked in the closet. I was told it was only for a few minutes and dismissed as a drama queen for complaining. I don't remember time, only darkness, crying and pounding on the door to come out. I believe this is the point at which my claustrophobia took hold. My mother took my brother into the kitchen to play cards while I cried and screamed. It's interesting that until my aunt suggested it to me only a few years ago, I never considered that this experience must have been damaging for him as well.

The guttural screams, cries, and curses were inescapable. Coming at me and grabbing my arms and biting into me. She never drew blood with her teeth, only with her claws. And I was always reminded that other children really suffered so I had nothing to complain about. I certainly had nothing to cry about, nor would it be tolerated. Crying and showing weakness in the middle of an attack would only earn ridicule. I was tough. It was okay. I could take it. To this day, I am largely unable to identify or connect with any emotion when I am under attack. Something in me broke.

I would learn to fend off hits from baseball bats, brooms, whatever may have been handy. I would only restrain my mother. I never hit her back. And I never cried. My godmother knew something was wrong. She had lost her 7-year old daughter to leukemia and her world collapsed. Two weeks after the funeral, she met my mom in the street and was completely distraught. My mother's impatience obvious, she asked "aren't you over it yet?" My Aunt Anna was unable to reconcile the words with the reality. When my mother bragged to her about how she threw me down a staircase, she began to advocate for my mother to seek counseling. I have no memory of being thrown down the stairs.

Along the way, the line separating which physical scars were earned and which were self-inflicted began to blur. The psychological scars, however, were well defined. Being told I was worthless, useless, a burden, an object to be abandoned and ridiculed... those things contributed to a seriously-compromised core. Any opportunity to embarrass me in front of other people was never foregone. It was as if my mother needed to demonstrate to the world what an utter burden she was saddled with, a horrible little child, and what a self-sacrificing saintly mother she was to endure her misfortune. I was never encouraged to succeed, only to appear well-behaved, intelligent, and clean. Only as an adult would I begin to understand that my mother was seeking external validation, albeit at my expense, for something that was lacking in her. I believe she did the best she could with what little tools she had available. I harbor no ill will or resentment. She simply passed on to me that which was imparted to her. I wish she could have been happy. I wish she could have been whole.

In retrospect, there was this fantastic paradigm in which I was nurtured -- know you are worthless and deserve nothing yet appear successful and worthy. I was browbeaten with the mantra "you can't" from my earliest memories through adulthood. I knew that arguing or debating my own abilities was futile as well as demeaning. When I was told that I could not accomplish something, I simply did it and let the results quiet the taunts. As a result, I've never been concerned in the least with how others embrace impossibilities. For me, anything I set my mind on is possible. I can do anything... with or without anyone's encouragement or consent.

At about 10 years old, while my mother dragged me by the hand through a local store; I grabbed a box of *Sudafed* and shoved it in my pocket without incident. It was the 1970s and I was extraordinarily curious about the hippie drug culture. My mother, while drinking her whiskey every night with the alcoholic neighbors and popping prescribed Valium, vehemently condemned drugs and the happy carefree people who did them. Back at home, I took a handful of Sudafeds. They made me drowsy mostly. But I was happy that I was *high* and largely removed from my life. I didn't have to care about anything. For the next several years, I would always be high when we went to visit relatives. I would run and hide when I was little so I wouldn't have to talk to or interact with anyone. I was a burden and just wanted to disappear. But now at 10 or 11, I could be around my family and be in my own world at the same time. It was good to escape. When I was 14, we were in my Aunt Anna's backyard for a Fourth of July barbecue. Concerned that something was wrong with me, she asked me to help her with a chore in the house. I had taken so many Quaaludes that I couldn't walk up the staircase. I tripped over my own feet twice. My aunt cried. I laughed.

By 13, I could no longer be controlled. I could take a punch, a kick, I could take a blow and walk through it without reacting. I found solace in marijuana, alcohol, and cocaine. Quaaludes, however, were the first love of my life. I always preferred sedation to stimulants. But if I could remain impaired, I wasn't a snob about it. And like-minded kids gravitate to one another. Many of the boys I considered brothers are dead; one was shot in the spine at 17 and has been in a wheelchair ever since. Unlike my friends, I was never a fan of hallucinogens. LSD and mescaline trapped me inside my own head. And that was someplace I didn't want to be.

As I explored the streets, I began to appreciate everything that was around me. I couldn't have my own father but being an Italian-American kid growing up in Canarsie in the 1970s, you were connected. It was a simple fact of life. The only family history I ever knew was about my maternal grandfather carousing with racketeers and infamous figures in the 1930s Brooklyn crime syndicate, Murder Inc. Apparently, my grandmother, who I loved dearly, was available to have kids -- 8 live births out of 16 pregnancies from what I've heard -- and cater to my grandfather's friends. Perhaps the most prominent name in my home growing up was that of the notorious contract killer, Frank "The Dasher" Abbandando. Before he went to the electric chair in 1942, the married gangster romanced my mother who was 19 at the time. I remain fascinated by my elusive family history. My grandmother raised her children on Pitkin Avenue in East New York, about 15 minutes from my childhood home in Canarsie. Groomed by criminals and growing up with the one-day-to-be-infamous Gottis, there was a palpable mentality within the family that permeated generations. Whether it was in my own home or out in the street, the one thing I knew how to do was keep my mouth shut.

I was 11 when my Aunt Anna lost my cousin Angela to leukemia. Her guttural screams at the wake were chilling. I would not hear those sounds again until over three decades later when I saw a dairy cow's baby calf ripped away from her. The mother's milk meant for her baby is then stolen to sell to humans for profit. Those identical shrieks of a mother's loss are etched on my soul. I chose my Aunt Anna for my godmother when I received the Catholic rite of confirmation. She has always been like a real mother to me. I'm not sure if it's because of her loss and my situation at home, but the bond between us is one that endures to this day. My aunt always wanted me to come live with her. I wanted to. But I loved her too much to burden her with me. Her son, my cousin Frankie, was one of my best friends growing up. We were the babies of the family and were very close. But it would be decades before I would begin to understand the devastation in my cousin's childhood that paralleled my own. I will never intrude on his privacy either. That is his story to tell, not mine.

We would spend a lot of time at my Aunt Anna's growing up. One of her best friends was Rosie Serpico, known within the family as "Rosie the Twin." There is a story about how she was at a doctor's visit one day and the physician jokingly remarked, "you have a very famous last name." There was a New York police officer named Frank Serpico who exposed police corruption and gained national notoriety in 1973 when Al Pacino brought his character to the movie screen. He was no relation to anyone I knew. But the amusing part was that Rosie thought to herself, "you should only know my maiden name." Her maiden name was Gotti. I never met her brother, John.

In my neighborhood, we all knew where the mafia congregated, who they were, and I always felt very safe on the streets, even though murder was all around us. The infamous Fountain Avenue Dump was notorious for snitches being found dead in the trunks of their cars... or not found at all. Down the street from me was *The Bamboo Lounge*. In the movie, *Goodfellas*, this is the bar that Henry Hill (played by Ray Liotta) and Tommy DeVito (played by Joe Pesci) set on fire. It would reopen as *The Regis*. The gangsters owned this corner of Rockaway Parkway and Avenue N. My friend, Gloria, lived two houses away. After my mother was passed out at night, I would sneak out at about 10 pm and Gloria and I would meet up and run the streets. Behind the romance of the goodfellas on the corner, we were able to blend into the night unnoticed.

Right around the corner from me on Avenue L was where all the up-and-coming Italian street gangs gathered. A catering hall called *El Doro's* demanded respect, with neighborhood royalty spilling out into the streets in their tailored suits and pinky rings. My mother would always warn me not to embarrass her at certain Avenue L landmarks because it would get back to my father. It was nice to imagine that I had a father or that he would actually care.

When I was 14 I fell in love with a man in his 20s who had

just been released from Elmira State Prison where he finished serving two years for armed bank robbery. His muscled arms were tattooed and he was dangerous. His family was among the Avenue L elite. He asked me out officially on July 15, 1979, 10 days after I turned 15. We were inseparable. We would sneak away whenever we could to be together. Even though I somehow maintained a 4.0 grade point average in high school and was in all advanced placement classes, I would cut school regularly to be with him. I lost my virginity one September morning when I cut school and he stayed home from work. I was 15 chronologically. But I didn't think there was anything wrong with our relationship then and I don't think so now. At 15 and 22, we were perfect. He was my protector. My mother hated him. I'd fight her out in the streets. She came after me with a shovel once. I had had enough. I grabbed it, ripped it out of her hands, and threw it into traffic. We lived on a very busy street. The shovel missed a bus by inches and I'm very lucky that it didn't hit any cars. My life was a sideshow and I was the reluctant star.

Joseph* (the names of incidental characters that have been changed are denoted with an asterisk) and I never made it to our one-year anniversary. Where only months earlier I wanted to drop out of school, have his babies, and run away with him, by early 1980 I had finished with being controlled by or answering to anyone. We argued in his house one day and I got up to storm out. He grabbed me, threw me down on the bed and, each time I would get up and fight back, he'd throw me back down. The final time he threw me down, he raped me. I did not identify it as rape at that time. I'm sure he didn't either. This was my boyfriend, not a stranger. But that was the turning point for me. I got tired of playing games where we would go punch for punch with one another to see who could take more. I never flinched but got tired of walking around with black and blues. A woman who noticed my bruises stopped me at a phone booth one day and, with great concern in her voice, asked me who was hurting me. I remember being annoyed by the intrusion.

When I broke up with Joseph, the violence escalated. He tried to run my mother over. He broke my friend's window. No matter

13

where I went, he was there. Popping up. Stalking me. Sitting outside my house while I was a prisoner inside. I finally had to call the cops. He was arrested. I got a restraining order, but it was obvious that that piece of paper wouldn't stop a bullet. If I went to meet my friends, he was there. If he couldn't find me, he would call everyone I knew. The law couldn't protect me and I knew it. I eventually found another girl who was in love with him and, luckily, his obsession with me wound down. It would be more than 3 decades before I had any more experience with restraining orders and then I would be the one being served. It makes no sense to me that every restraining order issued against me has been granted by a number of courts to protect abusive men from my words. This is such a perversion of domestic violence laws and an insult to any woman or man who has ever been harmed by a partner. Joseph and I are in contact as adults on Facebook. We talk on the phone occasionally. He's married. We're both in Florida now. I recognize that we were both young and products of our environment. Before it got out of control, I can't deny that I have never felt about another man the way I felt about him. I still have a little place in my heart that will always hold those days dear. I know he does too.

Poverty was a constant in my life. We lived in filth. I still have a uniquely-high tolerance to dirt. I always understood that money was what separated those with power, control, and respect from bastards and welfare babies. It was reinforced in us every single day of our lives. Money and the power I perceived would come with it became my reason for being. My brother, incidentally, sits on the board of a major international bank today. I know for a fact, though, that while it's better to have money than not, money cannot buy peace or happiness. A family friend, Harry Jones,* owned a moving company on Rockaway Parkway. He gave us a small apartment above the business that we could afford, he let my brother earn money as a moving man while he was in high school, and my Uncle Sonny worked for him when he needed money. At 15, Harry gave me a job answering phones in the office on Saturday mornings. I sat there for 4 or 5 hours and left with $20, sometimes $25 if I earned it. And it felt amazing to have my own money. I could buy an outfit, or pizza, or ices, or whatever I wanted. I didn't have to watch my friends spend the money their fathers would give them and pretend I didn't want anything because I didn't have money to buy anything.

The fact that Harry would molest me every Saturday was our secret. He was in his 60s I think, fat and sloppy, and not even remotely attractive. Yet, when he started touching me and kissing me, it felt as good as it was repulsive. I liked being touched. He would sit with me and we would look at his *Hustler* and *Penthouse* magazines. That's how it started. I didn't understand that I was being groomed. I didn't even know the word for it or have any concept to associate with what was happening. I only knew that I would earn an extra $5 sometimes. And who would I tell anyway? My boyfriend? My uncle? I didn't want to see anyone go to prison on my account. And I liked the money.

My uncle would be executed in a phone booth in Sheepshead Bay, Brooklyn the following year. I loved my Uncle Sonny. He was beautiful. He was carefree. He was tough. But it was a fairly standard event. His friends took him out one night, lured him into the phone booth outside a restaurant in Sheepshead Bay, and he was shot through the eye. I saw his body under a sheet on the news, blood pooling around him on the concrete. I was 16. I remember the New York Post story being entitled "Another Brooklyn Hood Rubbed Out Gangland Style."

I lost my uncle. I broke up with my boyfriend. I had absolutely no roots or grounding. And I was always looking for something, even if I couldn't define exactly what it was. Where Harry repulsed me, I was very attracted to his 40-something-year old son, Danny*. He had scruples and wouldn't touch me until I turned 18. I would drink my Jack Daniels, he would smoke his weed, we'd go to a motel in Sheepshead Bay called the *Windjammer* and spend a few hours together. Then he would drop me off on the streets with my friends and drive back home to his wife and kids in an upscale enclave in New Jersey. Although I don't remember much through the drug-haze in which I existed, I remember I really liked being wanted.

Skeletons in My Closet

I skipped the eighth grade and graduated high school at 16. Since my brother graduated when he was 16 as well and his birthday was in November, my accomplishment was trivialized. I turned 17 about a month later. Louis wasn't in the house by this time. He went to live with one of my aunts while he was in college because I caused too much of a disruption. No matter what I did to please my mother, nothing was ever good enough. I completed my first semester at Brooklyn College before I graduated high school. I was allowed to matriculate as a psychology major in college while I finished 12th grade. My professor told us that everyone who chooses psychology as a major generally does so because they're trying to understand themselves. I wondered if everyone else in the class was as confused as I.

Growing up, I considered my Uncle Mikey to be the patriarch of the extended family. We became close in my 40s after my mother died. My uncle and I would talk about all kinds of things. And although I know it was foreign to him, after I became vegan and took up my political struggle for Animal Liberation, he told me on more than one occasion that he was proud of me. I desperately wanted to hear those words my whole life and, in midlife, I finally had a protective paternal figure. We would communicate on the phone and on Facebook. And it was becoming clear that I was incurring the wrath of some very powerful industrial animal abusers. Jail was in the immediate realm of possibilities. Uncle Mikey would always tell me that if I ever needed him to come to Florida to just let him know and he'd be here. After my first arrest in 2012, he suffered a massive heart attack and died while I was in jail. He never knew I was arrested. He would never live to see the absolute betrayal by someone I once considered a close friend. He would never see me take a felony on this person's account, he would never see this individual sell me out to the state, and he would never see my former friend, a *snitch* in activist parlance and a simple garden variety *punk* in the streets of Brooklyn, declare a cowardly and treasonous war on me. He would never see me crumble. He would never see me regain my composure. But I've thought on occasion that if things had transpired at a different moment in time, it would have been an exercise in poetic justice if an escorted visit to Fountain Avenue could have been arranged.

My godfather would always tell me to "keep smiling." Never let them break you down. And after over a dozen arrests, 2 extraditions, 1 raid on my house, being well into my second year banned from the internet as I type today, spending over a year behind bars, and living under unrelenting attacks, stalking, and sabotage, my detractors have remarked several times that they don't understand. "She smiles!" "She laughs." "She doesn't care." And every time I've heard or read those observations by my tormentors, all I can think is, "Thank you, Uncle Mikey. I love you."

If I hadn't graduated at 16, I never would have. I was a certified truant. I had little interest in school and I would never measure up to my brother. I just wanted to make money and have fun. When the fall semester started in 1981, I was 17 and legally able to sign myself out of Brooklyn College. I had a job in a supermarket where I was earning over $100 a week while I was in high school. Now I could work full time. And if I was a good student, I excelled when I entered the work force. I've always been extreme in my behavior, good or bad, and very few were ever able to compete. But I figured out very quickly that I was taking orders from people who I questioned had the intelligence to tie their shoelaces. Manhattan was where the beautiful people, the money, and the fast life was.

Before I would leave Brooklyn, one night after work my friends and I were standing around in the Waldbaum's parking lot when my mother ran down the street charging at me with an ice pick. She was screaming from inside of one of her incoherent rants. I was so sick of her. I physically restrained her, took the ice pick from her, threw it somewhere, and laughed. It wasn't funny, but it was the only emotional mechanism available to me. My friends and I all piled in a bunch of cars and headed to one of their apartments where we drank, smoked, and got high. I remember that night well; at least until I don't remember anything else.

My first job in New York City was as a secretary at a publishing house. I hated that title, the embodiment of female subjugation. I didn't intend on taking shorthand from some man for very long; of that I was certain. My next job was working for a woman. I asked for $175 a week. She laughed in my interview and told me I would start at $225. She became something of a mentor. When Thomas Cook Travellers Cheques moved to New Jersey, I needed to find a new job and entered the male-dominated hedonistic world of investment banking.

I reveled in the attention of all the men who wanted to wine and dine me, impress me with their money and nice things. And I was impressed. Morgan Stanley was a premier investment bank, rivaled only by Goldman Sachs in the 1980s. I had another life at night, however, that was fast and dangerous and drug-fueled. The dichotomy from childhood had followed me. I appeared the consummate professional by day; by night I was stoned. The world that opened up before me by day was foreign. The contrast between the blue bloods with their Ivy League degrees, old-money pedigrees, country club memberships, and Connecticut or exclusive suburban addresses and my Brooklyn roots was never so defined as in the awkward silence of the elevators. The executives and managing directors would never be seen conversing with staff or secretaries. In our own areas, we were friendly, went out for drinks, flirted, and sometimes dated. But the elevators were a strange microcosm of the elitist misogynist atmosphere that permeated investment banking houses. I was unimpressed with the attitude. And despite the odds, I fully intended to compete and succeed in their world. I enrolled myself in Pace University at night to become a professional, a CPA, who had my own secretary. Interestingly, I chose a profession that was the antithesis of who I was -- rigid and artificial. I've always had a lot of self-discipline. If only I could have had some inkling that I deserved to do something I enjoy.

Somewhere along the line I took a semester off to become a stockbroker. Morgan Stanley sponsored me for my Series 7 and Series 63 and I became a licensed broker in New York State. I did not have the Ivy League education, however, that would have allowed me entrance to their trading floor. I quit my job and went to work for a *boiler room*, a penny stock outfit called Stuart James. We were rigorously trained in how to get rich selling worthless financial instruments to people who couldn't afford them. I loved the fast track, the drugs, the beautiful people, all of us dressed to play our parts; everyone immaculately groomed and fast-talking. Except for the part about swindling people, I was home. It was all about appearances. It fit. And I loved it.

My first day was October 19, 1987 -- Black Monday. The markets crashed, people went bankrupt, some jumped out of windows. No matter. I plugged along and made my first sale. It was an amazing adrenaline rush. I made $3,000 in a 10-minute phone call. We drank champagne. We celebrated. I closed it. The money and excitement were intoxicating. But I wasn't a liar; I couldn't exploit people in good conscience and I didn't like sales. I wound up reversing my own sale. I contacted the client and made some excuse that the transaction didn't go through. I told my supervisors that the *fish* had changed her mind. After 30 days, I quit. I had no income and nothing to fall back on. I had an apartment, a car, my cat (I adopted Baby when I found her living in my garbage can), and myself to support. With student loans, credit card invoices and other bills pouring in, I went back to interviewing for a straight job.

Intercontinental Capital Associates (ICA) was an investment banking boutique. It was a partnership of three tax attorneys and two others who simply were good closers. ICA created custom tax shelters for businessmen; one product called an NOL (net operating loss) Regeneration actually allowed a shell company that operated at a loss to shelter all the profits of the real company. And many of the financial vehicles were simply too sophisticated for me to fully understand. But with my stockbroker's license, I was able to sign on as a principal and get us Securities & Exchange Commission (SEC) authorization to buy and sell. It was amazing. One of my bosses was 48, he was tanned and wealthy and was proud of his friendship with Donald Trump and other celebrities. My friend at work and I invited him out for drinks after work one night and we had a threesome. Jeff and I continued our secret affair for about a year or so. We'd sneak away to his penthouse apartment on Fifth Avenue, intoxicated by the excitement that is the domain of the illicit rendezvous.

There were always call girls for out-of-town clients, money, cocaine, drinks, limos, celebrities, theater, parties, catered affairs and, because ICA was small, only 6 of us in the New York office, we were a family. I was the manager in title and had my own office. One of the assistants that was hired was one of my boss's call girls. Pam introduced me to the life. I had graduated college and was in Fordham University School of Law at night by this time. I had an apartment on the Upper East Side, on 72nd and York, around the corner from Sotheby's. I lived between there and my boyfriend's apartment in Brooklyn. I had freedom that I'd never known and to say I was living beyond my means is an understatement. No one was paying my bills and I answered to no one. The first time I took home $1000 for Pam and I spending an hour with a client, I was hooked. It was fun. And Pam and I were in control. Although neither of us were bi-sexual, it was a huge turn-on controlling men and their money. I would go out for lunch hours and meet with executives, lawyers, bankers, and one judge who was my regular. My rate was $300/hour with a 2-hour minimum. These calls rarely took more than 20 - 30 minutes. I was always safe. I always knew with whom I was interacting. I'd have dated any of these men for free. It was empowering.

To this day, when I see a judge, I can see right through their long black robes that are meant to hide their fallibilities. The judge, we'll call him Bill, liked to meet at his penthouse. I would entertain his fantasies during our encounters. He talked a lot about seeing me with a black man and he liked to speak about how much it turned him on if I would seduce little boys. His predilection for pedophilia disturbed me but it was my job is to give the client a safe and discreet outlet and I'd go back to work with $600 cash for a lunch hour. One day while I was visiting Bill, the bell rang. He told me he had a surprise for me. He had invited his friend, a black attorney, to join us. I was not pleased that he sprang this on me, but it was fun and I returned from lunch with $1200 that day. It disturbed me, though, that I was no longer in complete control. That was my last job as an escort. The line between fantasy and reality had blurred.

Whether Sol spent the night with me in Manhattan or I spent the night at his apartment in Brooklyn, we were essentially living together. Eventually we took an apartment together in Brooklyn and started a life together in earnest. He never knew about my extracurricular activities or side jobs. I was making $70,000 a year at ICA and frequently got $5,000 bonuses when a deal closed. Having a few extra $1000 here and there was not suspicious. On March 9, 1993, Sol took the motorcycle out while I finished getting dressed. He was going to pick me up in 30 minutes. He was never late. After about an hour I knew something was wrong. I identified his body in the morgue and then I just have spots of memory here and there. I remember going home, opening the safe in our bedroom, taking out a few thousand dollars, and calling one of our drug dealers. I remember my friends being in my apartment. Then I remember waking up out of a coma on March 17. I was completely paralyzed from the neck down, couldn't speak, my eyes were crossed, I couldn't even hold a pen if I wanted to communicate. I had no idea that Sol was dead. Inside my hallucination, I was sure that I had woken up in an S&M club called *The Palace* and that I was in some kind of sexual restraints. I tore the tubes and devices from my body as the medical team sedated me. I would learn later that such violent reactions are a routine consequence of brain damage.

I learned that no one had heard from me for days and someone eventually broke down the door to my apartment. I was in bed naked and comatose. My friends had robbed about $40,000 from the safe, and all of the artwork and antiques that Sol collected were stolen. I learned that I had spent at least $2000 on a baggie of cocaine and a lot of pills. For over two decades, I have simply told people that I was in a motorcycle accident. I do not know whether my drug overdose was intentional or accidental. I listen with interest as others fill in the blanks to suit their own agendas. The only truth of which I am certain is that I lived with a death wish and was on a perpetual mission to destroy myself. Where my mother left off, I took over. The distinction between accidental or intentional is arbitrary.

Skeletons in My Closet

At 28 years old, I had lost the man I loved, my job, my apartment, my ability to walk and talk, as well as any semblance of independence. My beloved stilettos became a distant memory. My mind was intact, but I was imprisoned inside a body from which I could not communicate. I listened to my mother and the doctors discuss my profession, my salary, my potential, and how sad it was that I had thrown it all away. I listened to everyone. It was as if no one ever knew me. My long-suffering mother was at the hospital every single day to care for me. I heard her tell me that I never loved Sol anyway and that I should have died too. I eventually learned that Sol had ridden the motorcycle into a truck on the Gowanus Expressway, his chest was instantly crushed, and he died on impact. The choices that were being negotiated for me were to either go into a nursing home or be released to my mother's care. I wanted to roll my wheelchair up to the roof and throw myself off, but I was physically unable to do so. After 3 months, I was to be released to a long-term care facility. While I was incapacitated on this floor with elderly stroke victims and others who had serious neurological issues, I met a man who had fallen out of a 2-story window and was basically in a body cast. We were both under 30 and he would come to my room and talk to me, even if I couldn't respond with anything other than one- or two-word garbled statements. Then one day he turned me onto heroin.

He wheeled me into the bathroom in my hospital room. He cut the lines for me, held the straw as I had no motor control, let alone fine motor skills, and all I had to do was inhale. We went back out and sat on my bed. Within minutes, my eyes uncrossed. My speech became markedly less garbled. My vision came into focus and I was able to move my pinky finger. I decided right there and then that I had some kind of neurological connection with my body and no one was putting me into a nursing home at 28. It didn't matter if they all wrote me off and said I was never going to be normal again. No one ever knew me. Why should this be any different?

With my new-found ability to minimally communicate, I was able to convey to my brother that I wanted to go back to Brooklyn and live on my own. I did not want to go into a nursing home. He was the only other person in the universe who understood that living with my mother was not an option. As I was basically homeless, he got me an apartment and I went home to a foreign life as an invalid, although I never saw myself as such. Fortunately, the only friends I ever had were like-minded drug enthusiasts so I found that heroin was readily available in the projects once I made it a point to look for it. Once the poison would hit my system, it was instant euphoria and my muscles would come alive. I set my wheelchair up at one side of the room and in the privacy of my own apartment, walked across the room over and over again, falling repeatedly, trying to teach my feet to land one in front of the other; my knees banged up, bloodied, and bruised each time I fell. And finally, I did it. I walked from one side of the room to the other. It would be a year before I was able to walk to the corner store. In between I worked out, walked on the treadmill my brother bought me, rode my stationary bike, and, except for being a heroin addict with no muscle control, I was in tremendous shape.

As I improved physically, I eased into this new life where money was no longer my god. Everything for which I had striven in the past, worked to become, thought I wanted out of life, became so glaringly artificial. I was very aware, maybe for the first time in my life, that I had no clue what life was about. I didn't want children, never saw the point. Money no longer held much of an attraction for me. I guess I wanted to be happy although that was something of an elusive concept. Something was missing. I didn't know what. When I regained some semblance of normalcy, I moved to another apartment where, with my disability insurance that I had paid into while I was working, I was able to support myself and be independent again. I ran into my friend, Mike Crandall, with whom I'd grown up; we met as teenagers on Avenue L in Canarsie and 2 of his brothers were among my closest friends. We had had a lot of fun together. Our first official date was exploring the infamous Manhattan swinger's club, Plato's Retreat, when I was 19. He was 26. And now, a decade later, we became a couple. We've been together since around 1994. Marriage means so little to me; it is an institution I simply don't understand. But we were officially married about ten years after we got back together. I have no idea when. I think it was in April.

When I came out of my coma in 1993, I didn't see any white light. My hallucinations were about a devil behind a curtain in my hospital room, waiting for me to succumb so that he could presumably take my soul. I wanted to define this brain jumble, to find some meaning. More than a decade after leaving the hospital, I renounced my atheism and became a born-again Christian. I conscientiously brainwashed myself with the mythology scribed by patriarchs and misogynists. I walked through the streets reciting psalms in my head, subjugating myself to the son of a god that made absolutely no sense to me; I married Mike because I didn't want to live in sin. But rational thought won out. I am an atheist through and through, a free thinker who was married for all the wrong reasons during an extended lapse in judgment. My sentiments have nothing to do with Mike. He is my dearest friend and will be for life. He is a good man. But the artificial institution of marriage is contrived; it's a manifestation of humans trying to create structure and control in a chaotic universe that is transitory. We own nothing; not land, not people, not animals, not life. Yet we are forever trying to assert some kind of dominion over the planet and each other.

Mike succumbed to my addiction and we were unable to quit snorting heroin. As long as I knew where to get it, the temptations in New York were too great. I wanted to be clean. I wanted to be strong. I wanted no shackles or addictions. And where this drug had provided me with the vehicle to transcend my physical paralysis in the beginning, it now paralyzed my mind and spirit. I could not function without it. I could not quit. It owned me. I had to leave New York. On January 3, 2008, with my mother in tow, Mike and I landed in central Florida to start a new life.

The time will come when men such as I will look upon the murder of animals as they now look on the murder of men. -Leonardo da Vinci

Old MacDonald's Farm

From time to time, various animal rights campaigns would interrupt my reality and I would generally dismiss the subject while the evening news soundbite was still in progress. I was repulsed by the gratuitous chest-pounding violence of those who hunted for sport. Every hunter I'd ever known, without exception, found killing animals a convenient excuse to go get drunk and fire weapons. I thought it poetic when fur-draped women were introduced to red paint in the middle of Times Square. Later on, when I would learn of the networks of activists who, in the spirit of Harriet Tubman liberating African-American slaves via the Underground Railroad, risked their own freedom to liberate enslaved animals, I would look upon these men and women with admiration and respect. But that was still a few years off.

I ate meat, but I didn't murder animals. I simply bought my food in the supermarket. After all, I'm Italian. It's my culture. It's my tradition. It's how we celebrate and bond. It's how we mourn as well as comfort one another. Spaghetti and meatballs, veal parmagiana, anything smothered with gooey, dripping cheese.

Old MacDonald's Farm

I looked forward to autumn in New York when I could cloak myself in stylish leather jackets and coordinated boots. One year I bought a little light pink calf-skin baby-soft tailored leather jacket for about $500. It was beautiful. At Peter Luger's, the famous steakhouse in, Williamsburg, Brooklyn, ordering well-done, medium, or rare was not in my vocabulary; my hundred-dollar steaks had to arrive on my plate "still mooing." I was visiting a friend once in Williamsburg one day. Actually, he was my heroin dealer. A refrigerated delivery truck arrived at Peter Luger's. When the doors opened, it was packed with sides of beef and other cuts of meat. It was slightly disturbing. But I didn't let it ruin my day. I turned my back away from the offensive display and continued with my transaction in blissful oblivion.

And as far as activists go, the one slogan that I found somewhat redundant and annoying was "Meat is Murder." Did they think they were telling us something we didn't know? I've known my whole life that my steaks came from cows, pork chops from pigs, and, obviously, chicken came from chickens. On Old MacDonald's Farm, nonhuman animals ran free, laid in the sun, played with little children, and were cared for by decent country folk who loved them. Then they were gently put to sleep and butchered, their body parts needed to sustain us. Unpleasant perhaps. But lions and all carnivorous species stalk and kill their prey too. I assessed the meat-is-murder activists to be nothing more than a bunch of peaceniks who probably needed to get a job and do something constructive with their lives instead of bothering people who eat meat.

One day, however, my life would change and it will never be the same again. It was as if the blinders were removed. Everything that had been in front of my eyes forever suddenly came into focus. I was shocked and horrified. I could never unring that bell. I would mourn for my ignorance from time to time; but I couldn't unlearn what I now knew. And simply as a function of who I am, unlike the meat-is-murder crusaders, I knew there would be absolutely zero ambiguity in my message going forward.

My message, whatever it would be, would be born of immense

introspection, turmoil, and awakening.

In January 2008, Mike and I were beginning a new life in Florida. We moved my mother down here too, my brother bought her a house, and I took care of her to the best of my ability. I am comfortable that I fulfilled my obligation. We would drive over every day or I would go alone, check on her, take her shopping, argue, fight, take her out to eat, then go home. My mother would become ill in February. I believe that with nothing left to complain about and no one but me left to malign, she largely lost her purpose. And, obviously, there is a degree of isolation in Florida compared to Brooklyn where she lived for 86 years. She would be hospitalized and go into a rehab where she contracted a contagious staph infection called MRSA, was dehydrated to the point of organ damage and dementia, and, even though I was there every day, I was wholly unaware she was being neglected. All I witnessed was her rapid decline. She remained in the nursing home until she died in May. The day she was dying, I was unable to kiss her goodbye. Or say goodbye. I had nothing to say.

During her decline, which thankfully was relatively fast, I would show up some days and she'd be throwing her diapers at the staff. Other days she would be happy and waiting for me to take her home. Some days she was lucid and simply annoyed with me. I did all I could to protect her and keep her comfortable. But I also learned to take care of myself, go swimming, exercise, and stay mentally clear. If I was not in a good place myself, I would be of no use to her or anyone. After her death, I learned that it was nearly impossible to sue a nursing home for neglect. Between the paperwork that is signed when the subject is admitted, where neglect is built into the business model and elderly patients' *failure to thrive* is endemic, there was no recourse.

I should say that I didn't hate my mother. I didn't love her either. We simply coexisted in this universe inextricably tied together by obligation and blood, resentment and guilt; by pretense and appearance cultivated so outsiders would know how close we were. When my mother finally passed away, I went home and let out a guttural scream, uncontrollable sobs, it was as if my body was being purged. There was a sadness and loss I had never experienced. And then it was over. I was free. But while I was her primary caregiver, being drug-free, surrounded by sunshine, clean air, trees and the beauty of my new surroundings, I turned my attention to losing weight and being healthy, mentally and physically. I bought a weight bench, an aerobic step, some other gadgets and I started looking into a vegetarian diet. I have always valued my appearance. It was clear to me that if I could just stop eating meat and eat more fresh fruits and veggies, I would be healthier and look better. While searching for information, I stumbled upon an undercover video of a dairy farm. By the time that video was over, I was vegan.

I always knew milk came from cows. It never occurred to me that female cows had to be repeatedly raped, euphemistically called insemination, to produce milk. If her milk was to be extracted and sold for human consumption, her calves were being deprived of the milk meant for them. These anemic babies, a by-product of the dairy industry, are what I had known my whole life as "veal." How had I not connected the dots? It's all so utterly obvious.

In the first video I watched, the wobbly day-old calf was ripped away from his mother's teat and chained up in a crate across on the production floor of this *humane* family farm. The mother's heart-wrenching screams and cries tore a hole in my soul. It was my cousin Angela's wake all over again. The helpless calf's wide eyes peered out from a little hole in his darkened enclosure where he would linger for several weeks until he was killed and sold to be eaten. This little baby literally went from the womb to a tomb fashioned for him by a heartless deviant dairy farmer. I had never associated the word murder with killing nonhuman animals. But this is exactly what we were doing. That baby was murdered. And then his little body parts were sold for profit.

The grief-stricken mother's engorged teats were infected with bloody pus from mastitis, a painful condition with which dairy cows live. According to the Mayo Clinic, "mastitis is an infection of the breast tissue that results in breast pain, swelling, warmth and redness... also might cause fever and chills."[3] The video explained that the cow herself was pumped up on hormones to produce more milk and antibiotics to fight the persistent infections to keep her viable. Bellowing for her child, she was hooked up to a machine that would extract her baby's milk from her body three times a day. All of the misery, heartache, and impurities would then be pumped into tanks, homogenized, and sold for profit. The sight of her grotesquely engorged udder which was the size of a basketball and dragged on the ground shocked me.

A cow's normal life span is about 20 years. But dairy cows are so depleted that many cannot even stand on their own feet or produce milk after roughly 5 years. They are called downer cows and are routinely dragged by a forklift to be slaughtered for food, even though downer cows' flesh is not approved by the United States Department of Agriculture (USDA) for human consumption. I hoped that this horrific video was isolated. I had to know for sure. I braced myself and clicked play.

In another video, the used up dairy cow, a downer cow, was not being ground up to be sold off in McDonald's hamburgers. She was dragged out and disposed of with the trash; left lying in the hot sun without water for days, unable to move, unworthy of any respect or dignity. She was discarded like the broken machine she was to her abusers. I couldn't cry. I only felt anger pulsating inside me. Activists found her and called the police. They could do nothing. The cow was the farmer's property and was not protected by any welfare regulations that would protect a dog or a cat. The activists brought her water and tried to comfort her. Finally, after two days, one of them shot her in the head to end her misery.

I watched video after video. It seemed that the next atrocity would dwarf the last. I researched factory farms. I was horrified. I felt guilty. I felt helpless. I was angry. I was also nothing if not naive. I wrote to PETA, People for the Ethical Treatment of Animals, to tell *them* about factory farming and demand we do

3   Mayo Clinic Staff, "Diseases and Conditions, Mastitis," http://www. mayoclinic.org/diseases-conditions/mastitis/basics/definition/con-20026633

something about it. I learned quickly that mainstream activism was nothing more than a pervasive business model of donating money to animal welfare organizations as animals kept dying. They would then send me a weekly or monthly reminder about more suffering animals and ask me for more money. Desperate to help the animals, people give their money. And the animals are never helped. I realized this quickly.

I watched a documentary called *Meet Your Meat* that was narrated by Alec Baldwin. It explored factory farms and how animals were brutalized. But it was produced by People for the Ethical Treatment of Animals. I wanted a less biased perspective. I found a documentary called *Earthlings* that was narrated by Joaquin Phoenix. It explored five animal-use industries: food, pets, entertainment, clothing, and scientific research. It became obvious to me that there was a hidden holocaust. I had known of it my whole life, I had been an active participant, but I had never seen it. The unmitigated torture to which we subject animals for our use was unconscionable. It was sick and disgusting. Then I watched a video called *Behind the Mask* which documents the stories of the underground Animal Liberation Front; it reiterated everything I had seen thus far, except this film focused on the heroes who risked their own freedom to save the animals. It filled me with a respect and sense of purpose I had never known.

I shared the videos with my husband. We watched every excruciating scene together. Chickens living in cramped filthy cages, their wings broken, no room to move, their beaks seared off so that they couldn't peck each other's flesh as insanity set in. They were then thrown into trucks, taken to processing plants, hung up alive on hooks, dunked into scalding water to remove their feathers, their body parts chopped up to be sold. Simply by virtue of the sheer quantity, chickens are by far the most abused animals on the planet. Female pigs spent their lives in gestation crates, unable to move, extend their limbs, or even turn over. The male babies had their testicles literally hacked off with scissors, the discarded body parts thrown into a macabre trash pile. The screaming, bleeding babies were thrown back into their enclosures with no pain relief. The testicles are removed to eliminate the musky smell that would ruin the taste of their flesh. The females were repeatedly raped to produce babies that could be fattened up and murdered. I cried when I read Hansel and Gretel as a child. The thought of fattening up children to eat them scared me. Real life for these animals was no fairy tale and there was no happy ending.

I couldn't imagine ever participating in this nightmare that was everywhere. But I had. Animals enslaved and tortured for their fur, wool, or leather. Dogs and cats being bred and sold like commodities, while shelters put millions of homeless animals a year to death using cruel and painful methods. Circuses and SeaWorld that cage animals, tear them from their families, and beat them until they perform tricks for humans. It would be just and correct if aliens came down to earth and caged humans as pets for their children and trained us to perform tricks for their entertainment. The holocaust permeated society. It was so pervasive that it remained invisible.

I was now vegan and had a lifetime for which to atone. It was inconceivable to me that anyone could see the misery, the injustice, the pain, fear, terror, and horror in which we imprison nonhuman animals and not be compelled to rage against it. My husband turned to me and said, "I'm not like you. I don't think I can change the world." In that split second, the fabric of our relationship tore. We'd been together over 10 years by then but I was alone. I couldn't understand how he could continue eating animals. It changed the way I saw him. I eventually moved out of our bedroom. My entire life was disrupted by this new-found knowledge. I was struggling with my own inner turmoil and a corresponding disbelief that no one else cared.

Despite my own revulsion, I acquiesced and bought a barbecued chicken for my mother who was in the nursing home. My husband was in bed. I was up alone. And the chicken was in my fridge. In the past, one of my favorite things to eat had always been cold chicken. I wrestled with myself. It wasn't food. It was a corpse. It was a once-sentient being that lived a miserable life, was tortured to death, and was now sitting in my refrigerator. But I wanted to

31

eat it. In one of the most shameful moments in my entire life, something I have never shared with another living soul, I took that corpse out of my refrigerator, laid it on the counter, and with tears streaming down my face, I tore it apart and ate it. Limb by limb. I was horrified. But I couldn't stop myself. The guilt consumed me. But who could I tell? I told myself it would never happen again. But it did... One night my husband left a sausage-and-peppers pizza in the fridge. I wound up eating a slice. I hated myself. I went online to find someone to whom I could talk. There had to be another person in the world who understood. I found the PETA forums that were full of vegans (and meat-eating trolls). I confessed my sins; well, I confessed about the pizza. I never told anyone about the chicken incident. How could I? And they understood.

If we put a baby in a playpen with an apple and a chicken, they will eat the apple and bond with the chicken. But we had all been indoctrinated from birth to view dead animals as food. Our own natural inclinations have been socialized out of us. And most people have absolutely no connection with the source of their food. For me, it became apparent that I had to re-establish those connections. I watched video after video, I read books, I considered what I ate and why. Within a few weeks, it was no longer a battle to abstain from eating animals. I became repulsed by the incessant commercials and nauseated by the smell of barbecued corpses in the supermarket. When I saw a glazed chicken, I no longer saw food; I saw that being with a broken neck who stuck his head through the cage in a desperate and futile attempt to escape his enslavement.

I was vegan. And I had found my community online. I wasn't alone anymore.

I am no longer accepting the things
I cannot change; I'm changing
the things I cannot accept.
-Angela Davis

The Internet

I found community online. I found others with whom I could communicate; share ideas, frustrations, and anger. It was a lifeline out of the increasingly-foreign reality in which I lived. Here others understood the urgency, the desperate situation on which animals' lives hinged. One of the most admired, respected, and vocal advocates of achieving Animal Liberation by any means necessary was Dr. Steven Best, a professor of philosophy at the University of Texas in El Paso. For more than a decade, he had been advocating underground direct action and encouraging breaking unjust laws in pursuit of justice. He was vegan and he had a reputation for his non-negotiable stance on animal enslavement. In 2005, Dr. Best was banned from the United Kingdom. The Home Office described his rhetoric as intended to "foment, justify or glorify terrorist violence... [he] seek[s] to provoke others to` terrorist acts; [or] foment other serious criminal activity or seek to provoke others to serious criminal acts."[4] This

---

4   Donald MacLeod, "Britain uses hate law to ban animal rights
    campaigner," The Guardian (August 31, 2005) https://www.theguardian.
    com/education/2005/aug/31/internationaleducationnews.highereducation

man gave voice and context to everything I felt and believed and he had been censored for doing so. Like many other progressive activists, I was humbled by his intelligence and courage. He was a movement patriarch.

There were others who had liberated animals from fur farms in the states, others who had penetrated labs in the UK and exposed the savagery of animal experimentation; some had simply walked onto factory farms and engaged in open rescues, liberating animals from their confinement in broad daylight. All had served prison time. None were apologetic. All of these veterans were active prior to 9/11. Thereafter, the United States citizenry obligingly began to relinquish our civil liberties to the manufactured political boogeyman of the 21st century, *terrorism*. If we were active in the 1950s, the vehicle the corporatocracy used to perpetuate itself and squash dissent was communism – the red scare. Animal and environmental activists would rapidly find themselves persecuted as terrorists as the green scare evolved. Nonetheless, I felt connected to others who lived and breathed honor and integrity, conscience-driven actors. Unfortunately, these seasoned warriors were largely retired; idolized by many, most appeared only on lecture circuits. I looked to established activists for direction. I needed to know how to be effective. I had gained the unwanted knowledge of a holocaust and the weight was burdensome. I needed to relieve my own conscience and make a difference. I needed to make up for a lifetime of ignorant participation.

Mainly through the PETA forums, I was welcomed into the online movement and lovingly neutered into impotence. I followed directions well. I sent away for all of the leaflets, bumper stickers, and posters I could find. I went to parks, to schools, to supermarkets, anywhere I could find a living breathing body to listen to me. If I saw a pickup truck with a sticker that said "beef, it what's for dinner," I would place a "go vegan" sticker over it. I leafleted. I proselytized. I was an utter success at contributing to a litter epidemic. I excelled at cultivating that glazed-over blank stare from those I engaged who politely waited for me to shut up. I had no clue how to research abusers, how to follow the money, or what to do. And the only advice I was able to secure was "research, research, research." Okay, but how? No one would share anything that mattered. Everything was a big secret guarded by those whose donation base depended upon their monopolizing data. I didn't understand this at the time and couldn't fathom what data existed, let alone how to access it or what to do with it.

I spent a lot of time online debating trolls and abusers, from meat-eaters to Canadian seal hunters. I listened as my peers preached moderation and explained to me that I was too confrontational. It took about 8 months, but it became glaringly obvious to me that the moderates were more of a problem than the actual abusers. I organized my first protest at the Lake Square Mall in Leesburg, Florida. The Cole Brothers circus, which has a lengthy 20-year long resume of animal abuses and crimes, was coming to town. Four people showed up including me. The police moved our little demonstration to a *free speech zone* a block away where we wouldn't disturb the patrons. I was shocked that I was the only activist who was incensed at being relegated to a sidewalk where we would remain unseen and unheard. I was told to smile and never use profanity. Fuck that! I threw out my sign, bought a ticket, and went right inside the circus where I spoke to people one by one about the sick and abused animals as well as the pedophiles and drug addicts employed by Cole Brothers. I was ejected from the circus in about 30 minutes, but at least I had ruined the experience for a lot of people. Hopefully they'd save their money next time.

The next day I was castigated online for buying that ticket and giving the circus money. It seemed that everyone was advocating doing nothing rather than infiltrating the venue. These people spewed sanctimony online while a war raged in factory farms, labs, circuses, bear bile farms, puppy mills; in every corner of the earth, in everyone's backyard, there were suffering voiceless victims. Yet, here we met daily to listen to the gospel of moderation; to debate about what was wrong and how slavery had to be abolished. It was evident that only some appallingly-few advocates ever left their computers long enough to do anything about it. Animal Liberation seemed to be an exercise in online entertainment. And I was part of it. I was maybe the most impotent of them all. I had no idea what to do.

This was my community. I found a social network in the midst of a world from which I was becoming increasingly alienated. Eating meat began to look like a form of flesh-eating psychopathology. I saw friends and family differently; a Master Race of humans who felt justified by a birthright of privilege to dominate, entomb, murder, and exploit every nonhuman on the planet. Injustice permeated our entire culture, I just never recognized that it extended to animals. Americans observe Columbus Day in honor of a murderous, genocidal savage. Thanksgiving became the iconic emblem of the American psychosis: a celebration of the imperialist genocide of indigenous Americans with the corporate-motivated genocide of billions of genetically-engineered birds. I felt like I woke up one day and realized I was living in the twilight zone. Everyone agreed that I was the odd one. I was no longer one of them. There was not another human being in my real life with whom I could communicate anymore. I both clung to my new online social network and despised myself for being a part of it. We were all only there because animals were dying horrible deaths, the inevitable end to their suffering. There is something inherently wrong with finding happiness with others and a meaningful existence all built upon misery and death. I think I'm the only person who felt this way or even recognized the issue. I had to find my own path. For the time being, though, I was on my own in a sea of well-meaning closely-knit wholly-useless individuals who sickened me. I sickened me.

I started volunteering in shelters. The local no-kill humane society (never to be confused with the Humane Society of the United States) was a relatively nice place. Yes, the dogs and cats were prisoners. But they were safe. They had volunteers to walk them. They were fed and cared for. I could not make the difference here that I needed to. I tried to volunteer on Animal Control's death row. But they would not allow civilian volunteers in any meaningful capacity. Mike and I would go there and adopt our first child, Max. He was an awkward little white puppy with droopy skin. He was just a beautiful, ugly little guy. I really wanted an old dog that no one else would ever adopt. But Mike wanted Max and today he's 7 years old. My first-born son who I love dearly.

I began working with a local German Shepherd rescue group. In my little manufactured home with pristine beige wall-to-wall carpeting, I volunteered to foster the big, scared and abused dogs. They needed love, they needed a home, and here was somewhere I could really make a difference. My carpeting was rapidly destroyed. My little home began to resemble more of a warehouse. I rehabbed about 5 or 6 dogs who were placed in allegedly stable homes. But I never knew for sure. I trusted the group with which I worked. I knew they did meticulous home visits before placing a dog, but I just don't trust people. They present themselves one way to the outside world and you never see the monster until it's too late. I would grow to love the giant dogs. We would trust each other. Then they'd be placed. It tore my heart out every time. I had to take solace in the fact that I gave them a chance they might not otherwise have had. My last foster was a nervous, scared little black dog. She was not a German Shepherd, so the rescue was going to have difficulty placing her. She was terrified to eat. I don't know the exact nature of the trauma she suffered, but she shook easily. I've now been *fostering* my little girl, Jasmine, for 7 years. She is Max's little sister and they are inseparable. Max intuitively became her protector from the day she arrived. Some things transcend language, like fear, terror, love, and safety. Jazz knows she is safe now. Jazz is home.

I was sincere but scattered, trying to find my way. While I would rescue or liberate any animal I could in a heartbeat, this was not the arena in which I belonged. If every vegan, every animal activist, every well-intentioned individual went out and started rescuing nonhuman victims, we would forever be running behind the machine that simply spits out terror and desecration with exquisite precision. I needed to get in front of that machine and stop it from churning out victims. This has been my vision since the beginning. But figuring out how to run sideways around an omniscient, omnipresent slave-based infrastructure is daunting.

While I found my way in the real world, I basically reveled in the community of those who provided camaraderie online. And it very much became a playground for me. I enjoyed confronting abusers, hunters, especially the knuckle-dragging seal hunters from Canada, meat-eaters, and trolls. I found that I excelled at confrontation. But I kept getting censored and deleted from Myspace and other public forums. If I ever actually sat down to figure it out, I am guessing I hold some kind of record for the most YouTube accounts, Facebook pages, and blogs censored and deleted by the corporate overlords of social media. Finally, I bought a domain, negotiationisover.com, and put up my first website, Negotiation Is Over (NIO) in 2009. In early 2010, Iceland was poised to become a global free speech haven.[5] With laws that were crafted in part by Julian Assange, founder of Wikileaks, moving NIO to Iceland was only natural. Now that the censors were removed, I pulled no punches. Unlike many who hide behind keyboards, I have never said anything online that I would not say straight to someone's face. This is a point of pride for me.

In the early days, I was already so hated by trolls that they erected a website called *Negotiation is Done* (https://negotiationisdone. wordpress.com/) devoted to ridiculing me. I was honored by the derision of my adversaries. A site called Peta Sucks still has myriad posts about me. Encyclopedia Dramatica hosted a page that ridiculed and tore me apart. Those things were a badge of honor. It was an acknowledgment that I had penetrated their comfort zone and the vindication was intoxicating, although I always remained painfully aware that this was not helping animals. We despised one another. Negotiation Is Over started getting hit with Distributed Denial of Service (DDoS) attacks – generally bots are programmed to flood a site with traffic to shut it down – within my first year of being online. They complained regularly to my offshore host to take down my site. My host in Iceland would forward to me the emails and say "don't worry

---

5   Mark Tran, "Iceland plans future as global haven for freedom of speech," The Guardian, (February 12, 2010). https://www.theguardian.com/world/2010/feb/12/iceland-haven-freedom-speech-wikileaks

about it."

As I became fairly well-known online, I noticed that other like-minded vegans gravitated toward me. My circle never exchanged cupcake recipes. We were more inclined to discuss the best way to rid the world of abusers. I was flattered that some of the most influential and seasoned vegans in my movement were becoming known to me. Dr. Steve Best began to occasionally like a Myspace post or comment on Facebook. I was flattered and humbled. I'm pretty sure I giggled. Although I knew deep within myself that I was doing absolutely nothing worthy of any praise or admiration, it became clear that I simply had the courage to say what everyone else was thinking... or so I was repeatedly told. The truth is that there is no courage involved whatsoever. I simply don't have a filter. I never have. If it's in my head, it comes out of my mouth.

Channeling my inner adolescent, I took a picture of my butt in little white boy shorts and put it up on my site with the headline "Kiss My Vegan Ass!" I knew I looked good. I was working out hard every day on the stepper. And I enjoyed all the comments saying "that's not you," and "whore." The meat-eaters suffering from high cholesterol, diabetes, acne, and obesity hated me even more. But there was one other unforeseen consequence of this stunt. For the first time, Dr. Steve Best sent me a private message on Myspace. I could hardly contain my excitement. It was wholly innocuous and, not wanting to sound like the 14-year old groupie I felt like, I responded with a simple "how's it going?" His response confused me. "It's lonely out here in the desert." I thought he lived in Texas and had no idea to what desert he referred. Was he traveling in the Middle East? He was clearly leaving the lines of communication open if I wanted to engage. And I genuinely wanted to know this man. I wasn't at all interested in a fling.

A week or so later on a Sunday we started to communicate in earnest by email. He told me that he considered himself a well-dressed and professional man who liked women to be "girly girls," arm candy essentially. It struck me as somewhat pretentious. I still very much take pride in my appearance, but I had outgrown artificiality in my 20s. I don't think anyone ever responded to him using the word "pretentious." It immediately changed the tone of our conversation although he remained very much a gentleman and very charming.

Drugs entered into the discussion from our first series of exchanges. I had been getting high for 30 years. They say that when you start getting high, you stop growing emotionally. So maybe there's a reason I was comfortable in the role of adolescent groupie. I had finally achieved sobriety. I had to leave the state of New York to do it, but it worked for me. So, when Steve confided in me that he wrestled with drug addiction, I understood. I understood his pain. I understood the cycle. I wanted to be his support system and help him overcome the demons that plagued him. I told him that if he could visualize what he wanted, where he wanted to be in life, then we could work toward getting him there. I began to care deeply about this man and was honored that he trusted me. We became very close, very fast.

You can discover more about a person in an hour of play than in a year of conversation. -Plato

Sibling Rivalry

In 2009, I saved my money and flew across the country to Los Angeles where I attended my first National Animal Rights Conference. It was great fun to meet my online friends in person. It was wonderful to have a sense of community. But the 3-day party was simply the outgrowth of the online social network that I enjoyed. And, again, in real life, I didn't see or hear anything much of value at the conference that translated into effective action for Animal Liberation. A few speakers were inspired in their rhetoric and I felt the excitement. But when it was over I still had absolutely no idea what to do with my energy. A lot of speakers were simply advocating the necessity of being vegan to a cheering crowd of vegans. It was fairly ridiculous. Others were welfarists as opposed to abolitionists (or liberationists, my preferred self-identification).

In 2009, I had no real understanding of the two schools of thought. Basically, welfarists advocate for bigger cages and better conditions for enslaved animals. Liberationists advocate tearing down the cages and freeing animals from their restraints. One might be inclined to agree that animals deserve big cages and to be treated humanely. But with a modicum of thought, it

41

becomes apparent that advocating for better working conditions for African-American slaves rather than the complete abolition of slavery would have been a perversion. Only a racist would advocate for well-treated black slaves. And only a speciesist would advocate for humane treatment of enslaved animals.

Having had to identify and own my 43 years of being a speciesist, I learned to figure out what I believed early on. When there was an apparent misalignment in my thinking about the animal holocaust, I would simply replace the nonhuman animal with a human baby – both autonomous beings, both able to experience pain and pleasure identical to any human adult, both innocent and vulnerable individuals over whom we can be said to be stewards, both morally equivalent. And my own speciesist inclinations rapidly receded. No one would advocate cages for babies, experimenting on them, making them live in filth, misery, beating and starving them to perform tricks or otherwise use them for our own purposes. Only a pedophile might view a baby as a resource to be exploited. And only a speciesist might view a nonhuman as a resource to be exploited. It became entirely black and white for me. I was uninterested in fighting for better conditions for entombed animals. I wanted to smash their cages and chains, incapacitate their captors, and liberate them.

As I came into my own as a liberationist, I grew to despise welfarists. They allow the public to believe that welfare laws actually provide some semblance of welfare for animals; in fact, the only thing welfare regulations do is regulate and legalize their unmitigated abuse. The laws are written by industrial exploiters and enforced by a state beholden to corporate interests. Our own movement welfarists promote this insidious idea while collecting donations. They are doing more to promote a feel-good holocaust than the actual industrial propaganda networks.

But I partied, drank, networked, ate a lot of vegan food, spent money on a "Fuck Speciesism" t-shirt and flew home from the 2009 national conference no clearer about my direction than I had been a week earlier. When I returned home, the welfarist/ abolitionist schism began to take shape for me. I was honored to be included in a series of emails with Steve Best and others. Although Dr. Best derided the conference for years and would never have attended, he was very critical of the speakers for their positions. One speaker in particular, Karen Dawn, was the focus of Steve's derision. I knew nothing about Dawn and was fairly unconcerned about her presentation. But I learned that she had shunned Steve's advances in the past. And she was also aligned with Wayne Pacelle, Steve's former friend who went on to become president of the Humane Society of the United States (HSUS). I would come to understand that the HSUS promotes welfarism, actually has agri-business tycoons sitting on its Board of Directors, and in coming years would take on Michael Vick, the notorious NFL dog fighter, as one of its spokespeople. But at the time I had no feeling about it one way or another.

In one of the emails, Steve asked if anyone wanted to do an attack piece on Dawn and indicated it would make him happy. I inferred that his motivation was more personal than professional but immediately dismissed any critical thought. Who raises their hand and says "oooh, me, me, me"??? Me, of course. I'm a writer. And I wanted to ingratiate myself with this iconic individual who was allowing me access to his universe. I wrote what I thought was a sarcastic parody about Karen Dawn drinking too much and preaching for bigger cages. The image I used for the article was of a drunken woman passed out on a park bench. The picture made me laugh. Steve edited my article and then it was published on my site, NIO, under my name. He loved it. We laughed. Our bond grew stronger.

It is vital that I examine myself and my own motivations as my story unravels. I really believed that Steve had been victimized by Karen Dawn and many others. He told me about all of his former friends who had betrayed him. He told me about his last best friend who was also a woman. She was in love with him and became jealous when he would date other women. She developed a fatal attraction. And his male best friends would always be jealous because of his prowess with women. They would try to sabotage him; he called it "cock blocking." He was forced to sever relationships with everyone he had ever thought of as a friend. He was hurting. He was damaged. I felt his pain and wanted to take it away. I wanted to protect and defend him. I did so with an utter ferocity and unwavering loyalty. I wanted Steve to know that I would not betray him as every other friend he'd ever known had. I was his soft spot. I was the person on whom he could count. To me, that is what friendship means. And it was my privilege to have him accept it.

That explains why I was extremely protective of him and maybe why I was willing to defend him against others. It does not, however, even begin to explain why I would allow myself to be used, to be a mindless tool, to vehemently attack others without provocation. No one can manipulate another person unless they allow themselves to be manipulated. And at this point in my life, I had no inkling that there was something really wrong inside me, a giant black hole was being filled by the validation and pats on the head I got by pleasing this man. I was blinded by his reputation and eloquence. He was brilliant in my eyes. He was charismatic. He exuded confidence. I valued him. I valued him far more than I ever considered valuing myself. And, sadly, I would learn in years to come that for whatever inner demons drive others, I was not unique. I would eventually be cast in the long procession of Steve's friends who had betrayed *him* and become the subject of his obsession. I was to learn that I was simply a disposable commodity, not a friend, easily replaced by a seemingly-endless parade of groupies seeking an Animal Liberation messiah.

I guess it's true that we reap what we sow. And I'm very careful these days about what I sow. Sometime in 2010 I came to my senses and was extremely embarrassed by my attack on Karen Dawn, a woman who I never met and still know nothing of other than that she is a seasoned animal advocate who enjoys the respect and admiration of the mainstream movement. But Karen Dawn was only the minor leagues. I was about to move into the major leagues of character assassination with gleeful abandon. Gary Francione is a law professor at Rutgers University. He is unrelenting in his non-negotiable stand about veganism constituting a moral baseline, a necessity if one is to conduct themselves as a decent human being. He is probably also the most vocal critic of welfarism in our movement and on these issues, he has my complete and utter support; even my admiration for his unflinching courage in addressing the movement plague that is welfarism.

But Professor Francione is also a critic of violence and all actions on behalf of Animal Liberation other than peaceful vegan education. It always makes me chuckle to think about what the opposite, violent vegan education, might look like. I envision vegans with baseball bats taking swings at the heads of non-vegans yelling "Go Vegan." This law professor's stance against activism and campaigns is troublesome because he commands a cult-like following. The last thing on this planet that anyone should be advocating is less action. But, truly, I am unconcerned with Francione or anyone else for that matter. As my own path began to illuminate before me, the paths others chose, inside or outside of activism, became irrelevant. My philosophy has always been to keep my eyes on my own paper and not allow myself to be influenced by anyone else's performance. It applied to test-taking in school, it applies to my career as an activist, and it applies to my journey. My path is the only one with which I am concerned.

It became apparent very quickly, however, that Steve had been engaged in a competition (a *pissing war* as many activists far more seasoned than I observed) with Francione for over a decade. It goes back to the days when Gary Francione started out with PETA, when Steve Best supported PETA, and then as is common in our community, their paths diverged. It was clear to me that he felt overshadowed by Francione's professional success, academic recognition, and influence in our community. But he also made a strong and unrelenting case for how Francione was *the worst thing to happen to the animal rights movement* and how he was an enemy of the animals.

Steve was wounded. I wanted to help him heal. But the animals continue to live in a state of emergency. Under siege by a human population, animals are the subjects of an indefensible globally-enforced genocide. And if the far-too-scarce human resources the activist community enjoys were being diverted and neutralized by Francione, this was outright treason. It never occurred to me to challenge Best on his convictions. He was forceful, powerful, and coherent in his arguments. If Francione was the worst thing to happen to animals then he needed to be stopped. So, when Steve suggested we go after his nemesis, I jumped on the opportunity. At the time, another of Steve's proteges named Jason Miller would regularly use his site, *Thomas Paine's Corner*, to launch critical pieces on Francione. It was largely like being granted access into an exclusive club.

Jason and I would simultaneously publish negative articles about Gary Francione to Steve's great enthusiasm. But Jason was not pleased by my growing friendship with his mentor and, while I looked up to him, he became more intent upon trying to neutralize me. This was the first time I had been the target of another activist and was clueless about his resentment. Eventually, Steve intervened and defended me against Miller's attacks. In retrospect, embarrassing as it may be now, that situation was not unlike a parent having to mediate a sibling rivalry. Jason Miller exited the movement shortly thereafter. And Steve and I became closer.

For weeks, almost every day, attack piece after attack piece would be published under my name on NIO. When Steve would call me from his car after he crossed the border on his way home from Juarez, his ideas for new angles would spill out faster than he could talk. From the first word or two he spoke on the phone, I could easily identify whether Steve was impaired; he would be excited and his ideas would pop. I was honored to be his closest confidante. And we were nothing if not funny and creative. We laughed and laughed until I was crying. Then another attack on Francione would go out. At my peak, NIO had between 30,000 and 40,000 hits a day. When a blog went out, it would saturate our community fairly well. Steve once called me laughing that Professor Francione probably had a bell that went off every time something was published on NIO and that he was probably on tranquilizers by now.

My focus on Francione created tension with some of my former allies who broke ties with me. I was a little uncomfortable, but I dismissed any misgivings. I had a real friend now and my loyalty was absolute. About a month into the Francione campaign, I told Steve that I was distressed; I was not proud of what I was doing and I wanted to move on from targeting Gary Francione. I fully expected him to sever ties with me and move on. But he didn't. He understood and was okay with it. At that moment, from my perspective, our friendship was cemented.

He still called me every day. But not wanting to intrude, it took some time before I felt comfortable enough to initiate our conversations. Then he asked me one day why I never called him. Once I felt welcome, we would be on the phone all day long; whenever either of us needed a friendly ear, the other was there. Dr. Best taught me a lot. He filled in the blanks for me about the history of animal rights. He created a context for the movement in which I existed. He challenged me to rethink everything I knew. One of the pivotal books that redefined the way I saw the world was Howard Zinn's *A People's History of the United States*. The oppression of animals and humans was endemic; both justified and excused because it was the oppressors themselves who wrote history. Suddenly, my own indoctrination became glaring.

Steve's videos, his speeches, his history in the movement were nothing if not inspirational. In one of his discussions of Animal Liberation he spoke about how it was conceivable that the animal rights movement might one day find itself fighting a war not unlike the IRA (Irish Republican Army). My colleagues in Ireland ridiculed his audacity in private discussions; I defended his ideas. He had coined the term *extensional self-defense* which essentially promotes the same idea upheld by every court in this country: it is acceptable to use violence or any necessary amount of force to defend another person from harm. Except Steve's powerful theory extended our duty to defend others to nonhuman others as well – those excluded from our legal and moral sphere of consideration. One of Steve's infamous videos that spoke to me was recorded around 2010 on one of his European tours. He told his cheering Italian audience that "every motherfucker who hurts animals is gonna feel the fear." He explained that it is not jail cells we should fear. It is the prison in our own minds that holds us back; that is the only thing we should fear. Steve was known for his quotes like "feel the fear and do it anyway" and "if the law is wrong, the right thing to do is break it."

We were exactly on the same page. Everything I felt, he spoke. Everything I believed, he gave intellectual context and credibility. We shared a philosophy. We shared secrets. We shared fantasies about exterminating entire populations. It was telling that I would always envision walking into a conference of vivisectors and blowing us all up. He would share similar fantasies about his academic colleagues. No one has ever done anything to me in my life that could inspire such enmity. I simply think the world would be a better place if animal abusers were dead. It really isn't personal. I couldn't equate the mission with professional rivalry, but I never questioned Steve about it. I could have. I felt comfortable that we could talk about anything. But there was also always an uneven balance of power that I chose not to disturb. It suited him to have an acolyte. And, although it would take years before I would realize it, it served my own lifelong void to have an authoritarian male accept me. The relationships I've enjoyed with most men in my life have been either sexual or romantic. It was different with Steve. We shared a deeper connection.

How can you have a war on terrorism when the war itself is terrorism?
-Howard Zinn

Domestic Terrorist Watch-list

Steve had a long-time girlfriend, his one-time student, 30+ years his junior. Theirs was an ongoing saga. I never acknowledged the imbalance of power between them either. I only listened as he told me of their sexual escapades and then basically spoke of her with derision. He had cut off all communication with her for a year while she had someone else's baby. It seemed to me that he used silence as a weapon. She lived on a trust fund and received an allowance of $10,000 a month. Yet she didn't pay his bills or spend as much on him as he thought she should. There were other issues between them to which I was privy, unsolicited as the information was. A paradigm was constructed where Alicia Rodriguez* and I were pitted against one another. Alicia grew to dislike me because of the bond Steve and I shared. She resented me. In turn, I disliked her because Steve would relay to me the endless ways in which she abused him. He would call me the second she would leave his house. He would call me while they were on dates. I felt like he called me at these times because he valued me. I grew to understand that he would call me when he was with Alicia to hurt her.

Steve would call me if he was happy, if he was in distress, he'd call all hours of the night and wake me up, he'd call if he just found some video that he wanted to share with me. One night, Steve accidentally posted a compromising video to his Facebook profile. When I woke up in the morning and saw it, I logged into his profile and deleted it. Then I called to wake him up. Neither of us had any idea how long it was there. But it was a major mistake for something so sensitive to leak out of his private world into the public. It could do irreparable damage to the persona he worked so hard to cultivate. Fortunately, I was able to delete it before too much damage was done.

During one of his and Alicia's off-again periods, Steve began dating a woman named Martha who was his contemporary. I would have to encourage him to get dressed and go out on their occasional dates. When Martha would come over to clean Steve's house, he would take his laptop outside and he and I would be laughing and playing on Skype. He wouldn't even look at her when she was at his home. There was a procession of meaningless, transitory women in Steve's life. I was the only constant along with Alicia who came and went. It was more than tedious to deal with the verbal spats they had on a regular basis, followed by the incessant email exchanges and texts. I felt privileged that Steve would share Alicia's messages with me, but I had zero interest in their toxic association. It rattled me the first time Steve shared others' private emails with me. This behavior, however, became normalized in the context of our friendship and was indicative of our shared trust. It never occurred to me that he shared my private emails to him with others.

In the summer of 2010 and again in the summer of 2011, I spent four weeks at his house taking care of his cats while he was in Europe speaking. I was happy to leave Florida and spend time with Steve before he flew off to Europe. And since Alicia wouldn't housesit, I assumed the responsibility. On my first trip across the country, I discovered that I had been placed on Homeland Security's Domestic Terrorist Watchlist.

My boarding pass dated June 17, 2010 was designated *SSSS* for Second Security Screening Selection. This allegedly-random stamp is routinely found on the boarding passes of Muslim Americans as well as animal and environmental activists. I was pulled out of the security line at Orlando International Airport and taken to an area where they ran a complete background check. They examined every item in my luggage, swabbing them for nitrates or bomb residue. I was physically scanned and my hands were also swabbed. After about an hour, I was finally allowed to board my plane. In the air, I logged onto my computer and sent an encrypted message to a colleague with the subject line *Emergency*. I told him what had happened and that I was afraid they were going to confiscate my luggage. I would be stranded for a month with no clothing or personal belongings. He wrote back immediately and told me everything was going to be fine, that they weren't going to take my property. Then he said "you must be doing something right. They only do that to me on international flights." I was relieved. From that day, every boarding pass issued to me has been stamped with SSSS.

A month before I was scheduled to fly out the following year, I was on a date one afternoon and saw animals imprisoned in a tourist spot, kept in a filthy tiny pool, and others who were being used to take pictures with tourists. I could not leave the state without freeing them first. One Sunday afternoon when the business was closed, a colleague and I wandered in as if we were lost tourists. We had a driver drop us off. With adrenaline pumping, we wandered until we were out of sight of the cameras. Then we took out our bolt cutters and started cutting open cages. We freed five animals that day and waited from a safe spot while we watched them make their way back to their home in the ocean. I texted the code word to our driver. Committed to our roles, we wandered back out snapping pictures of the scenery until our ride arrived and we all drove away. Two days later, the anonymous liberation was posted and being hailed all over the internet. It was an amazing feeling. I had joined the ALF. The next day I flew out to New Mexico.

51

Everyone sees what you appear to be, few experience what you really are. -Niccolo Machiavelli

Behind the Scenes

During the winter between house-sitting in New Mexico in 2010 and 2011, Steve received a series of three anonymous emails disparaging him, Alicia, and even me. They appeared to come from a dummy email out of Russia. At the time, I knew nothing about VPNs, proxies, the dark net and didn't understand how it was accomplished. The author was clearly someone close and knew very personal details about the three of us. Given what I now know about how no one's privacy was sacred, the list of individuals who knew intimate details about Alicia or me is unlimited. But those emails were angry and I thought they were written by someone who was hurt and confused. Steve thought they were meant to break up him and Alicia. I remain unconvinced of that. On other days he would accuse Alicia of having authored them. I am uncertain about his rationale.

I believe they were written by one of his conquests, a victim who he seduced, discarded, and hurt deeply. But the weeks and months of listening to him obsess about the author and the author's intent was mind-numbing. At one point he made Alicia and me talk to one another on the phone; he used to joke that the three of us were in this relationship. I was abrupt with her and

52

annoyed, more so because I was engrossed in my work and didn't appreciate the distraction. In the preceding months, I had found my calling fighting against vivisection and my free time became scarce. Interestingly, I would find out in the next few years that Steve Best remained obsessed with these anonymous emails. In 2012 he named *me* in court papers as having authored them!

At the time he received them, however, I had no compunction about being his *wing man* and helping him find available and, from my perspective, hopefully-compatible, women in our movement. I had yet to identify them as his victims. As he began focusing on my friends and I realized he was just using them for sex, for bragging rights, I became something of a *cock blocker*. I believe that when I began to object to him going after certain women that he interpreted this as jealousy. Between the anonymous emails and my objections to him victimizing my friends, Steve Best began to convince himself that I was developing a *fatal attraction* to him... just like his former *best friend*.

I found his sexual proclivities a little disturbing; nonetheless, I enjoyed that we shared everything. As my marriage broke apart and divorce papers were on the table, I was openly dating. I never lied to Mike. Even though we'd grown apart, he's been my friend since I was a teenager. I was dating and Steve was still serial cheating on Alicia. And I earnestly hoped he would find someone who would make him happy. He was in a hotel in New York with a woman who was a friend of mine at the time. Alice* and I worked together on many occasions and our association was important. She passed out in her lingerie. He texted me a picture that should have bothered me a lot more than it did. Alice had been the victim of a sexual sadist at one point and did not want to bare her breasts. The situation became emotionally abusive. He described it to me and she described it to me separately; the only difference in the two versions was that he blamed Alice for causing his outburst. She would later claim that he was physically abusive and threw her to the ground. I believe that was an exaggeration. To this day, I still believe that Alice authored the anonymous emails.

At one point, I began seeing a South African man who was

chivalrous, protective, handsome, and had a very exotic accent. I began to develop feelings for Anthony* after a few dates. Steve would call when we were together and chat with him. It made me feel like he was protective over me and I enjoyed that, even though I found it odd that he usually called to discuss Gary Francione. Oh well, just one of his endearing eccentricities. There was a slight problem with Anthony though. On about our third or fourth date he introduced his fetish into the discussion. Although I'm far from a prude, Anthony's fetish turned out to be bestiality. He enjoyed watching women have sex with dogs. And I am the last person in the world with whom you want to have that discussion.

Needless to say, that relationship expired as quickly as it began but not without some disappointment on my part. Until I learned he was a deviant, he seemed like the perfect man. Steve and I each explored various trysts and would share the details with one another, but I simply didn't have the energy to keep up with his dalliances. The competition was fun but it just wasn't that important to me. Sharing our salacious details with one another was the fun part. I began to invent encounters; the more daring and exciting, the better. Actually, all I really did was bring some of my fantasies to life or draw upon my past. It saved me so much time.

I know many things about how my one-time mentor exploited and demeaned Alicia; she is an abused woman. When she finally extricates herself from that situation, she will have enough wreckage with which to contend. I will not compound her abuse by discussing anything of a personal nature that is not essential to this story. I shouldn't have this knowledge anyway. But I also know so many things about several activists, what they did with whom, intimate details, and gossip I had no business knowing. I loved that Steve and I were so close that he would trust me with information he would never tell another soul. I never even entertained a fleeting thought that he would betray me and tell anyone else about my sexual adventures. So, making up stories about one-night stands, gang bangs, negotiating my way out of speeding tickets with cops, whatever came to mind, was easy and fun. And while sometimes he would say "TMI" meaning "too much information," when it came to sexual romps, his mantra was "TMM" or "tell me more." This was a mutual condition. Not one sided. I enjoyed reporting or making up sordid details as much as he enjoyed hearing them. He enjoyed telling me every last detail about his encounters. Neither of us were Puritans. But I had less and less time to be distracted by such frivolity. Steve was my outlet. Even though he officially became my mentor and a Managing Editor of my website early in 2009, he was never able to impart any wisdom or practical direction about how to launch a campaign, what tactics or strategies to employ, or how to be consistent or focused. I learned those with time, effort, and many arrests. Distinct differences developed in our approaches to Animal Liberation.

Steve is a vocal advocate for a school of thought known as intersectionality, a long-standing tradition of egalitarianism among leftists that recognizes commonalities of oppression which cross over all marginalized populations, human and nonhuman. Steve repackaged this theory and called it *Total Liberation*, holding that alliances must be forged between oppressed groups if we are to have a successful revolution of the people against capitalism and the oppressive state. It sounds good in theory and my website promoted this popular crowd-pleasing philosophy while we were colleagues. In fact, as my mentor, Steve once told me that if I did not tout his Total Liberation politics that "you're going down that road alone." This theory, however, does not have any practical application in reality. The human species meets the definition of both a parasite and a virus. We proliferate exponentially, destroying the planet and everything in our path, and we feed off of others. While Animal Liberation will likely not be achieved until we are extinct, I told Steve privately that it is treasonous to divert our precious scarce resources to enriching those who oppress animals. We needed to make our own movement formidable if we want to win the respect of other revolutionaries. I didn't say it publicly, however.

In truth, my mentor had experience with stunts, not strategy. He told me once about jumping up on the counter in Burger King and getting ejected or standing at the corner of a circus with a sign that said "we're sorry, the circus has been canceled today." I still like that tactic, but it will never save a single animal. And he even appeared in a hilarious Penn and Teller video protesting dog food.[6] I totally agree with his message. But the irony of a college professor orchestrating this fairly inane action was not lost on the bombastic comedians.

NIO espoused a zero-tolerance animal abuse philosophy. Theory and philosophy, however, are utterly useless if they cannot translate into practice. I always believed that this is where our combined genius lay. Steve was a brilliant and articulate orator who gave a great deal of legitimacy to our by-any-means-necessary philosophy while I had a vision of small cells of like-minded activists rising up around the globe to confront the purveyors of death. My taglines have long been "the time for civil discourse has expired" and "Animal Liberation will be achieved when the detriments of animal abuse outweigh the benefits." I have yet to deviate from this vision. NIO in the Streets was born in late 2009.

With a solid minimum of 20,000 readers on a very bad day, I became a lightning rod that galvanized activists across continents who were fed up with mainstream civility, deference to the guilty, tolerating apologists, and seeing zero results. I never saw myself as a leader, nor did I seek such responsibility. But in retrospect that is what I became. In Australia, several countries in Europe, Israel, South America, Canada and at home, small cells of activists came together calling themselves "NIO Canada," "NIO Germany," my group was "NIO Florida" and we boasted about 2 dozen other locations. Still in my infancy as a strategist, I tried to effectively focus these resources to the best of my ability. In Germany, they tore down and destroyed tree stands. In Florida and New Jersey, we gained access to slaughterhouses, filmed the murderers, posted their names, pictures, cars, and addresses on NIO. In Arkansas, they sabotaged trappers going into the woods and destroying their equipment. In Canada there were several activists who went into supermarkets and relabeled meat with

---

6   Penn & Teller: Bullshit – PETA (April 1, 2004) http://www.liveleak.com/view?i=6c1_1361968754

truth-in-labeling stickers.

Steve even took to the streets and had Alicia film him confronting a woman and child whose husband allegedly poisoned cats. Steve wanted the video deleted after he was criticized for being a "coward" and bullying a woman. I conceded. But I do not concur with the criticism. If one wants to harm innocent animals I believe they have divested themselves and their families of any right to peace of mind. Period. Steve Best was justified. I wish he had stood his ground.

I was accumulating a wealth of human resources. I was very much a dilettante, however, lacking both depth and focus. And while I was already well-known and hated by animal abusers in general, 2010 would bring me face to face with those who perform cruel experiments on animals.

Revolutionaries do not make revolutions. The revolutionaries are those who know when power is lying in the street and then they can pick it up. -Hannah Arendt

NIO In the Streets

I've always been unapologetic about pushing boundaries and coloring outside of the lines. If the state wants to define the parameters within which we may act, thereby keeping the abusers safe and rendering activists confined and ineffective, then we have a mandate to open up new frontiers. Along with Steve's characterization of Gary Francione as the worst thing to happen to our movement, I've had detractors from way back in 2009 assigning to me the same label. I still am unsure whether I am more hated by animal abusers or moderate vegans. Some individuals legitimately challenged my tactics, but they were a scarce minority. It would take me a while to realize that my critics were largely composed of those who viewed me as their competition. I was no one's competition. Practically speaking, the only factions within my own community with which I have ever concerned myself are the actors that are focused, committed, and willing to escalate effective action to achieve Animal Liberation... my friends and colleagues. And NIO became our own community.

In late 2009, I received a message from Gabby* who was leading a campaign against a puppy store in South Florida. The abusers down there hated her as much as the rest of them hated me. They had begun to harass her young daughter. She asked me to identify them on NIO so our community could return the favor. We published the pictures, addresses, and contact info for these integrity-deficient individuals who were exploiting animals as well as targeting a young vegan girl. We called for our colleagues to feel free to contact them with their thoughts. That was the beginning of a valued friendship. Twenty years my junior, I considered Gabby a sister. We thought alike. We conducted our campaigns alike. We believed that if we weren't going to confront the guilty, then we may as well stay home. We each had a lot of confidence, were very independent women, and had big personalities. Once we came together the abusers took notice.

We were contacted separately by activists who were distressed by the condition of sick birds being sold in a store in South Florida. Everyone who had tried to intervene was intimidated by the loud, overbearing individuals inside Bills Birds. Everyone, but Gabby and me. I drove down one weekend to do surveillance. I took some pictures inside the store and was accosted by one of the owners who tried to take my camera. Gabby jumped to my defense. A yelling match ensued. Then a huge, filthy-looking man blocked our exit at the same time a female, I thought she might be the large man's mother, was trying to throw us out of the store. Undeterred, we turned our attention to him. They called the police. Gabby's friend John* was with us. An intelligent man whose conversation I valued, he was mortified. Outside the store, John distanced himself from us and sat with his face half covered in the background. It still makes me laugh to think about this episode. The police came. Gabby and I received our first Animal Enterprise Terrorist Act warnings for disturbing an enterprise that profits from animal exploitation. We were trespassed and immediately posted everything on NIO, calling for a protest.

Bills Birds realized that we were not intimidated and were

prepared to battle it out in the court of public opinion. This was a fight they did not want and they conceded. While we didn't actually shut down the store (and it was neither of our intentions to devote the time and energy to a sustained presence there), we did arrange to have an activist visit once a week to make sure the birds were fed and received proper veterinary care. We also negotiated to have this shop become a vehicle to re-home rescued birds, making them available for adoption. This was a small victory.

NIO was no longer a blog. It was becoming a weapon. In another situation, I was contacted about horses that were being starved on a farm in Florida and the authorities did nothing. (I don't recall whether it was animal control or the ASPCA at issue.) I published pictures of the horses, the woman who was starving them, her contact info and, this time, I published info about the individuals who were allowing it to happen. I was contacted the same day by the director of the agency in question who told me she was unaware of the situation and promised to make sure the horses were cared for. Allowing me to report on the progress of the investigation daily, I was relieved that within days the horses were removed and the woman was going to be prosecuted. I repeatedly posted info about individuals who were chaining their dogs up outside, suspected of dogfighting, or any other variety of abuses. In most situations, by taking matters into our own hands, activists were able to rescue the animals and exact our own brand of justice. Abusers are cowards. We see it over and over again. When exposed and confronted, they either take a gun and shoot you or they run for cover.

In early 2010, Mercy for Animals (MFA), an animal welfare organization, released undercover video from inside Conklin Dairy Farms in Union County, Ohio.[7] The video showed the owner, Gary Conklin, punching, kicking and beating cows. But it was a farm worker named Billy Joe Gregg who was seen kicking and stabbing calves, cinching cows to metal bars through their noses to restrain them while he beat them over the head

---

7   Mercy for Animals, "Ohio Dairy Farm Brutality," http://ohdairy.
mercyforanimals.org/

with crowbars and other tools; the sadism that Gregg, who was to become a police officer, inflicted upon his victims was gut-wrenching to watch. It was sickening. Petitions and angry chatter permeated my universe. MFA collected donations. NIO was prepared to be a bit more proactive.

Gary Yourofsky is a vegan educator and a celebrity within our community. His lectures convert thousands to veganism annually. In the '90s, he was arrested 13 times for acts of civil disobedience in the furtherance of Animal Liberation and labeled an *international terrorist*. He is banned from entering 5 countries and is considered controversial by some. He and Steve had a long-standing association and, through him, I met Gary when he lectured in Florida in 2009.

Gary allowed me to use NIO to call for an action he led against the Conklin Dairy Farm:

> *"I am asking everyone who cares about justice and injustice to bring bolt cutters, bats, crowbars, pitchforks, hammers and wrenches to help destroy every piece of equipment the farm has and tear down the sheds."*

My friends, Alice and Jennifer*, accompanied Gary and his wife on May 31, 2010 as activists descended upon Union County. One-hundred fifty officers in riot gear and with tanks ready greeted them. The town spent $50,000 to protect the abusers that day.[8] The police presence assured that no property damage was possible and no animals would be liberated. Undeterred, Alice was able to sneak onto the property and gain some more footage. This was a small victory for revolutionary action. When we are able to instill the fear of god in abusers, it's a good day. When we stand up and take the fight to their doorsteps, it's a good day. When activists are willing to lay down in front of slaughter trucks, defy injunctions, court orders, get arrested, or do whatever it takes, it's a good day. My only regret about this action was that I was

---

8   WBNS-10TV News, "Dairy Farm Protest Prompts Massive Police Presence," (May 31, 2010) http://www.10tv.com/live/content/local/stories/2010/05/31/story-plain-city-dairy-farm-protest.html

unable to be there. I was allowed, however, to report live on NIO and Facebook as events transpired.

Alice and Jennifer had each started their own NIO In the Streets cells in their communities in Toronto and New Jersey, respectively. And the three of us became close. We shared a vision and ideology. We understood that Billy Joe Gregg was only a symptom and by no means an isolated actor; the same atrocities take place at every single industrial farm and lab across the country. Alice, Jennifer, and I understood that the real problem was the dairy industry itself.

Consider that a loving caregiver can occasionally get overwhelmed and frustrated by the responsibilities of parenthood caring for their own human or nonhuman children. Now consider what kind of individuals take low-paying jobs in slaughter houses. These are not the most well-adjusted specimens society has to offer. They are largely drug addicts, the uneducated or intellectually-challenged, they are violent felons who cannot find employment along traditional avenues.

The people with whom we entrust the most innocent and helpless are the most desperate, easily frustrated and overwhelmed, sadistic, and violent. This is why we see cows, chickens, pigs, turkeys, and every other commodified animal being raped, beaten, burned, dragged, punched, kicked and unspeakably mutilated during the normal course of any given day whenever an undercover video is smuggled out. The workers are burdened by the cries and needs of the sentient beings over whom they simply tend until they're murdered. And they are the sole beneficiaries of their captors' frustrations.

Enslaved animals are given the same care and consideration one would give a footstool. This is why the agricultural industry is trying to pass *Ag-Gag* legislation across the nation. It criminalizes taking pictures inside factory farms. The abuse is endemic. The industry's response is to conceal the horror and put those who expose it behind bars.

Indeed, the courts were quick to exonerate Gary Conklin finding "no probable cause to believe Conklin committed any crime."[9] With little attention or media coverage given to the owner's abuses, we decided that when Gregg went to trial on September 26, 2010 we would put the entire dairy industry on trial in the media. We would all meet up in Ohio and chain ourselves to the courthouse doors so that no one could enter the building on the day Gregg was to be tried. We thought we had everything planned perfectly. Without announcing our intended action, I used my NIO networks to broadcast to thousands of activists that we were going up for the trial and encouraging others to join us. We were hoping that we would have a healthy group of protesters in the background while we handled the interviews and were escorted off to jail. We got a hotel room and made our signs, we bought gray sweatshirts on which we wrote slogans. We bought industrial chains that we hoped would take some time to cut. Then we went and bought some vegan Subway sandwiches and Starbucks coffee.

A day or two before the trial, we took the neon green Beetle that Jennifer rented and we drove out to Gary Conklin's home. We took pictures of his estate, his mailbox, how it was situated, we took a picture of him in the doorway, and we gathered other information that would be useful to publish on NIO. As we entered the highway to drive back to the hotel, we drove by a road block. All of a sudden, the flashing lights and sirens glared and we were being pursued by two police vehicles. A little stunned, we quickly sent our info to our emails, deleted our images, and pulled over.

I had never been arrested in my life. My only interaction with law enforcement had been over a few speeding tickets. Imagine our surprise. The officers surrounded our vehicle, asked us what we were doing, and told us "it is against the law to take pictures in front of that house." The fact that the police force in Union County mobilized to harass civilians at the behest of Gary Conklin speaks to the money and power agribusiness commands

---

9   This Week Community News, July 10, 2010 (http://www.thisweeknews. com/content/stories/marysville/news/2010/07/10/conklin-cleared-of-abuse-allegations.html)

in their own regions and, collectively, within the composition of the state. They wanted to seize our phones and cameras. There was nothing of value left readily available on our devices and we were able to talk our way out of it and keep our phones. We were relieved that we were not arrested prematurely. We went to survey the courthouse to make sure we knew where we were going and exactly what had to be done.

The morning of Billy Joe Gregg's hearing, we sent out press releases at about 4 am and left our hotel an hour later. Alice and Jennifer dropped me off across the street from the courthouse where I waited with the chains and signs. They dropped the car off at a parking lot where it would be safe if we ended up in jail for a few days. Our hotel was paid so we had a base to which to return when it was over. We had a throwaway cell phone that only had the two phone numbers, Steve's and Gabby's, who would report on events as they happened. In a few minutes, Alice and Jennifer met me and we headed across the street to lock down the courthouse and make a stand for the animals. When we arrived on the doorsteps, we were shocked to see the lights on and a lot of police activity inside the building. In this small little Mayberry-type town, the entire police department had its headquarters inside the courthouse. We were devastated. We actually discussed whether we should go ahead with our plan and ultimately decided that getting 20 years each for taking the police department hostage was not an optimal action.

We tried to pull Plan B out of a hat. We moved over to the steps and chained ourselves to the railing. It was utterly humiliating. When the courthouse opened, people simply walked by us and over us. The cops actually came out to look at us sipping their coffee and went back inside. At one point I dropped my sign. I had to unchain myself, walk down the stairs, pick it up, get back in position, and re-chain myself. We were hoping no media would show up. We were hoping there were no video cameras outside the courthouse that were recording us for a YouTube bloopers reel. We did one embarrassing interview and never read the report for fear our message about the dairy industry would be dwarfed by the ridiculousness of our action. We ultimately unchained ourselves and tried to walk away as inconspicuously as possible. We had failed the animals in a magnificent way! We tried to console one another with encouragement for at least trying. We all followed through and took some solace in our loyalty, but the screams of the cows in our heads that we failed to amplify for the mainstream were deafening.

When we got back to the hotel, we decided we were going to make the most of the time we had left and destroy whatever we could on the night before we flew home. We drove around and surveyed the torture floors of the factory from a distance. We knew where to go. We knew what to do. We waited. We drove out there at midnight after the town was asleep. And the diary was actually operating in the middle of the night. What the fuck!

We drove as close as we could without getting shot by one of the men who stopped abusing his bovine victim to come outside with a shotgun and watch us. We weren't armed. We were three women faced with a death chamber of violent degenerates and their helpless victims in the middle of the night in the middle of nowhere. With no chance left of achieving anything remotely effective, we filmed the operation to publish in the hopes that other activists could use our information. We caused some slight property damage on the periphery of the farm. And we flew home in the morning utterly dejected. We never published an update on our trip and never spoke of it again.

At around the same time the dairy farm video was garnering donations for Mercy for Animals, one revolutionary vegan would take matters into his own hands and demand the world's attention. On April 30, 2010, a fire engulfed a sheepskin factory in Denver, Colorado.[10] The uninsured building was destroyed, the fire having caused $500,000 in damages. On June 5, the Tandy Leather Factory in Salt Lake City, Utah went up in flames causing extensive damage.[11] And on July 3, a restaurant in Sandy,

---

10 ABC News Denver, "Fire Destroys Glendale Sheepskin Factory," (April 30, 2010) http://www.thedenverchannel.com/news/fire-destroys-glendale-sheepskin-factory

11 Biteback Direct Action Info, June 11, 2010 http://www.directaction.info/news_jun11_10.htm

Utah that served foie gras was set ablaze. *Tiburon* incurred approximately $10,000 in damages. An anonymous Animal Liberation Front operative calling himself "The Lone Wolf" claimed responsibility for these actions.[12] With each successive act, the Lone Wolf gained my admiration and respect.

The North American Animal Liberation Office (NAALPO) acts as a media outlet for underground ALF actions, publishing their anonymous communiques. An incarnation of the original press office that formed in the UK in 1991, Steve is credited with having founded NAALPO with Dr. Jerry Vlasak, a former-vivisector-turned-outspoken activist, in 2004. Since becoming an activist, I have never known Steve to make any contribution to NAALPO other than in name. Both veterans, Jerry and Steve shared a long-standing friendship. It is only my suspicion, but, largely due to his drug addiction, Steve was unreliable and inconsistent. I don't believe he possessed the personal discipline necessary to effectively participate in the highly-secure information hub that NAALPO demands.

The press office published the Lone Wolf's final communique on July 5, 2010:[13]

> *"The ALF is watching and there is nowhere to hide. The arson at Sandy, Utah, at Tiburon, was done because of their sales of foie gras and other quote, unquote, wild game. Animals exist for their own intents and purposes, not human ends. Go vegan. -ALF Lone Wolf*

Unbeknownst to him at the time, the FBI had been contacted by an informant on July 1, 2010. For a few measly thousand dollars, a snitch named Trapper Zuelke told the feds that his brother,

---

12 Animal Liberation Frontline, "A.L.F. Takes Credit for Fire at Utah Foie Gras Restaurant" (July 7, 2010) http://animalliberationfrontline.com/alf-takes-credit-for-fire-at-utah-foie-gras-restaurant/

13 North American Animal Liberation Press Office, "Foie Gras Restaurant Burned by ALF Lone Wolf," (July 5, 2010) https://animalliberationpressoffice.org/NAALPO/2010/07/05/foie-gras-restaurant-burned-by-alf-lone-wolf/

Walter Bond, was the Lone Wolf. On July 22, Zuelke arranged a meeting with Bond at a Ramada Inn in Denver that was recorded by the ATF. Interestingly, Trapper Zuelke was a meth addict that Walter had tried to protect in the past. For targeting his brother's drug dealer, he had already served time in prison. Before Zuelke was identified as the informant, another former underground activist, Peter Young reported:[14]

> *"The suspect also served prison time in 1997 for an arson at a meth lab in Iowa. Bond received notoriety when the vegan straight edge band Earth Crisis wrote a song about Bond and the arson titled ' To Ashes ' for their 2009 album 'To The Death.'*

With tribal tattoos covering the right side of his face and the word "vegan" tattooed boldly across his neck, Walter Bond would be arrested as he left the Ramada Inn. I strongly believe that if we celebrate the actions of our underground operatives when they are free, it is our duty to support them in any way we can if and when they are arrested. I rallied our community to support him, write letters, be present at his court appearances going forward, and contribute to his legal fund and commissary. Walter and I became friends while he awaited trial. He related to me that he met Trapper because he was looking forward to spending some time with his sibling as well as his brother's family. Walter was deeply touched that he found the loyalty and trust he needed in his brother. The betrayal cut like a knife. As he left the hotel, he was swarmed by federal agents and thrown to the ground. In his backpack was a copy of *Declaration of War: Killing People to Save Animals* by Screaming Wolf. Walter has been in custody since that day.

NIO in The Streets continued to grow with new cells popping up and monthly events where we would all go out into our own communities. It deeply disturbed me that I had to call for a day of action in order to get activists to leave their computers, but,

14 Peter Young, North American Animal Liberation Press Office, "Breaking News: FBI Makes Arrest in A.L.F. "Lone Wolf" Arsons Informant used in arrest of Walter Bond," July 23, 2010.

if that's what it took, I was glad to provide the direction. I was learning as I went along. Surely there were others more seasoned and accomplished than I. But it seemed to me that while so many in my movement were theorizing, giving speeches, debating, critiquing, and writing books, no one was doing a whole lot of anything for the animals.

Walter and I would talk frequently and he and I co-authored several essays. While we had divergent views about issues like abortion, when it came to Animal Liberation, it is very fair to say that we saw eye to eye. Walter Bond became someone whose ideas, perspectives, and opinions I grew to value. He once told me to not do anything to get myself arrested because mine was a voice that the animals needed. Maybe I understand better what he meant now that I've been momentarily silenced.

Steve and I never made a move without consulting one another. At least in name, he was my mentor; more importantly, he was my friend and was probably the only person who knew the whole story of the Conklin Dairy Farm disaster. He was very supportive. He told me that most activists never even leave their homes, let alone take it upon themselves to take the struggle to the abusers' doorsteps. This is something on which we wholeheartedly agreed. Steve was the academic, I was the actor. I was abundantly fortunate to have the counsel of Steve in one ear and Walter in the other. We all believed that the time for civil discourse had long expired.

With Walter, however, I felt I shared something unique, but also elusive and intangible; an understanding. I always acknowledged that it was easy for me to remain defiant and non-negotiable from my sofa. Steve, on the other hand, had no equivocation about using the most militant of rhetoric from his armchair. I slowly began to challenge Steve to live up to his words if he believed them. We both advocated "bringing the fight to the abusers' doorsteps." We both advocated civil disobedience. Steve would make YouTube videos where he quoted Martin Luther King, Jr.'s words: "we will fill the jails with singing children." He seemed oblivious to the fact that Dr. King led the way to those cells. I enjoyed having Steve's arguments lend legitimacy to my actions. But I was becoming fairly insistent that he needed to begin to practice what he preached.

Walter, on the other hand, had already taken revolutionary action for the animals. And I continued to push every boundary I hit. Throughout the world, anonymous actors liberated animals from confinement, damaged slaughterhouses and fur farms, targeted vivisectors, whether by blowing up their cars or sending them razor blades in the mail, and, occasionally, physically attacking a deserving abuser. The fringes of my movement were teeming with dedicated activists. I remain proud to be a part of it.

Atrocities are not less atrocities when they occur in laboratories and are called medical research. -George Bernard Shaw

The University of Florida

Michael Budkie founded an anti-vivisection welfare organization called Stop Animal Experimentation Now (SAEN) in the 1990s. In the summer of 2010, the veteran activist came to Gainesville to lecture at the University of Florida. Vivisection comes from the Latin words *vivus* which means "alive" and *sectio* which means "cutting." A vivisector is one who cuts up live animals, either human or nonhuman, and subjects them to cruel experiments. The term is generally understood to describe anyone who uses live animals in research. Josef Mengele was a vivisector. James David Jentsch, Donal O'Leary, and Raymond Joseph Bergeron are vivisectors too.

From the first video I saw on YouTube, ending the nightmare became my mission. Vivisectors in the University of Pennsylvania filmed themselves laughing while they beat the brains out of baboons with hydraulic devices and flicked cigarette butts on their victims. Like something out of a demented horror movie, they laughed about PETA as they surveyed their beaten, battered, and bleeding brain-damaged victims. That was in 1984. Animal

Liberation Front activists broke into the labs and found the recording. While not involved in the break-in, Gary Francione is credited with having run with that footage to make sure it got to PETA who ultimately published it. That video is now a four-part YouTube series called *An Unnecessary Fuss*.[15]

Chillingly unimaginable, however, I was to rapidly learn that these University of Pennsylvania researchers were not unique. On April 29, 1985, the ALF broke into the labs at the University of California, Riverside. A monkey named Britches was liberated along with 700 animals that were enduring experiments funded by taxpayers.[16] A UC vivisector removed the baby monkey from his mother and put him in an isolation tank within days of his birth. Britches' eyelids were crudely sewn shut and an object was affixed to his head that emitted loud high-pitched sonar sounds. When the ALF took the little macaque into their arms, he trembled and shook uncontrollably. This experiment was alleged to produce information about blindness in children. Of course, no one was ever supposed to see the actual experiment. After an eight-month investigation conducted by the vivisection complex itself, crudely sewing Britches eyelids together with a needle and thread as well as putting the sonar device in place to drive the little monkey mad were found to be "appropriate."[17] No corrective action was taken. The experiment was found to be in full compliance with federal animal *welfare* standards. Britches was ultimately placed in a sanctuary by his anonymous liberators where he lived out his life. From time to time, I still watch the images of this little individual enjoying the freedom and joy he so deserved.

The only thing that has changed since the 1980s is that it has become almost impossible to penetrate underground, windowless labs that are now protected by cameras and security alarms. In

---

15 YouTube, "An Unnecessary Fuss" (1984) https://www.youtube.com/watch?v=-MbqYLOJBdI

16 YouTube, "Britches – Baby Monkey Rescued from Vivisection Lab" (1985) https://www.youtube.com/watch?v=zd95gVyFo5U

17 Wikipedia, "University of California, Riverside 1985 laboratory raid," https://en.wikipedia.org/wiki/University_of_California,_Riverside_1985_laboratory_raid

addition, through the American Legislative Exchange Council (ALEC), the industry crafted a convenient piece of legislation called the Animal Enterprise Terrorism Act (AETA) which passed through Congress in 2006. ALEC is a non-profit organization composed of corporations and elected legislators who work to maximize profits for its members; it embodies Mussolini's definition of fascism – the marriage of corporations and the state. The AETA designates the ALF as *terrorists*. In fact, the language of the bill says that anyone who affects the profits of an animal enterprise can be tried as a terrorist. Therefore, I am a terrorist. Every effective animal activist in the United States is a terrorist. Anyone who wants to save an animal from the grip of a sadist who profits from harming his or her victim is a terrorist. Oh, and the sadist in this equation has the full authority of the federal government to prosecute anyone who tries to stop him or her.

In conjunction with the federal government, states are quick to protect animal abusers and criminalize dissent as well. This is because our laws exist to protect profits, not life. Take, for example, the notorious UCLA researcher, James David Jentsch; he has been addicting monkeys to methamphetamine and other street drugs for decades.[18] Monkeys do not become schizophrenic as human beings experience the illness. But with his mad-scientist, tattooed-on eyebrows, Jentsch is accomplished at driving these innocent beings insane until they mimic what schizophrenia looks like in humans. His work has earned him millions of dollars in taxpayer-funded grants and has yielded nothing other than papers boasting his name, accolades from his abhorrent community, and a succession of security-alarmed mansions. Jentsch earned himself a target on his back long before I came along. In 2009, some progressive activists firebombed his car. Sadly, Jentsch was not in it when it blew up.

The protests and home demos by colleagues in California were consistent. In an effort to escape, in 2010 Jentsch quietly moved to

---

18 Progress for Science, "David Jentsch: Turning monkeys, rodents into drug addicts," (June 23, 2012) http://progressforscience.com/david-jentsch/

a new mansion with no media coverage whatsoever. A colleague embedded in a university on the east coast had a line into the vivisectors' cesspool. From coast to coast, these individuals conduct themselves like a single psychotic organism – the move was a well-guarded secret. My associate passed Jentsch's new address along to me. I was able to secure pictures of his security gate and did a blockbuster post announcing Jentsch's covert move, complete with his address, pictures of his home, and instructions on how to disarm his alarmed gate. Within 24 hours, Jentsch's security and peace of mind were a distant memory. Thousands of activists shared the information all over social media and left their thoughts on his site. The home demonstrations immediately moved to his new address. We emailed him. I never threatened him. I did, however, wish him a "very hot housewarming." Days later I was served with my first restraining order in Florida. It was out of California. It prevented me from contacting the mad scientist directly. Even though I had never set foot on the UCLA campus, I was banned from there as well. Jentsch's restraining order would stay in effect until October of 2013.

I have PTSD from some of the nightmarish experimentation videos I forced myself to watch. Puppies being beaten if they wouldn't accept the poison they were being fed, a dog who was restrained in a chair and fed alcohol until his stomach became swollen and distended, monkeys being restrained and having their skull caps removed, being blinded, having electrodes placed in their brains, animals having limbs sawed off, being starved, dehydrated, and then resuscitated... only to continue the lucrative horror. This is all happening in the United States at this very moment. Taxpayers fund it almost exclusively. One clip that haunts me, however, was out of Israel. A vivisector was in the lab with her monkey victim. He had a metal box implanted in his head, presumably to monitor his brain activity as painful stimuli was introduced. With his arms restrained, he tried in vain to swat at the object in his head. When the woman was finished torturing him and measuring his responses, she put him in a dark box with no food or water, left him alone in his pain and misery, and went home for the weekend.

The University of Florida

That scene epitomizes the plight of these doomed beings. Was the best part of his life when he had the companionship of his tormentor, or was the best part of his life when he was left alone in his dark prison, in isolation and distress? There is no other aspect to an animal's life in a lab. I was nothing if not determined to stop this cruelty. I always loved horror movies. My favorites were the original *Texas Chainsaw Massacre* and the first *Hostel*. I cannot even look at this genre anymore. The gore that once gave me a cheap thrill now horrifies me. It's not fantasy. The reality of vivisection labs makes horror movies seem like scathing jokes.

I was excited to meet Michael when he arrived in Florida and he was welcoming in greeting me at his lecture. He invited me to hold the SAEN banner at the protest the following day. After the protest I was invited to learn more about the animal experimentation industry inside UF at *Jungle Friends*, a local primate sanctuary. A few of the monkeys there were released by UF vivisectors with the stipulation that they never speak publicly about their history in the labs. One of the individuals at this meeting who gave a presentation had been a lab tech while he finished his college career. He never released the images he showed us that day for publication, but inside UF's labs were every species imaginable, from horses to alligators to dogs to lambs to sheep to monkeys to species of which I never heard. All were enduring grueling experiments which enriched the university with hundreds of millions of federal grants dollars annually. We learned about sheep being subjected to the same experiment for 20 years with absolutely nothing to show for them except profit. A few babies were born accidentally within the confines of this study that year and had to be quickly murdered before anyone saw their deformed bodies or learned of their existence. Animals were being blinded, starved, and routinely maimed.

Harrowing as they all were, the most heartbreaking first-hand account was about a macaque monkey named Louis. Louis had stopped eating, was steadily deteriorating for a year, he was sick, he was in obvious pain, and he was diagnosed as being anorexic from the mental and physical stress. Deprived of every natural inclination – grass, fresh air, friends, exercise, stimulation – all animals negotiate madness in a bare barren cage. A lab tech named Bob* begged and pleaded with UF to release Louis to the sanctuary. The sanctuary pleaded with UF to release Louis. He was far too sick to be experimented on so he was only languishing in despair and misery. But his little body was far too deteriorated and would create a public relations problem were UF to release him. Bob returned to school from a vacation break to learn that Louis had been murdered and incinerated in his absence. That weekend, the atrocities taking place an hour and change from my home came to life.

At his lecture the previous evening, Michael explained that they were conducting brain mapping experiments on monkeys inside the University of Florida. The National Institutes of Health (NIH) was granting a researcher named Ming Zhou Ding hundreds of thousands of tax dollars to saw off monkeys' skull caps and plant electrodes in their brains. Typically, the subject of brain mapping will be restrained, deprived of food and water to make him or her more compliant, then introduced to painful stimuli and/or mutilated to measure brain responses. I had no idea that vivisection was thriving in my own community. That night I spoke with Michael and I took it upon myself to start a community-based initiative. I protested with SAEN that Saturday and met Lisa Grossman who would become my partner in NIO Florida's campaign at UF.

I went home and tried to figure out where to begin. The University of Florida had a pristine reputation. When I Googled them, other than the singing serial murderer, Danny Rolling, who had made UF his playground in 1990, I could find nothing even remotely damaging. An occasional article appeared in the Gainesville Sun about a welfare violation filed by SAEN, but the reader was allowed to believe that the violation was an aberration and the balance of animals were happy and healthy; the truth was confined inside this tomb of higher education. Lisa and I made fliers. I used my website to publish our information, and we went into Gainesville to begin protesting and going door to door around Ding's home. We found his address in the property appraiser's records. I was fairly well-known by this time, my website was notorious, and I was already tracked routinely on my site by the Florida Department of Law Enforcement (FDLE) and the Federal Bureau of Investigation (FBI). When I moved into the streets in Florida in a meaningful way, the radio and print media took notice. From the beginning, Lisa felt overshadowed.

I had a phobia about public speaking and the last thing I wanted was to go into the mainstream. I asked Jason Miller if he would do the interviews for me. I asked Steve to do them. They told me that if I was going to be a voice for the animals that speaking in the media was an integral part of it. I stepped out of my comfort zone and engaged anyone, any media outlet, any investigative reporter, anyone who wanted to challenge my philosophy or tactics. On my first radio show, I was asked why I was intent on personally confronting Ding and other vivisectors when it wasn't personal to them. And my response was that "it's very personal to the animals they torture." And then the first print article about our campaign came out in the Sun quoting me discussing Ming Zhou Ding.[19] The article implied that I didn't know what I was talking about. There were no brain-mapping experiments happening inside the University of Florida. I felt foolish. Their spokespeople insisted Ding was only accessing public information. The opportunity to begin to paint me as a terrorist, a stalker, and a criminal as demonstrated by Jentsch's restraining order was not forgone. An article rarely appeared about me that didn't mention Jentsch, his car being blown up, and my restraining order, as if they were somehow connected. My position quickly became and still is that if they're getting money to perform these experiments, then they are equally, if not more, guilty than the butcher who is directed to take his knife to a live sentient animal. But I really didn't understand.

Michael Budkie was nowhere to be found and didn't answer my emails. I accept that this was an amateur mistake on my part. What was Budkie's excuse? I checked the NIH Reporter that maintains a database of all of the federal grants awarded for

---

19 Nathan Crabbe, "Activists Mount Protests of UF Researcher," The Gainesville Sun, October 8, 2010 http://www.gainesville.com/news/20101008/animal-activists-mount-protests-of-uf-researcher

vivisection. According to this government database, Ming Zhou Ding was awarded $259,528 that year under Project Number 5R01MH079388-04. In fact, the database indicated that he had collected exactly $1,297,418 since 2007 to perform neurological animal experiments inside the University of Florida.[20] I filed my first public records request to take possession of the university's data about these experiments. I had to figure out for myself what was going on; and the battle began. Eventually, through painstaking research, I discovered that the actual brain-mapping experiments were conducted in New York and Ding was getting hundreds of thousands of dollars annually to simply access the public data. In order to get this information disseminated outside my community, I began circulating articles in alternate news media.[21] I never learned exactly how many institutions may be enriched redundantly at taxpayer expense from any single experiment; but I was hoping that even if one was not inclined to care about an animal suffering, s/he might have a stronger response to being defrauded via taxation.

Since Michael Budkie had been privy to all the public records for all the monkeys in the labs all along, he had to have known the experiments were not happening inside UF. But sharing his records with me was not part of the deal. Unlike Budkie who has a relationship with vivisectors and only focuses on violations of federal welfare laws, I couldn't care less about their regulations. And we all knew it. So UF refused to give me access to their public records. Budkie was not pleased with this situation because I think he foresaw it becoming more difficult for him to gain access to the public information. In addition to sustaining his donation base, the welfare violations he publicizes also serve to promote the idea that these incidents are isolated events and that the balance of animals in labs are well-cared for. While nothing could be further from the truth, it was clear to me that Michael

20 National Institutes of Health Reporter, Research Portfolio Online Reporting Tools (https://projectreporter.nih.gov/project_info_history.cfm?aid=7905763&icde=30600662)
21 Camille Marino, "The Science of Public Deception," Dissident Voice (November 27, 2010) http://dissidentvoice.org/2010/11/the-science-of-public-deception/

The University of Florida

Budkie and the vivisectors shared something of a symbiotic relationship, each perpetuating the other. I fell outside of their paradigm. I was stuck.

We kept protesting. If there was an alumni event or a football game, Lisa and I were there. When the church right off campus held services on Sundays, we were there with bullhorns and protesters. At Christmas when stores throughout Gainesville were setting up trees and ornaments in their displays, we would replace the ornaments on the trees with fliers about the monkeys. We once found an empty table at the mall where Goodwill seemed to have gone home. We co-opted the space, set up our posters and had people come over to the table to sign our petition. I've always used petitions solely as a vehicle to educate and involve the community. Otherwise, I maintain that they are wholly useless. On many occasions with only the two of us, Lisa and I went door to door to get signatures or simply to talk to people about their vivisector neighbors. We never missed an opportunity to tell them to keep an eye on their dogs.

Michael and I maintained a working relationship at arm's length. When he would focus on a university in a given area and needed protesters, he would write me to connect him with my NIO in the Streets activists in that region. I was glad to do it. I believed there was strength in unity. Budkie explained to me that he couldn't have a public affiliation with me because I was too confrontational and controversial; he needed to maintain a mainstream respectability. Steve told me Budkie was using me. I didn't care as long as we supported each other's efforts. I was a little taken aback when he contacted me one day to ask me how many hits NIO got daily; he was concerned because he was losing supporters. Steve told me that Budkie saw me as his competition. It made no sense to me. I told Michael I was getting between 20,000 and 40,000 hits a day and I told him how to use Facebook to maximize his exposure when he published material.

I was advised in mid-December of 2010 that the response to my records request was ready and I could pick it up at the UF Police Department. Lisa and I had bought tickets to a Christmas Gala for alumni at which our colleagues would stage a small demo outside while we mingled with UF's benefactors. On December 19, 2010 we picked up my package from the UFPD before we went to the party. Inside the envelope, my $566 check was returned to me. The University of Florida refused to honor my request and I didn't know how I was going to overcome this.

We went forward that night. At the gala, not a single guest, police included, left there without getting a comprehensive lecture about the animals inside UF; each received one of Lisa's elegantly-crafted *party favors* which contained the same information. We were ejected from the celebration and trespassed from stepping on campus property for the next three years. Our pictures were disseminated to students and faculty advising them that if they saw either of us to not engage us but to call campus police immediately. We were "dangerous." Public Affairs Director Janine Sykes sent out a letter to her Gator Clubs and other benefactors classifying us as criminals, advising that any communications with us be reported to campus police, and, obviously, discussing my restraining order from Jentsch.

While our detractors were quick to criticize us for being trespassed from the institution, we were only just beginning to put the prestigious university in full damage control mode. Our protests continued at the vivisectors' homes and at their churches, but I didn't feel like we had any substance. The toxic association between Lisa and me evolved and was becoming abusive. When I saw emails come in with her name, I would tense; I never knew what I did or said or posted that would irritate her. On my way to meet her for a protest in Gainesville one afternoon, I found a dog stranded on the highway. It took me some time to coax him into my car and I was going to be a little late. I decided to bring him to the protest for a couple of hours and then find his family when I got back home. She started screaming in the phone telling me to surrender the lost dog to animal control. When I wouldn't do it, she said it was totally irresponsible to bring a dog to protest in the hot sun. When I told her to "go fuck yourself" and turned my car around to head home, she said there never was a dog; that I was simply making up excuses to not show up. I could feel her contempt and animosity more and more. I wondered how delusional she must be to imagine that I needed to invent excuses for her benefit. I was relieved when I returned the little dog to his family.

I know Lisa had self-image and control issues. I tried my best to not exacerbate her vulnerabilities. And she had a talent for things like finding venues for demos and creating our propaganda. I was the writer and strategist. And where I tried to encourage her in the areas in which she excelled, there was always an underlying current of her trying to tear me down. Nonetheless, I believed the mission was far more important than the friction with which I had to contend.

Then a vivisection student contacted Gabby one day and Gabby contacted me. After a night of re-*education* by our combined contingents in Florida – emails, intimidation by some, education by others – Alena Rodriguez denounced vivisection and issued a public apology on NIO the following day:

Alena Rodriguez – March 23, 2011

> *"This is my public announcement denouncing animal testing and my involvement in it. I haven't really even started any animal research and after reading all of the information and watching the videos you have all sent me, I have had my eyes opened. I was truly unaware of these horrible things going on to animals behind closed doors. I love animals with all my heart and I would never do anything to harm them. I apologize for my original message to Gabby, and I'm sincerely apologetic. Please accept my apology and I wish you all luck in your crusade against Scripps. I will be looking for other career choices. Thank you."*

Clearly a weak link in the chain had been identified. The vivisector blogs polluted the cybersphere with reports about me being an "abuser"[22] and about our "Soviet-style"[23] tactics. I took this small victory and ran with it. It was clear to me that while we couldn't penetrate the fortified dungeons of the vivisectors themselves, student vivisectors were soft targets. And I went on my merry way offering rewards to the student body for information on fellow students performing animal experiments. I showed them no deference. Their names, addresses, and images were posted on NIO.

Much to the industrial abusers' dismay, several NIO in the Streets groups followed suit. NIO Michigan took on a parallel campaign. NIO New York and NIO Florida went out in tandem to "Welcome [students] to Your New Curriculum." We infiltrated several universities' sciences buildings, orientation events, and any festivities we could find. Inside administration buildings where jobs were posted, we replaced their announcements with our reward fliers. We took all of the newspapers out of their dispensaries, inserted our money-making opportunity, and returned the newspapers for their early-morning readers. In a private email from a colleague, I learned that three vivisection students at UCLA had reconsidered their career paths. With vivisectors' cars being blown up and now students being publicly identified, some determined that the detriments of a career in animal abuse were beginning to outweigh the benefits. And I know of one other student at UF whose plans were permanently derailed. This was success. This was victory!

I believed Steve had a responsibility to confront animal experimentation inside his own university but, of course, I never challenged him. At least he was my biggest supporter.

---

22 Janet D. Stemwedel, "On the targeting of undergraduates by animal rights extremists (and the dangers of victim-blaming," Adventures in Ethics and Science, (March 30, 2011) http://ethicsandscience.scientopia. org/2011/03/30/on-the-targeting-of-undergraduates-by-animal-rights-extremists-and-the-dangers-of-victim-blaiming/

23 Orac, "Animal rights terrorists target students as the 'soft underbelly of the vivisection movement,'" Respectful Insolence (March 30, 2011) http://scienceblogs.com/insolence/2011/03/30/animal-rights-terrorists-target-students/

When I published several articles identifying student vivisectors as soft targets, he edited in rhetoric about running through the administration building rioting. I believed his rhetoric on my campaign announcements was an expression of his own feelings about his own university and entirely irrelevant. But it made Steve happy to have it published and I was glad I had a platform to oblige.

Steve was preparing to write a chapter in his book-in-progress about my *war on students*. He even used his PayPal account to secure donations for NIO Florida's campaign. The vivisectors had a field day[24] when they figured out we were doing this. He panicked. We removed any reference to him from NIO to protect him. I was genuinely grateful for his counsel considering the fact that I came under attack from vivisectors and educational institutions around the world for simply stating the obvious: student vivisectors should face the same consequences as their professional counterparts. Having gained the attention of threat assessment outfits, Jacquie Calnan, president of a vivisection lobby group called *Americans for Medical Progress (AMP)* denounced me an "evil genius"[25] in one of their Security Management alerts. I had it on good authority from inside Florida Atlantic University (FAU) that there were top level meetings with the heads of various institutions to figure out how to stop me. Infiltrators always being an issue in any political movement, my colleagues in South Florida were approached by agents and told that they weren't interested in harassing them; they were interested in stopping a "higher up with international connections." We assumed they were referring to me.

As was becoming standard, in conjunction with the outcry from

---

24 Speaking of Research, "Best of Friends: University of Texas Professor helps to fund Extremism," (December 20, 2011) https://speakingofresearch.com/2011/12/20/best-of-friends-university-of-texas-professor-helps-to-fund-extremism/

25 Matthew Marwood, "Animal Rights Extremists Target Medical Students," Security Management (November 2, 2011) https://sm.asisonline.org/Pages/animal-rights-extremists-target-medical-students-009208.aspx

animal abusers, the backlash from the moderates in my own community was deafening. I was summarily denounced by vegans and student activists. The not-for-profit anti-vivisection groups who haven't made a dent in the vivisection industry over the last 100 years apparently figured out that I was bad for their business as well. And since the animals don't care whether it's an amateur or professional carving them up, I don't either. It still makes absolutely no sense to me that anyone would concern themselves with such arbitrary distinctions. Disgusted by the backlash from vegans whose only form of *activism* is eating, Steve came to my defense in UF's student newspaper.[26] His contempt was palpable:

> *"Utterly enfeebled in spirit and creativity, the only 'activism' that potluck passifists [sic] can undertake is to attack those who grasp the urgency of planetary crisis, to malign (in the discourse, no less, of the corporate-state complex) someone who stopped baking cookies and started cooking up resistance; a woman (Camille) who possesses the courage and vision to elevate this war against life to something other than a tea party and parlor game."*

Lisa was soft about how we should approach students, wanting to coddle and educate them. And with no support outside of Steve and a few other progressive thinkers who encouraged me, I moved on.

In 2011, the Sierra Club made headlines when they sued UF for failing to disclose public records about their agriculture programs. And there it was. The answer I knew was out there. I called the Sierra Club's lawyer who put me in touch with the person who would become my attorney in Gainesville, Marcy I. LaHart. I saved $400 to retain her and officially sued the university in October of 2011 to gain access to their lab records. On December 30, 2011, I actually won! Still in disbelief, I called

---

26 Jared Misner, "Radical group does not accurately represent animal rights activism," The Alligator (June 20, 2011) https://www.alligator. org/opinion/letters_to_the_editor/article_083abc92-b34c-11e0-8a69-001cc4c03286.htm

The University of Florida

Steve as I left the hearing in Gainesville; we shared an excited and celebratory chat. He was ecstatic. This was real. I even called Michael Budkie who was very supportive and maybe even happy for me. This was my first substantial victory over the vivisection complex. I went to South Florida to spend New Year's Eve with my friends, Ron Roberts, Josh Durden, Gabby and a few others, and celebrate. On January 1, 2012, I woke up and wrote my *First Victory of 2012* post and published it on NIO.

I drove home the next day and on January 3, I would take possession of the University of Florida's lab records, pictures of their victims, the daily charts of the progressive, intentional harm they forced the monkeys to endure and, unlike the ALF, I gained access to their labs legally. There were many redactions in the records, including names of vivisectors and lab workers as well as the locations of the animals. Marcy would file an appeal on my behalf citing the illegality of redacting public information on these documents. Having won this first huge legal battle, the university's campaign to discredit me escalated. UF's spokesperson, Janine Sikes, was now publicly labeling me as an "animal terrorist" in the news.[27]

I was very fortunate that I had several scientists within our movement as well as an informant from inside UF's labs who graciously analyzed the lab data and made sense out of it for me. First and foremost, I found out that Louis, the little monkey that was intentionally murdered inside UF, had a broken hip. He was diagnosed with this injury exactly one year to the day before he was exterminated. He was given zero care. He was given zero pain relief. He was left to languish in agony and die where no one would ever know he lived. His anorexia was pain-induced. And *that's* the reason they refused to release him to a sanctuary! *That's* the reason he had to be incinerated. Now the world would know their secrets. I held back nothing.

It irked me that Michael Budkie allowed Louis to live and die

27 Nathan Crabbe, "Camille Marino of Wildwood, who founded the group Negotiation is Over, received the records last week," The Gainesville Sun (January 9, 2012) http://www.gainesville.com/news/20120109/judge-orders-uf-to-give-animal-rights-activist-records-on-primates

with no exposure whatsoever and, even though he had the lab records at least a year before I, he never even filed a welfare complaint. But since he was proficient at writing them, we agreed that he would file it with the USDA now. Withholding pain relief from Louis was a federal welfare violation. I would have done it myself but Michael assured me that it was too complicated. He also asked to talk to my informant. I introduced them. I understood by now that Michael Budkie would use my information and contacts to usurp me and promote himself if he could, but I didn't care. I wanted to effectively attack the university from any direction possible and their days of pristine publicity were quickly fading away.

The records I won indicated that Stephen Roberts, a 42-year old toxicologist, was responsible for Louis' confinement. His picture, images of his home, address and contact info were published along with a less-than-glowing bio.[28] The post dedicated to Louis began:

> *"In August of 2010, we learned about a monkey named Louis. A lab tech pleaded with UF to release him to a sanctuary and stop his suffering. While the lab tech was on vacation, Louis was murdered and incinerated on July 9, 2010. UF wanted to ensure that the world would never see his deteriorated condition or know his story. In October of 2010, NIO's campaign against UF commenced. Now we know that Louis was allowed to languish in torment with a broken hip and never given any pain relief. His records document callous neglect, violations of the law, and incompetence. In death, Louis has a voice."*

Our report ended by quoting UF's own disturbing words:

---

28 NIO Florida, "A Monkey named Louis: UF gave him no pain relief for broken hip, made him suffer and deteriorate for a full year," Eleventh Hour for Animals (January 12, 2012) http://universityofflorida.us/a-monkey-named-louis-uf-knew-was-in-excruciating-pain-made-him-suffer-and-deteriorate-for-a-year/

The University of Florida

"The only consequence of Louis' agony for the vivisecting sadists appears in a rather chilling entry on the vet records dated April 26, 2010: '...Long term, this monkey has been unable to be used...'"

In weekly calls to action, hundreds of activists wrote letters to UF's alumni and benefactors highlighting the information we published the previous week. Our community created both an annoyance and embarrassment for the university. Lisa also took the opportunity to educate them about technology and the alternatives available. We asked alumni to urge UF to ban primate testing. We urged them to withdraw their support until the school conceded. I would publish the emails of those alumni who denounced UF. And if they wrote back cursing me out, I would still publish their statement except I would replace my name with UF's. If Lisa or I had sent one alum 100 emails, it would have been spam. But if 100 activists send each alum one email, it is simply freedom of speech. Lisa was the person who primarily put the mailing lists together for the Gator Clubs, UF's official alumni base.

The great thing about a big victory is that everyone wants to be on the winning team and so our campaign was building momentum. One colleague called for students to forego applications to the University of Florida; her article was republished on the universityofflorida.us website.[29] Floor plans of UF's vivisection labs were leaked to us for publication.[30] Everyone wanted to be on board. Hundreds of activists participated in our email blasts. When we published new information, it was rapidly shared, saturating cyber space. When I posted information on Facebook,

29 Linda Beane, "Cleveland Students Discouraged From Applying to UF," Eleventh Hour for Animals (January 21, 2012) http://universityofflorida. us/cleveland-students-discouraged-from-applying-to-the-university-of-florida/

30 NIO Florida, "Leaked Documents: Floor Plans of UF Vivisection Labs," Eleventh Hour for Animals (January 9, 2012) http://universityofflorida. us/leaked-documents-floor-plans-of-uf-labs-document-where-vivisectors-commit-their-crimes/

the first 20 likes and shares would come in under a minute. UF was in my sights and everything I had learned up to this point was finally coming together.

The next information we published in January of 2012 was about Stephen Roberts and his colleague, Raymond Joseph Bergeron, who had force-fed five monkeys toxic soil in another experiment. They collected arsenic-contaminated soil from five sites in Florida: an electrical substation, a wood preservative treatment site, two pesticide sites, and a cattle-dip vat site. According to our informant, these experiments were conducted on behalf of the Department of Agriculture who needed toxicity levels below a certain number so that they could legally build a playground for children in one of these locations.[31]

If that was not cruel and disturbing enough, the depth of the horror became apparent in the story of Monkey 24A.[32] He had been captured as a baby in the jungles of Guyana, his mother presumably killed and the baby stolen from her arms. He was shipped across the world into a laboratory inside UF where he had spent 17 years inside a cage the size of a dishwasher. The cages used in labs are called squeeze cages. The terrified animal, in this case a monkey, panics and tries to run to the back of his tiny cage as his or her tormentor approaches. A lever on the cage pushes the back wall up against the front wall, literally squeezing him in between where he is restrained and can't move. Then he is *knocked down* with Ketamine, taken from his cage, and put in restraints to be mutilated or fed poison or operated upon. Sometimes they will be burned or blinded. "Knocked down" is a term used by vivisectors which means drugging their victims

31 NIO Florida, "Bergeron & Roberts forcefed monkeys toxic waste, gave okay for children to play in toxic dirt," Eleventh Hour for Animals (January 27, 2012) http://universityofflorida.us/bergeron-roberts-forcefed-monkeys-toxic-waste-gave-okay-for-children-to-play-in-toxic-dirt/

32 NIO Florida, "Monkey 2A4: Tortured in UF's Labs for 17 Years, Died at the Gloved Hands of his Tormentors," Eleventh Hour for Animals (January 13, 2012) http://universityofflorida.us/monkey-2a4-tortured-in-ufs-labs-for-17-years-died-at-the-gloved-hands-of-his-tormentors/

to render them unconscious. They can then inconspicuously transport their unconscious subjects in a box through hallways unnoticed. Any imaginable horror the human mind can conceive is perpetrated upon lab animals and funded almost entirely by taxpayers. Little 24A was repeatedly used by Raymond Joseph Bergeron in this manner for 17 years, enduring dose after dose after dose of poison.

Sia and Shane Barbi, known as the *Barbi Twins* gained celebrity in breaking sales records as the cover models for *Playboy* magazine in the 1980s. They had successfully used their celebrity to bring worldwide attention to animal rights issues about which they were passionate. The Barbi Twins were big fans of Steve's and he introduced us. Sia and I would talk for hours on the phone and we shared a lot on a personal level as well as professionally. Shane struck me as being the more thoughtful and cautious of the twins. Sia was more like me. And our concern for the animals was genuine. In early 2012, the Barbi Twins came on board to be the spokespeople and ambassadors for the UF campaign to Free the Monkeys. Although they graciously allowed me to use their names to elicit online support, my real vision was to bring them to Gainesville and have them lead protests.

We had announced a protest to take place on February 4, 2012 at a huge UF Gator Gala at which its benefactors would gather to support their alma mater. Against their celebration, we would dress in black and hold a mock funeral for all the monkeys that had died and were still suffering. Michael Budkie was excited about maximizing my legal victory and the mock funeral was his idea. While he refused to make a public announcement, he sent out private invitations to all of his followers in Gainesville. This was the first time that he had reciprocated me directing my followers to support him. The Saturday morning before the demo, we spent a lot of time on the phone. He prepared the press releases, sent them out, and coached me about the talking points he thought I should emphasize. I disagreed that welfare should be discussed at all.

Lisa was always the person who had the talent for making signs, fliers, and organizing protest details. We bought a little cardboard coffin and she had some Halloween-type tombstones. We checked into our hotel in Gainesville that afternoon, making sure we had everything in order. We had major support now for our campaign, both online and in the community, and with the images secured through the lawsuit, we had finally cut through their lies. The images of the monkeys bandaged, scarred, and wholly despondent spoke for themselves. People who had once laughed at us and once said "they don't experiment on monkeys anymore" were outraged. But there were three relatively innocuous images that were the most profound for me. One set was of a small seemingly-healthy monkey being carried by his twinkling-eyed captors.

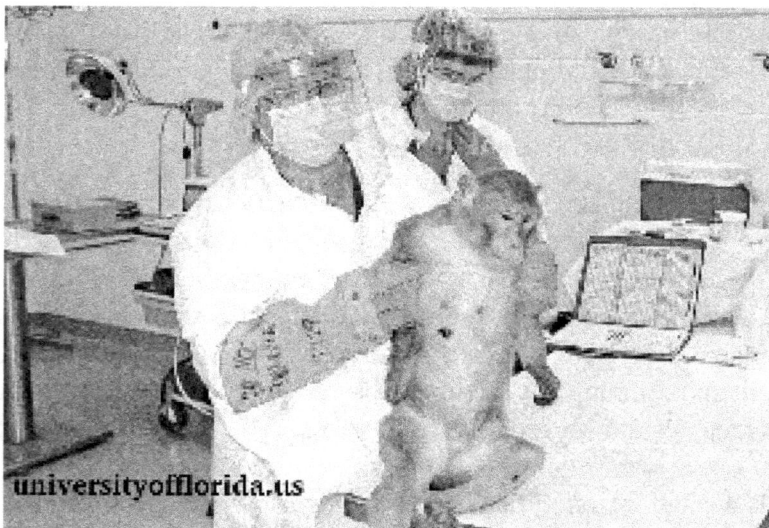

universityofflorida.us

It was followed by an *after* image of another monkey.

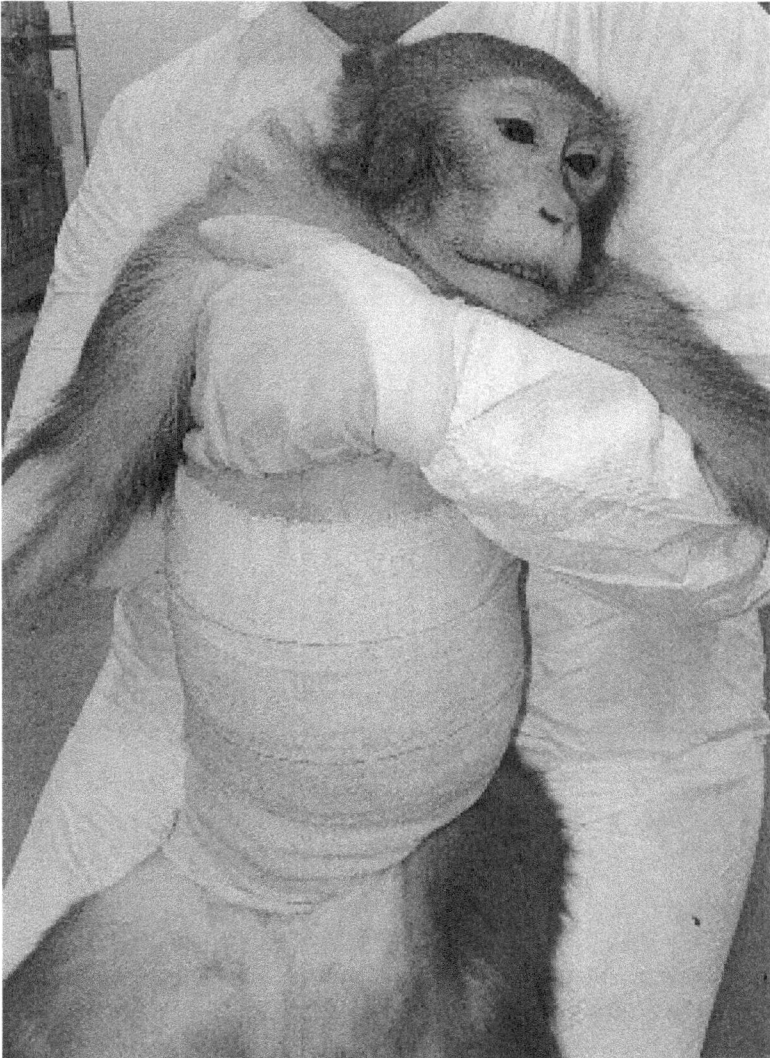

And a third image was of a small, unconscious monkey; his head fell to the side with a contorted facial expression. He was being tattooed for identification in the same fashion as Jews were tattooed in concentration camps in Nazi Germany.

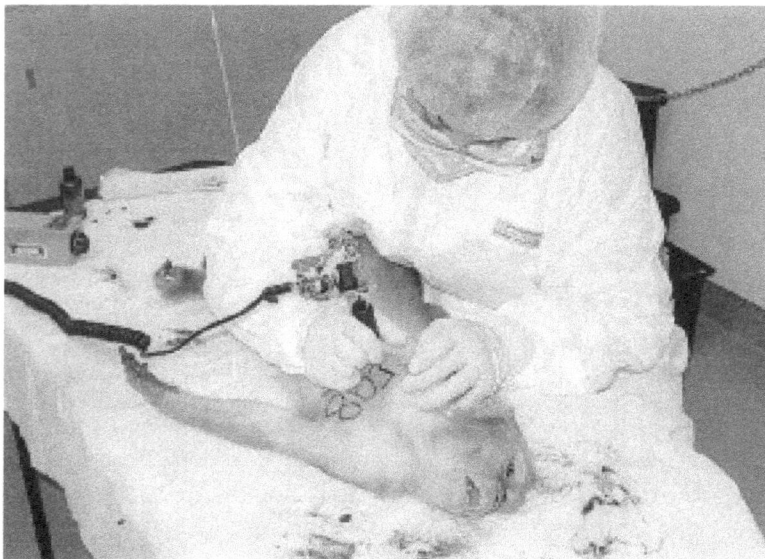

There were many images of burned, mutilated, emaciated, and dead monkeys. But, somehow, the pictures of these individuals at the beginning their nightmares disturbs me at a level I am unable to articulate.

On February 4, I left half a bottle of carrot juice on the night stand. Lisa and I packed up our gear, and we took a taxi to the Emerson Alumni Hall to set up for that evening's demonstration. We anticipated a good turnout. For some reason though, I was really focused on finishing up and getting back to my hotel room to finish my carrot juice. I also couldn't wait to change. I wanted to wear my jeans and be comfortable. But Lisa objected: "after all this, you better wear black!" It became a habit to concede on irrelevant issues to avoid having to waste my energy arguing. I wore black leggings and my giant *Support Walter [Bond]* T-Shirt that fit almost like a dress. I hate tights! But my wardrobe stress quickly evaporated and was replaced with excitement as I saw dozens of activists dressed in black coming toward us to take their places.

Once rights become privileges for any segment of a population, they can be revoked for the rest of the population. -Chris Hedges

The First Shoe Drops

Steve suggested I get a passport in 2010 so he could show me Juarez before he left for Europe. In July we crossed the border and visited Zips Pharmacy. I was fascinated by the tanks and armed soldiers clustered in streets of the Mexican border town. I was embarrassed because I couldn't keep up with his stride as we crossed the walking bridge. He walked faster and I tried my best to keep pace but couldn't. I struggle with residual challenges from my experience as a quadriplegic. One huge issue for me is that my balance is impaired; when I try to stand still my appearance is probably akin to someone trying to balance on one foot. My gait is somewhat compromised as well; I couldn't run if my life depended on it. While I rarely give a second thought to these issues, I suddenly felt very inadequate. At one point I tripped and fell hard onto my knee. It hurt. But I could tell that Steve was embarrassed by me and so I became even more self-conscious. Rather than stopping to help me, he walked faster as if he didn't know me. I remembered him ridiculing Alicia when struggled with a medical condition; she would have to hide from him until she was over any physical manifestations. He distanced himself from me at that moment just as he had bragged about having done to his girlfriend. I absorbed the emotional abuse. At that point I was seeing myself through his eyes. I hate that I didn't possess the wherewithal to challenge him.

At Zips, Steve bought Ritalin and HGH (human growth hormones). I bought Xanax and Percocet. He showed me how to smuggle drugs by hiding everything in his socks as we crossed back into the states. He told me that he had only been stopped at the border once and was able to convince them that he was just a college professor who filled his prescriptions in Mexico because it was cheaper. We made it back into the Texas without incident and went home to get high together.

He left for Europe in a day or two and I was stranded at his house without a car. I was upset when Steve failed to even check in. I knew I was being used at some level. His first terminally-ill cat died in my arms and I buried her in his yard. I was glad I was there to comfort Kayla in the end but did not appreciate his selfishness. He was aloof and unappreciative. And I was only there because Alicia refused to house sit. She finally showed up to take another of his sick cats to the vet. Chairman Mao died in her car on the way back. Alicia and I buried him together. She was terrified that Steve would blame her. Chairman Mao had not been noticeably ill when he left. But the vet said that by the time the cat's gum disease was finally treated, it was too late. When we got to know one another, I liked Alicia. She was intelligent, attractive, and thoughtful. I thought she was selling herself short.

I sent Steve off some angry emails. Then I relented and apologized profusely, especially after Chairman Mao died. Alicia told me that she "know[s] what he is" but that he "is like a drug to me." I understood. I tolerated his behavior because in some inexplicable way, he was like a drug to me as well. Steve once bragged to me that Alicia told him "you can leave me laying in the curb and I would still crawl back to you." I was uncomfortable with the satisfaction he seemed to exude.

I was at his house when I came under fire for working with Walter

Bond and publishing personal information about Trapper Zuelke. From jail, Walter sent me all the data he had on Trapper and I published the documents to expose this snitch on NIO. I found out that I could be indicted for tampering with a federal witness and that Walter might be looking at an upward deviation in his sentence for our collaboration. When I finally spoke to Steve and turned to him for consolation, he berated me and told me I was "stupid." He didn't want any of these problems happening while I was at his house. He demonstrated repeatedly that he wasn't a friend. He was on tour in Europe, speaking, having trysts, partying, and encouraging militant direct action. Extending any friendship to me while I was in his home taking care of his affairs or supporting Walter who *actually took militant direct action* was not his concern. Yet I stayed. On this trip, I was invited to be flown to New York to speak at a rally that was to take place in a few weeks. I was forced to forego the opportunity because I wouldn't abandon his cats.

Steve's house was isolated and surrounded with pig farms in walking distance, a huge dairy industry, and alleged back yard cock fighting rings. I learned this in 4 weeks. Certainly, there was something he should have been doing in his own community. Alice came to stay with me and we took it upon ourselves to explore and see what we could effectively do to sabotage local abusers. Aware of their prior relationship, Alicia got angry when she found out that Steve allowed Alice to sleep in his house.

Alice and I shared a vision, one of urgency where baby steps were simply not getting the job done. Before I met Steve in person, he liked to tell me that "I'm one step away from the Unibomber." At least in his mind, I'm sure that was true. And while his ranch house bore little resemblance to Ted Kaczynski's shack, there was an eerie isolation that reminded one of David Koresh's compound. In the solitude of our own Waco, we would hatch a 7-year plan. The 7 years would allow Alice and me to satisfy family obligations before we turned our attention to vivisectors across the country. Alas, like most progressive actions deferred, the 7-year plan was to die a sudden death two years later.

The First Shoe Drops

I didn't understand the malicious undercurrent I felt when I visited Steve; I only knew it left me feeling hurt, confused, and abused. The other 11 months of the year we were thick as thieves. I was a workaholic. I spent a good 14 to 16 hours a day researching everything, every cent that ran through the NIH into UF's coffers, the details of every grant, researching personal information about their researchers, always looking for an angle. Sometimes I wouldn't sleep for a night or two. When I lived in New York, I had suffered from a severe depression that kept me in bed for the better part of two years. I went to therapy weekly, spoke with both a psychiatrist and a counselor and was treated with every anti-depressant known to man, all of which exacerbated my symptoms or, at best, did nothing. My doctor and therapist ultimately decided that I was bi-polar. It never occurred to me or anyone else that I had sustained catastrophic injuries and that, in the blink of an eye, life as I once knew it changed forever. It never occurred to me or anyone else that I was snorting heroin and that might have been affecting my moods. But, indeed, while I was doing drugs my symptoms mimicked bi-polarity.

Once I was in Florida and drug free, my symptoms completely disappeared; I was no longer on mood-altering medications, but I still identified as bi-polar and shared that diagnosis with Steve and Lisa. She would use this information like a club to bash me whenever she was annoyed about something. "You need to be on meds." "Oh my god, you're so sick." "I can't work with you while you're like this!" Steve, on the other hand, was envious. He suffered from severe bouts of depression but without the periods of heightened creativity and euphoria. I am comfortable now that I'm not manic-depressive. I've simply been a workaholic my entire life punctuated with periods of drug abuse. If I was bipolar, I'd own it.

While I was focused to the point of obsession with finding a weakness inside the University of Florida, Steve was contending with his addiction and found it exceedingly difficult to be productive without Ritalin. At his request, I would regularly take his departmental compliance exams because he was constantly being reprimanded for being late. After a while, he didn't even ask; I would just get an email saying "it's that time again." Although he was tenured, this continuing education exercise was required to remain in good standing. I was glad I could cover for him. Once or twice, I helped him grade his students. I would simply count how many Xs they had under three categories; if I remember correctly, it was something like oral presentations, written presentations, and group projects. I counted up the Xs on his students' records in UTEPs database, made him a list, and he assigned a grade accordingly.

One night we were talking about how we were both in need of money. For my part, every penny I had was being consumed by my campaign, lawsuits, propaganda, gas, and having to host my website in Iceland. His money was absorbed by his vices. We had discussed turning NIO into a 501(c)(3) (a charitable corporation) but not with any degree of seriousness; it was highly unlikely that I would ever get not-for-profit status. One morning after one of these last discussions on the subject, I was getting the urge to get high with him again. I woke up and flipped off an email.

From: Camille Marino [mailto: negonegoplanetarenews.com]

Sent: Wednesday, November 24 2010 7:33 AM

To: steve18@up.n.com

Subject: appssss

I'm having a weak moment...

I need money. I need to move. I need a car and computer. I want high. And just to maintain nio on the new servers is going to cost $600+ a year.

My being active depends on my being independent, having transportation, and money to finance campaigns.

We could start accepting donations.

We're good at what we do and I bet we could generate a decent income if we tried.

And, seriously, NIO is you and me so it could be our own little personal dollar faucet.

Imagine...

Steve called me from his car on his way to Juarez. We laughed about my idea and never spoke of it again. I forgot about the extraneous email as soon as I sent it.

Around this time, he called me one day in a panic. He had hit Alicia in a restaurant and slammed her head into a wall. He was afraid he was going to be arrested even though she was not going to press charges. None of the patrons called the police. There was another instance where she woke him up and he threw something at her. And once where he threw her down to the ground, every time she would get up he would throw her down again. He laughed. As long as he was confident she would not involve the law, he was far more concerned that Alicia would confide in her brother. The brother apparently hated Steve.

On this occasion he called me frantically after the fear set in. He complained that Alicia's behavior was becoming progressively-more provocative. It was her fault he was having these violent outbursts. I allowed myself to be blind to many things. But this is where I began to draw the line. I was firm that no matter what Alicia said or did, he had absolutely no right to physically attack her. And his response was that she would be physical with him. "Steve, you are the only person responsible for your actions." I heard nothing more about physical fights for a while and I was hoping the situation would resolve itself.

The animal holocaust, however, never resolves itself. While animals are tortured in the most unimaginable ways, every so often one abuser will gain some public attention. In October of 2011, the Physicians Committee for Responsible Medicine (PCRM) was publicizing the brutal heart experiments being performed inside Wayne State University by a researcher named Donal O'Leary. His name has been deleted from their website but a timeline of events remains.[33] They were pursuing welfare violation sanctions against him, not for the brutality itself, but because of *welfare law* violations. One dog named Queenie died.

O'Leary was securing his victims through Class B dealers. When people surrender their dogs and cats to shelters or when animals are rescued, there is an insidious network that adopts these animals cheaply and sells them into university labs for profit. The scared family pets and rescued homeless individuals will then endure experiments at the hands of vivisectors. Queenie

33 Physicians Committee for Responsible Medicine, "Wayne State Campaign Timeline" https://www.pcrm.org/research/edtraining/waynestate/wayne-statecampaign-timeline

was secured through a Class B dealer. She was once a family pet.

According to the PCRM, when Queenie arrived in the labs, her tail was wagging and she was excited to be out of the shelter. She thought she had found a new home. After meeting O'Leary, Queenie would cower in the back of her cage, sad, scared, in pain. But there was nowhere to hide. O'Leary inserted catheters into her veins and heart. Some were hanging out of her, her body leaking fluids as she was made to perform. O'Leary would force Queenie to run on a treadmill to induce high blood pressure. I had an image in my mind of the corpulent vivisector sitting there laughing and eating a sandwich while his victim ran on the treadmill, her life draining as she tried in futility to keep up the pace. She eventually died at O'Leary's hands. He had been performing these experiments for two decades. The PCRM began circulating petitions to stop him. As of the writing of this book, the PCRM is still circulating petitions to stop him. I had other ideas about how to contend with this individual.

Overnight, Donal O'Leary ousted James David Jentsch as the prevailing face of vivisection. I published his information and called for my colleagues to feel free to pay him a visit and send pictures of his house and family into NIO for publication. I never asked anyone to do anything I wouldn't do myself. I sent him an email wishing him a "slow painful death." And I was sure to qualify it by saying "please do not interpret this as a threat. It is merely my fondest wish for you." I sent him a link to the post on NIO with all of his pictures and personal information with the closing "welcome to NIO!"

Like always, I blind copied Steve on my vivisector emails. But this time I called him afterward and told him I had a funny feeling and was concerned that I had gone too far. I was always pushing boundaries and was always something of a provocateur. Steve was not at all worried. That allayed my anxiety. His response was to write and publish the now-infamous Freddy Kruger letter on my site as a comment to my post:

"Dear Donal, welcome to your nightmare; it begins

The First Shoe Drops

now. As avid readers of NIO, we took immense delight in reading your profile and the list of crimes against the innocent today.

We are on vacation, a bit fatigued upon exacting just revenge on so many sick, sadistic fucks throughout the world. And vile vivisectionists keep us most busy. But we are leaving our beachfront condo here in hell just to come pay you a special visit.

We have good news and bad news for you. Really, since we are bad news, we only have bad news. The good news is that we are granting you powers of eternal life so that, like us, you can never die. The truly bad news is that we are going to kill you as many times as the milliseconds the innocents you tortured had to suffer. We are going to grab you in the middle of the night and bury you under a concrete basement floor in an isolation chamber Henry Harlow [sic] would have envied.

Don't worry about your nourishment. We will put a tube in your mouth and feed you human feces piped in through the sewers of a disease treatment center and pump pureed corpses into your veins mix with Drano to pump it through your veins smoothly. We will then strap you into a monkey restraining device and use industrial pliers to crack your testicles like walnuts. We will take sharp wire cutters and remove every hand and foot digit with slow and inexorable force.

After lunch, we will take our favorite dull rusty saws and slice through both your arms and legs before your first pathetic life is over. As you gurgle with blood-soaked lungs and shiver with death rattles, we will kick you raw red bloody stump of a torso stripped of all your hideous reptilian skin down 10 city blocks to the crossroads of starving dogs and let them devour what little is left of you, pieces of venal flesh flying into the air until nothing of your evil greedy heinous ugly sick sadistic puck-

inducing utterly worthless soulless fuck shit body is left.

And that is only payback for Queenie, one of the beautiful and innocent souls you murdered gratuitously and unconscionably, just as your demented mentors, more sleezy [sic] white coat whores of Big Pharma have trained you to do at Frankenstein Academy and the Institute of Dr. Moreau.

We will resurrect you for every canine victim you tortured and killed and each time we will fuck you up worse than the time before. We will record every nightmarish life and death you suffer for the next three years; and there's an eternity to pay after that."

He signed it "Freddy Kruger and the Grim Reaper." It was simply an artistic expression of everything Donal O'Leary justifiably deserved. It was a snuff fantasy no different than anything Quentin Tarantino has produced. And my response to the Freddy Kruger letter was to congratulate them, Freddy and Grim, for their brilliant activism and ask them to forward one of their films to NIO so I could publish it for the enjoyment of all our readers.

Steve called me. He had me laughing so hard that I couldn't breathe, tears running down my face. His graphic depiction of O'Leary's demise tickled us. I believed then and I believe now that one of the greatest contributions an activist could make to the struggle would be to strap on some explosives, attend a conference of vivisectors, and detonate in the middle of the festivities. Yes, I would wholeheartedly support an ASIL (Animal State in Liberation).

But Steve and I didn't stop there. The Freddy Kruger Letter needed a standalone blog. I formatted it to re-publish. Steve suggested we include his YouTube video, "every motherfucker who hurts animals is gonna feel the fear."[34] I embedded it in the post and told him to log onto NIO to do his edits. He was happy

---

34 Dr. Steve Best, "Every motherfucker who hurts animals is gonna feel the fear," YouTube (August 26, 2010) https://www.youtube.com/watch?v=xUoaY_ddrhc

with the finished product. I was happy with the finished product. I remember asking him "are you sure it's okay?" I was already apprehensive about having crossed some invisible line. But we were both comfortable with our work and I hit publish. Then I sent Donal O'Leary a link. We laughed hysterically on the phone.

The first shoe dropped about a week later. I was served with a restraining order out of Wayne County in Detroit prohibiting me from contacting O'Leary again and also directing me to remove his information from my website. I was also banned from the Wayne State University campus. I had never set foot in Michigan in my life. Everything I ever published about any abuser was retrieved from the public domain. Property appraisal sites are teeming with publicly-available personal information. Many sites are. I am the public. My readers are the public. And my freedom of speech is not contingent upon where public information is published or for which sector of the viewing public. I removed nothing. I was charged with civil contempt.

Steve completely supported my position. I'd already been through this with UCLA's David Jentsch for over a year. The county of the originating order would have to incur the expense to have me arrested in Florida, housed, and extradited into their jurisdiction where I would be charged with a misdemeanor, slapped on the wrist, and sent home. I was never summoned to California. Detroit was bankrupt besides. It was highly unlikely they were concerned with me and my blog.

There were plenty of others, however, who definitely were concerned with me and my blog. I completely underestimated the comprehensive and virulent campaign to discredit my work and eradicate my presence that was taking shape. The Southern Poverty Law Center (SPLC) which tracks racists and other hate groups had apparently been following me for some time. In a telephone interview with them, I made the following statement:

> *"There is a war being waged against animals and any*
> *act committed in the name of love and compassion*
> *against those who are waging the war I do not consider*

an act of terrorism. I've never committed a crime in my life. I've never done anything violent and I don't intend to. But if some unknown person took that step, I would support and applaud it... If you spill blood, your blood should be spilled as well."

The simple fact is that I make no value distinction between a human or nonhuman victim. I make no value distinction between a black or a white human. I make no value distinction between a man or a woman. They are morally equal, they are each sentient, they each have a right to live free from pain and exploitation. We recognize capital punishment for egregious crimes against humans. I recognize the same justifications for crimes against nonhumans. It's very simple and entirely consistent. The SPLC disagreed. On November 3, 2011, they came out with an article entitled *Animal Rights Activist: 'If you spill blood, your blood should be spilled,'* officially classifying me as an extremist and labeling NIO a hate group[35] right along with the Ku Klux Klan. The difference, however, is that I am wholly unconcerned with anyone's race, religion, gender, sexuality, or shoe size. I identify animal abusers because of their behavior – their violent actions. The SPLC clearly understood the distinction.

Every week another article would come out from some security shill or other doing a threat assessment on me. A 10-page letter with no return address except *Community Watch* was sent to all of my neighbors warning them that I was a terrorist and urging them to have me ejected from my development. My next-door neighbor, Agnes* gave me a copy and told me everyone had received one. At least when I communicated with vivisectors' neighbors, I did it face to face.

My first NIO blog, negotiationisover.com, had been DDoSed and hacked so many times that it simply became too expensive to keep hiring technical consultants to fix it. DDoS means Distributed

35 Leah Nelson, "Animal Rights Activist: 'If you spill blood, your blood should be spilled,'" Southern Poverty Law Center (November 3, 2011) https://www.splcenter.org/hatewatch/2011/11/03/animal-rights-activist-if-you-spill-blood-your-blood-should-be-spilled

Denial of Service and is a common attack used by hackers to overload a network, thus rendering the website inaccessible or useless. I bought a new domain, negotiationisover.net, redirected the first site to the second one, transferred any salvageable information, and the transition was fairly transparent. My NIO YouTube account was deleted after being repeatedly reported and flagged for rhetoric. Everything that I had recorded disappeared. There was a veritable move from every corner trying to silence me and erase my presence. Thankfully, Steve was always in my corner and the most vocal critic of the smear campaign and corresponding censorship. He had first-hand experience with censorship having been banned from the UK.

On February 4, 2012, five weeks after I won my lawsuit against the University of Florida, Lisa and I were setting up for our demo outside the Emerson Alumni Hall as activists began to gather. I was approached by four police officers, both campus and Gainesville police. A UFPD detective named Jeff Moran asked, "Are you Camille Marino?" "You know I am." "There is an out-of-state warrant for you. You're under arrest." I handed my phone to Lisa.

Outside UF that night, I was put in handcuffs for the first time in my life and led away to police cruisers that lined the corner. I was surprised when Lisa was brought over in handcuffs about 10 minutes later. Utterly aware of Lisa Grossman's identity, they asked her for ID. She produced an expired driver's license. Producing an expired driver's license for ID is a crime in Florida, especially when the subject in question is opposed to a multi-million-dollar animal abuse enterprise that functions as a municipality in the community. I firmly believe that if she had produced a valid license, they would have found another reason to arrest her. We were the campaign against UF. And law enforcement had a mandate that night to shut us down. We had become a true threat to UF's blood-money profits. Lisa and I were dismayed that we would not be present at our biggest protest to date. We worried that other activists would be scared away, no doubt an anticipated side benefit. But I was confident that when this was over, we'd be able to exploit the repression to our advantage and would ultimately attract a more militant following. We laughed and were in good spirits as we rode in the back of the cruiser on our way to jail.

Politics is the art of making people believe that they are in power, when in reality they have none. -Mumia Abu-Jamal

General Population

It was probably about 8 pm when we arrived at the Alachua County Jail. We were uncuffed, our effects like jewelry and hair ties were taken from us, pockets (if I had had any) and purses emptied, phones confiscated, and we were led into different holding cells. These concrete rooms have a bench, a bare light, a window through which the police can watch you, a toilet right out there in the open (except for a little 3-foot high wall), and nothing else. You sit. And sit. You pace. You sit. You fight the urge to relieve yourself in front of an audience. There are no clocks. You are fairly disoriented. I didn't have any idea what to expect. So here I waited. Occasionally another prisoner would be brought in and taken to their own holding cell. I would watch the process repeat itself over and over. Then I would watch the prisoners who had come in after me get fingerprinted and taken off to another area. But not me. I waited.

I was eventually taken to see a nurse as is standard procedure; my blood pressure was seriously elevated. They gave me some meds and took me back to my cell. Apparently, none of the officers understood why I was arrested or for what I was being held. I was told that they were uncertain whether I was staying or going home, but they had orders to keep me detained until further notice. I knew I had no charges in Florida and I was not in violation of my campus trespass order. Lisa and I were both on the public sidewalk, off campus property. Only our unencumbered protesters were squarely inside the campus perimeter mingling with UF's guests. I couldn't wait to find out if the protest continued after I was taken away. I fully expected to go home and touch base with the other activists. The officers were waiting for hours to see if they would keep me. The paperwork for an out-of-state hold from Detroit finally arrived.

I was taken out of holding, fingerprinted, my first mugshot was taken, and I was officially booked in as an out-of-state fugitive. They took me to change out of my clothes and into a two-piece striped uniform. My ID bracelet was red indicating my classification. When I changed out, I had to surrender everything. You may only keep your undergarments in this jail if they are white; mine were black. I was issued a white sports bra and ugly white granny panties. I slid everything through a slot in the window and stood there naked as she slid back my state-issued ensemble. I was actually glad to get rid of the tights. I wasn't sure whether or not the white panties were new and I considered foregoing them but thought it better not to draw attention to myself. I stepped to the side behind the wall and had a moment of privacy while I got dressed. From that moment I began to condition myself that no matter what they did to me physically, I would never allow them to penetrate the sanctuary of my mind. I would never react.

In my jail uniform, I was taken to housing in the infirmary because my blood pressure wouldn't normalize. I was put in a cell that was larger than the holding cell. The walls were the same blocks of drab-colored concrete and half the cell was bullet-proof glass that overlooked the guard's desk which was usually empty. That was a good thing. I was able to use my open restroom area when I had some privacy. I didn't know it then, but being in the infirmary is like being in isolation. Other than guards doing their rounds, you are generally locked in a wing where you are alone in your cell except for the two or three times a day when a nurse will do a perfunctory check of an inmate's vital signs.

The next morning, I was taken to a slightly larger cell to await arraignment. The two other women with whom I waited were clearly more comfortable with the accommodations than I. We talked about our charges and they told me what to expect in court that morning. An out-of-state misdemeanor is generally adjudicated with a slap on the wrist and a finger wag from the judge. They both were confident I'd be home in a few hours. And then while we were speaking, talking eye-to-eye, one of the women began to walk toward the toilet. She dropped her pants, sat down, and apparently had some strenuous business with which to contend. Our discussion continued uninterrupted. The third woman in the cell didn't even seem to notice. I adopted her nonchalance but I didn't know where to look. I laid down on my back on my concrete slab, my left knee bent, and my right leg crossed over my knee. I crossed my arms to rest under my head. Now that I was staring at the ceiling I had a second to process my environment. Was this what that word "institutionalized" meant?

In court, Lisa and I saw one another for the first time since the night before. With about 40 defendants that morning, the judge called individuals one by one, formally announced their pending charges, assigned a bail bond amount, and dispensed with each prisoner quickly. Lisa was allowed to go home on her own recognizance. A child pornography ring had apparently been broken up in Florida at that time. Several of the alleged pedophiles were allowed to post bond and go home as well. I was sent back to jail with no bond.

Back in the infirmary I had a TV, a phone, a cot and it was a little like being in a private hotel room. I was given a pencil and paper. I wrote my statement that I would dictate for publication. I sat on my bed in my cell for hours with my legs crossed in my lap thinking about all the revolutionaries who came before me. I thought about Martin Luther King, Jr., Malcolm X, and Leonard Peltier, who was approaching four decades in prison. I thought about Walter Bond and Nelson Mandela, both classified as terrorists. Mandela was considered an international terrorist and incarcerated for 27 years before he would become Africa's first black president in 1994. I was suddenly proud to be in jail.

Steve and I spoke daily, sometimes several times a day although not nearly as much as when I was home. He rallied support for me. My critics seized this opportunity to denounce me and use my arrest as proof that I was a detriment to the movement. The papers began churning out articles about my arrest and impending extradition. From global watch groups to Americans for Medical Progress to the National Association for Biomedical Research and every vivisector in between, the blogosphere was celebrating. My support simultaneously went viral. Facebook support pages and a dedicated website were launched overnight. My friends in South Florida, who by now had re-organized themselves under the anti-vivisection campaign Smash HLS, arranged fundraisers. Steve organized many of my supporters around my NIO Facebook group. Many seized this opportunity to work with him, their enthusiasm for my cause largely motivated by a desire to please my mentor and ingratiate themselves. But most of my staunch supporters had been with me from the beginning and we had been working together now in various capacities for years. I was achieving minor celebrity. Activists were applauding me and raising me up on a pedestal. I wasn't sure why. I was just sitting in a box and hadn't really done anything.

After three days, my door opened and the guard told me I was moving to general population. Suddenly every prison movie and every episode of *Lockup Raw* I had ever seen flashed through my head. I wasn't a fighter, not in the physical sense. I was a 47-year-old, disabled woman. And I had no idea what to expect. I don't think I betrayed my thoughts. I silently stood, gathered my things, and followed the guard through the jail. When she opened the door to my pod, I gathered every ounce of courage I had, stared at my writing pad for dear life, and walked as confidently as I could into the unit. I didn't want to look at anyone for fear that it would be a challenge and they would want to fight. I sat down and continued writing as if it was just an ordinary day. I must have stood out like a Martian.

A 21-year-old woman named Jessica Snook was the first person to sit down and talk to me. She had been arrested this last time when a meth lab blew up; her legs were badly scarred. She was all tatted up. She could tell this was my first time in jail. I told her why I was there and she was impressed that I was in there for my beliefs, that I was unapologetic, and her admiration and friendship put me at ease instantly. Then I met another woman in her 60s. I realized that if this woman was okay, I would be too. She was a fugitive on a federal hold. She had been a drug smuggler in the 1980s who was on the run for over a decade before they found her living abroad. One by one, the women learned why I was there and were intrigued. I was shocked at the friendship and camaraderie I found behind bars. I immediately began to cultivate a vegan outreach approach for inmates and began trying to recruit activists. Most of these women were in there for drugs and were in desperate need of guidance and direction. I was happy to provide both.

The worst part of general population was that it was an open dormitory with 32 bunks on two tiers that housed 64 women. Completely unexpected for the claustrophobe that I was, I found I preferred the privacy of sleeping in my own cell. Snook was in the lower bunk to my left, a few other new friends were in surrounding bunk beds, and there was one woman right above me who would experience night terrors, screaming uncontrollably in the middle of the night. Her cries were jarring. A big, strong inmate, a woman who I found intimidating in my first hours in that pod, I sat with her the next afternoon and found out she was homeless. I learned that there were impoverished black ghettos that remained largely invisible in the college town of Gainesville. I learned that while hundreds of millions of tax dollars were pouring into the pockets of UF's vivisectors every year, there were people living in the local streets who couldn't even afford food. My new friend would get herself arrested from time to time to have a place to sleep and something to eat. I was very curious to know the source of her night terrors, but I never intruded.

It was deliberately freezing in jail to keep the germs down to a minimum. But that didn't stop the lice. A week after I arrived, two bunks right next to mine experienced an outbreak. Fortunately, I escaped any contamination, but I learned to be very careful about sharing anything with anyone. You never share combs, drink from others' cups or use their plastic utensils. You never sit on other peoples' bunks; besides, if construed as a gesture of disrespect, such an act will invite an attack. I was horrified when they gave out old washed undergarments in the pod so that we would be able to change. I took to going commando as soon as I familiarized myself with my surroundings. Even though I had money and my supporters were extremely generous about putting funds on my books, I was unwilling to acclimate to incarceration. I refused to buy a sweatshirt or new granny panties from commissary. I didn't belong here and I was just waiting until someone figured out how to get me out.

A few days after I was there, I had a visitor. It was UFPD Detective Jeff Moran. He wanted to know why I was *targeting* college professors. I had nothing to say to him and he left. I had to suck up my pride and face him with unkempt hair and no makeup. I held my head high and did what needed to be done.

The phone was my most important tool. Since I had no idea when I would be free, I arranged to have the records that I won in court sent to Michael Budkie. I called him from jail and he promised he would do the federal complaint for Louis. He even defended me in the Gainesville Sun: "It's my opinion that these arrests took place at the protest in a concerted effort to stifle dissent against the university."[36] My goal was to orchestrate my campaign unimpeded despite being behind bars. I spoke to Lisa daily and she was happy to assume primary responsibility for publishing on NIO. As I delegated more responsibility to her, I began to understand that she resented me diverting the monkeys' veterinary records to Budkie. We both agreed that he had clear and obvious limitations as an activist. But he was the only one

---

36 Nathan Crabbe, "Two animal-rights activists arrested at protest," The Gainesville Sun (February 6, 2012) http://www.gainesville.com/news/20120206/two-animal-rights-activists-arrested-at-protest

of the three of us who was actually qualified to analyze the data. With me in lockup, Lisa contacted Michael and browbeat him into sending her all of the documents. Everything I was awarded was now with Lisa Grossman who fancied herself an analyst.

I was determined to make this work effectively. As long as we focused on the methods of torture and the monkeys' suffering, we would be okay. I just steered us clear of any scientific minutia. I didn't understand the science. And I couldn't care less if it held any validity or not. When vivisectors try to rationalize experimenting on mentally-challenged humans, on orphaned babies, or any other disenfranchised human, then the rest of the world can debate the scientific gibberish. Lisa would tell me what she found, I would write something up, and I then I would dictate our final article. At least the animals still had a voice. And given that my community was following NIO in unprecedented numbers now, anything Lisa published was reaching a substantial audience.

Gabby and I spoke frequently. One of about half a dozen people who had administrative privileges on my website, she was great about publishing my statements from jail on NIO. Ron Roberts and I would talk regularly also. I remember telling him that jail was like "day camp with bars." I wasn't being brave or self-sacrificing; I was being truthful. Steve remained my primary confidante. He would keep me informed about fundraising and the efforts to secure counsel. He also put together a wish list of book titles for people to send me. I was a little concerned because all of my calls were obviously being recorded. On more than one occasion, he would talk about needing to go get his "party favors" in Juarez. I knew my keepers would understand what he was telling me. I tried to steer the conversation to more benign areas.

Since I had never stepped foot in the state of Michigan, some of the lawyers with whom my support team spoke said that they couldn't extradite me. One of the inmates with whom I became friendly was a career criminal who had just been extradited from Wayne County to Alachua. She said to me "Detroit is full of street gangs and drug dealers and Wayne County is the worst jail in the country. Who do you think you're going to find behind bars?" She told me they were filthy, infested with rats and roaches, and extremely violent. My food had been reasonably good where I was. She told me there were no vegan trays where I was going. You ate the slop they gave you or you starved. She told me you couldn't even compare the bankrupt Wayne County Jail to where we were. Having gotten comfortable at Alachua, I was not wanting to go to Detroit. I had no idea what to expect and was more than a little apprehensive at the prospects. I would never be able to assimilate into the violent gang culture. I was going to get killed.

My team didn't have the money to retain a lawyer in Florida to prevent me from being extradited as well as retaining a lawyer in Detroit to defend me. It looked like I was going to Michigan one way or another. There were probably over a dozen committed people working on my team. They learned that I was to be extradited on a certain day in February. Normally, extradition dates are kept confidential because it presents a security issue. The post went out on NIO announcing my impending extradition date. I knew that my team had retained the president of the Michigan Lawyers Guild, John Royal, to represent me when I arrived. I tried to keep my anxiety under control while I waited. The day came and went without incident. The next morning, I woke up in the same Alachua County Jail. Maybe I wasn't going after all. I'm not a criminal. Maybe they were getting ready to send me home where I belonged. I called John Royal and learned they were intent on getting me out of Florida but this time they would keep my transfer date a guarded secret.

Our pod got to go outside for an hour, two or three times a week. We got to walk around or exercise in a small cage and get some fresh air and sunshine. I was laying on the black tar with my uniform legs rolled up to my knees and the short sleeves of my uniform rolled up to my shoulders enjoying the sunshine in my face. A guard came out and called "Marino, pack it up." I swallowed hard and began to rise. I said goodbye to all of my friends. I was surprised at how emotional I felt. I was only there for three weeks, but we lived together day and night. When I first saw the five toilets out in the open next to one another, I wanted to find a window and climb out. After a few days, we would regularly use the restroom area in groups. We watched out for one another. We had become sisters. They all had a greater understanding of vivisection and I introduced all of them to veganism. Some of the women cried. We all hugged. I didn't want to leave.

I walked out of the pod carrying my towels and dragging my mat behind me.

He who commits injustice is ever more wretched than he who suffers it. -Plato

Extradition

I turned in my uniform and got back into my street clothes. I had forgotten that I wore those awful tights the night of the protest and now I was about to travel across the country wearing them. I wondered if we would fly. I wondered if we would have to stop and sleep in a hotel. I was led to an area where the Alachua County Jail handed me over to the custody of a federal extradition agent named Billie. She was nice enough and I was put at ease. Then she handcuffed me and put shackles around my ankles. Both sets of restraints were affixed to a heavy chain that fastened around my waist. The ankle restraints made it extremely difficult to walk.

We entered the sallyport, a fortified garage that acts as an entrance to prisons. I was led to a van that was guarded by Billie's son, a young man who looked like he walked right out of the movie *Deliverance.* He slid open the van door and unlocked a heavy metal enclosure behind it that opened a cage. Inside the box, three women were sitting on a small metal bench that extended the width of the interior. They wanted me to climb up and squeeze in between them.

I felt myself starting to sweat. I was fully restrained, arms and legs,

Extradition

and now they wanted me to climb into this tiny claustrophobic space so they could seal me inside. It looked airtight! I was horrified. An image flashed in my mind of the monkeys that are stuffed in boxes and transported in the cargo areas of carriers like Air France. The terrified, voiceless animals are sealed up in these tomb-crates. Many die on their harrowing journeys. Those who trade in living beings consider this a cost of doing business. I wondered if I would suffocate and my death would be just a cost of doing business as well. I'd been fighting the University of Florida to shut down their labs. It's my job to get the animals out of their cages. Now Billie was helping me climb the step to seal me inside my own.

Open records requests filed during my incarceration would demonstrate that Jeff Moran had arranged my extradition with the Michigan prosecutor's office.

It cost the University of Florida a total of $526.50.

One of the women got out so that she could sit by a little window behind a metal grate in the door. I would be sandwiched in between them. I didn't betray my terror. I slid in next to one woman. The bigger prisoner slid back in next to me. The heavy metal door was slammed shut. We were squeezed tightly inside our burial vault. It was dark. The outside van door closed. The only light in this enclosure came from the windshield from which we were separated by a blackened partition. There were small cloudy windows, maybe 12" x 6" on either side of us. Over these bullet proof windows were metal plates with dime-sized holes through which we could see slivers of foggy daylight.

Sitting on this metal bench crammed up against one another, there was no room to move our arms. The partition in front of us was inches from our toes making it impossible to extend our legs. The ceiling was about one foot above our heads. Even unrestrained, one could not stand up straight. The pigs that are raised on factory farms flashed in my mind. They are repeatedly raped and forced to live in gestation crates, a creation of a profit-motivated soulless individual. This economical and space-saving chamber ensures that the pigs will never be able to stand up or extend their limbs. Just like this economical little van. They lay awake in their filthy tomb while their babies suckle at their teats. All caged animals are housed as cheaply as possible to maximize profits. Many lose their minds. I was now one of them.

The wall behind us separated the male prisoners in the back of the van. The same steel bench extended around three walls. The fourth wall of the box was the back door, also equipped with heavy steel doors. The enclosure held as many as 14 or 16 inmates if they were packed in tightly. The men could extend their legs in the middle of the tiny room. They could alternate maneuvering down onto the floor occasionally to lay down in the filth and stretch. What an absolute luxury I thought.

I was fighting to maintain my composure. I told myself I could hold on for an hour or two. *You're okay. It's all in your head. Don't panic.* I asked the woman next to me when we would stop to eat. "We eat here." Then I asked her where we would sleep. "We sleep here." My anxiety was rising with every response. When were they going to let us out then? I learned we made stops every 8 hours to relieve ourselves at jails along the way.

Extradition

And then I asked her how long she had been here. "Three days. They can keep you in here up to 14 days." That explained why it stunk so badly. Our mausoleum was packed with prisoners who hadn't showered, brushed their teeth, or seen deodorant in days.

I wanted to scream. Billie and her son were smoking up front. I couldn't breathe. I may have been back there for two minutes. It may have been two hours. I have no idea. I had no sense of time. I know the other prisoners were talking and laughing. My only dialogue was internal. *Don't panic. You can do this...* And then I couldn't do it anymore. I had to get out. I screamed that I was having a heart attack. I had pains in my chest and couldn't breathe. It's all I could think of. Let them put me in a hospital and go on without me. Then I'll figure out what to do. I'll buy a ticket and fly out to Detroit.

The van stopped. It seemed to take minutes to open the padlocks and manipulate the cylinders that secured this reinforced steel cage door. Deliverance Boy took out his shotgun and trained it on us to deter an escape. It's a good thing too. We were all planning to jump from the van and inconspicuously waddle away in our leg restraints! Billie asked me what was going on. I told her I couldn't breathe and my chest hurt. Undoubtedly not the first prisoner to feign a diversionary illness, she looked at me skeptically and called an ambulance. This was good. The door was open, I could breathe, and they were coming for me. The panic subsided.

The first responders arrived and spoke with Billie. I heard her tell them to just give me a fast okay so she could get on the road. They took me to a nearby hospital, checked my vital signs, gave me an Ativan for anxiety and I was sealed back in the steel box in under 45 minutes. This time they made all three women get out so I could slide to the totally sealed in side of the van by the window. They all got back in after me.

What the fuck was I going to do now?

The inmates were not pleased that they had to wait an extra hour for my little stunt, but I couldn't have cared less. Billie had given them cigarettes while they waited so this time the stale smoke in the back mingled with the underarm odor in a suffocating cloud. Then the Ativan kicked in. Suddenly the panic disappeared. I felt fine. It really *was* all in my head. I looked out the dime-sized holes over the window and relaxed. I didn't know it yet, but I had just permanently overcome my claustrophobia. My journey to understand what was happening, however, was only beginning. Everything suddenly became very real for me. I was inside the system. My freedom was gone. Others were in control and I had ceased being a person; I was simply a commodity; a package being shipped across the country. I represented a paycheck to my captors, nothing more. My words represented a threat to those who abuse animals for profit. The vivisectors needed to silence me. Watching the precision with which the system converged upon me to accommodate them was confounding.

The van stopped at fast food places along the way three times a day. Everyone ordered burgers and such. Billie bought me French fries, the most vegan-like food available. At one point, Deliverance Boy threatened to seal me up in an isolation cage within my tomb if I started preaching about veganism. I didn't respond. I had to focus all of my internal resources on myself. I wasn't doing any outreach. Every eight hours we would stop along the way to visit jailhouse restrooms, most of them dirty and many without any toilet paper. Billie's son trained his shotgun on us during each one of these stops; I wondered if the big, fat gun allowed him to compensate for some private inadequacy. On the second day, a diabetic inmate went into shock and lost consciousness. Billie pulled over and gave the woman an injection of something that might have been insulin. When she regained consciousness, the van continued on its course. Another inmate with an unknown condition was given a paper bag in which she would repeatedly vomit. We went on like this for days. My head would fall forward occasionally and I would nod off for a few seconds but I didn't sleep in the van. Billie and her son took turns driving while the other slept. No one bathed. My legs ached from not moving. Every bone in my body ached from the intensive confinement. Until that point I had empathy for the animals who live their entire lives unable to extend their limbs. Now I was given the privilege of glimpsing the world from their vantage point.

After three days of zig zagging back and forth across states to drop off some prisoners and pick up others, we were only in Kentucky. The Daviess County Detention Center is an extradition hub where we had to spend the night. While prisoners are in transit they are allowed no contact with the outside world. When I finally got booked in and got to the phone, it was shut off. We were stored in a small dayroom with our own cells. We watched TV in the common area waiting to finish our respective journeys across the country.

A hurricane hit shortly after we arrived. Vans and buses kept bringing prisoners in, but no one was going back out and the jail got overcrowded. The women were all broken up into groups of four and herded into tiny two-person concrete cells to wait it out. Only days earlier, I'd have been panicking inside this cement box. After the van, it was actually a relief to be able to stand and take a step or two, not to mention being able to shower once a day. On the fifth day the storm broke. I was anxious to get back in the van and simultaneously dreading it. I just wanted to get where I was going. The handcuffs and shackles went back on. This van had different drivers. They put the women's cuffs on loosely and told us not to let them catch us trying to slip them off. Wink. Wink. If we managed to slip our cuffs we would get an attempted escape charge. Once I was secured back in my new vault, I maneuvered one hand out of my cuffs ignoring the pain of squeezing it over my knuckles. At each stop I'd slip back into them before the doors opened. The woman next to me did the same.

Several days into the second leg of this trek, the little van pulled into the sallyport of the Wayne County Jail in Detroit. It was about 2 am on Sunday morning, March 4, 2012, when my handcuffs and shackles were removed. I was thrown into a dirty holding cell somewhere near yelling male inmates. I fell asleep on the floor face down in the filth, exhausted after enduring over 10 days of a torturous extradition. I was awakened to get my mugshot taken and get booked in. There was a time when I would have been mortified by that picture. But I'm glad that the washed-out, blank expression on my face and faraway look in my eyes, crowned by a dirty, dry, unkempt mane was immortalized.

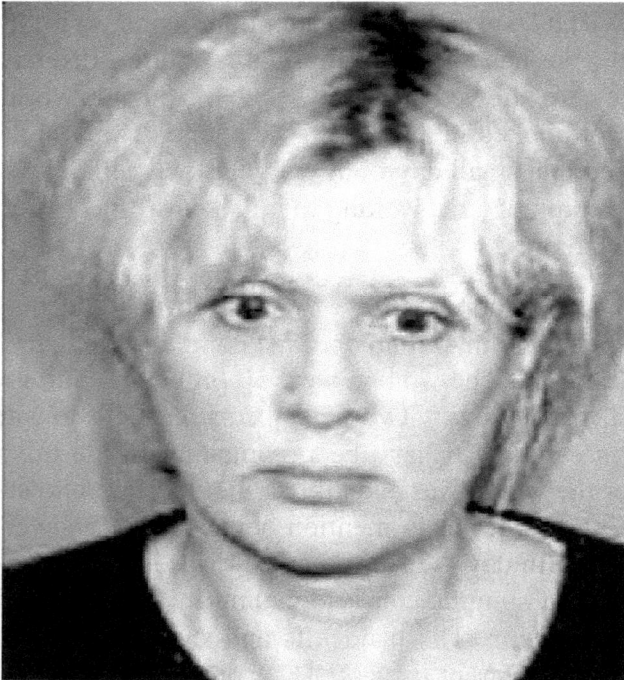

Camille Marino (March 4, 2012)

The vivisectors would use this picture frequently rather than the photos on my Facebook page. The fur industry issued a press release with this image. Any animal abuser or other individual with an agenda used that mugshot; some still do. But I own the face in this picture and am proud of it. It is the face of a prisoner of war. It is the face of an individual who was forced to experience intensive confinement, commodification, and injustice. It is the face of a woman who was allowed a mere glimpse of what nonhuman animals endure as a matter of course. And now it is my privilege and duty to convey my experience for the world.

Never was anything great achieved without danger. -Niccolo Machiavelli

Wayne County Jail

The dirty jail in Detroit was a world apart from the day camp I just left in Gainesville. The inmates called this place *the new jail* as opposed to the one that was condemned and no longer operational. But it was old. It still had bars on the cells instead of solid concrete and steel doors. I preferred the bars. It was so much more open. The holding cells here were filthy, some with dried blood or vomit on the walls, all of them had graffiti and green mold. And the guards here were different. Alachua County Jail officers were harsh and conducted themselves like drill instructors; the inmates were made to walk in single-file uniform lines when we left our housing unit, were not permitted to sit on tables or raise our voices within our pods, and there were bunk inspections twice daily. In Detroit, there was no charade. These guards were rude, abrasive, and abusive. The inmates were loud and aggressive. An element of street justice very much permeated this environment. I found it preferable.

After my mugshot was taken I was thrown back in my holding cell where I went back to sleep. When shift changed in the morning, I watched a big black woman with graying hair in dreads take her place behind the desk. It was obvious that she would be problematic. She was going to take her time. She was in no hurry to get me processed. And so, I sat. She ate. Shuffled papers. Talked on the phone. Chatted with the other guards. At one point, there was an emergency. Two male guards were wheeling a male inmate past my cell on a stretcher. A sheet was over his head. One of the male guards remarked about the man having been murdered on his shift and now they were going to be stuck doing overtime. The burly, dreaded woman said something and they all laughed.

When she was good and ready, this menacing sergeant opened the cage for me and the other women who had trickled in overnight. I was taken to see a nurse to get a TB test. Every time one is jailed, s/he is screened for tuberculosis. I learned in Alachua that if a prisoner says they're allergic, s/he is given a chest x-ray instead. I didn't want any more animal remains and poison injected in me so I told the nurse I was allergic. She called the intimidating woman, Ms. Graham, who started screaming at me. Then they both grabbed my arm and pinned it down to shove the four-pronged needle in. I didn't react. After the first two TB tests, administered in Florida and Kentucky, I started to develop an innocuous quarter-sized red patch around each test site. During the routine intake questions where they seek to establish gang affiliations as well as whether an inmate is suicidal or homicidal, I told her I was Buddhist and would need a vegan tray. She called over Graham. This time they laughed at me. I betrayed no emotion.

Then we were taken to change into dingy green WCJ uniforms. Imagine my surprise when Graham brought all four women into the change-out room, had us line up and strip. While we stood naked, she slowly shook out each piece of our garments. She went down the line and had each of us open our mouths, stick out our tongues, run our fingers between our gums and cheeks, and then lift our breasts Graham growled at us to turn around and face the wall and "squat and cough." "Lower!" "Cough three times hard!" Then while we were squatting at a level she found pleasing, she admonished us to spread our cheeks. I went into some robotic mode but felt a twinge of sympathy for the overweight woman next to me who was clearly humiliated, struggling to stifle sobs.

Finally, we were told to stand and lift our feet to make sure there was nothing taped to our soles.

The most disturbing part for me was yet to come. She threw our uniforms at us, allowed us to keep our own undergarments, and told us to get dressed. Then she directed us to a trash can where we were to go digging for a pair of filthy plastic jail slippers. At this I was horrified. I didn't want to touch them, let alone claim a pair as my own. I found two size-eight shoes which, because of some residual muscle loss in my feet, would fall right off when I tried to walk. We were led to a stack of smelly, filthy mats and told to grab one. We were given a towel, a blanket, a three-inch toothbrush, a little state-issued toothpaste, and a baby comb. Then we were to drag our things as we were led to our housing unit. My biggest challenge was keeping my slippers on my feet. And it was clear this jail was making no accommodations for anyone for anything.

I was taken to another floor and locked in another holding cell where I waited for another guard to get around to me. After what seemed like another few hours I was taken to my unit. There were maybe 20 women in there, everyone yelling and running wild. Some women played cards. A few stared at a TV that was impossible to hear above the noise. There was a bullet-proof guard's booth outside, but it was empty; the guards didn't interfere with the inmates. I liked the anarchy in the Detroit jail a lot better than the rigidity in Florida. And after extradition, there was simply no fear left. Through the grime on the six-inch-wide by two-foot-long windows, one could see people outside walking and driving. The Frank Murphy Hall of Justice was across the street. The pod itself was small and I just wanted to get out.

The next morning, I was called to get ready for court. They woke me at around 5 and dragged me out five minutes later. I sat in a holding cell for a few hours with all the women scheduled to appear. Finally, we walked under the jail, down a couple of flights of stairs, through a long, dirty corridor, to the courthouse across the street. I was taken to a block of holding cells underneath the building. They were solid concrete tombs. There was no one outside in the hallways, the toilets were stuffed up and clearly had not been cleaned anytime this decade; I could scream at the top of my lungs and no one would hear me. It was desolate down there. But I was with other women so I told myself that, surely, they couldn't forget about us all.

In my dungeon, I sat and thought. I knew exactly what the animals saw in theirs. They were built that way so that there is no escape and no access from the outside world. The only difference was that no one was going to come to this bunker to torture me. Being entombed alive must be the best part of their unfathomable odyssey. Maybe one day I would be able to use my experience to make people understand. Maybe I could make them see what we do to the innocent. Maybe I could make them care.

I was about to face the judge for contempt. I assumed that my flagrant disregard for their rules was not going to win me any favor. But I resolved to go through this with my head held high and without apology. I knew I had overwhelming support on the outside. Steve did an important interview with the Barbi Twins that gained a lot of exposure.[37] He spoke very eloquently about my victory over UF, my arrest being politically-motivated, and he successfully crafted the image of the repression that looms ominously over the Animal Liberation community.

John Royal came back to speak to me and told me what to expect. He told me we would go into court, plead not guilty, and then I would likely be allowed to fly home. He was right. When they took me to court, it was over in a few minutes. I was released on the condition I appeared in circuit court for my restraining order violation.

I was grateful that a colleague met me in Detroit and let me stay at her home. Two days later I appeared in court. The *Detroit Free Press* and other media were taping the proceedings. This was the first time I had seen Donal O'Leary in person. He looked older than his online images but arrogance and sadism dripped from his pores. He smiled contemptuously at me and I smiled back,

37 YouTube, "The Barbi Twins Interview Prof. Steve Best about Camille Marino," https://www.youtube.com/watch?v=W4tvwFVG654

entertaining an image of a baseball bat connecting with his skull.

John Royal was the epitome of professionalism. He was an astute, thorough, and competent advocate. But his affable and cordial manner in greeting O'Leary and his lawyers was jarring. O'Leary deserved no respect. My lawyer clearly disagreed. I pleaded not guilty to the contempt charge. A $5000 bail bond was set and my next court date was scheduled for May 2. I wasn't looking forward to having to defend myself in Michigan. But I wasn't at all rattled. Thanks to my supporters, I was able to post the 10% due on my bail bond and buy a ticket to fly home. In another two days I was back in Florida.

We are revolutionaries. True revolutionaries. And we don't make no apologies for that... We know that at this time more than any other time, revolution is necessary.
-Ramona Africa

Walter Bond

On February 11, 2011, Walter Bond was sentenced. He had avoided an upward deviation in his sentence and no repercussions for leaking the Trapped Zuelke information were visited upon me. I don't know whether or not he had anything to do with shielding me in that incident but I've wondered on occasion.

Walter and I spoke frequently. We were both of a single mindset when it came to Animal Liberation. He is very intelligent and articulate and could discuss just about anything. Where I've had a history of drug and alcohol abuse, he has always been straight edge. I admired that as much as I was in awe. We co-authored a few articles about vegan resistance and I rallied support for him. He would regularly allow me to post his comments and ideas on NIO or my Facebook page and I was glad to keep his voice alive.

Early in 2011 he told me he had his statement ready to read in court and he was excited for me to hear it. But he wouldn't

Walter Bond

read it to me over the phone. He said that as soon as he read his statement in court that it would be sent to me from his support people to publish. On February 11, 2011, Walter Bond delivered his statement in Denver, Colorado:

> *"I'm here today because I burnt down the Sheepskin Factory in Glendale, CO, a business that sells pelts, furs and other dead Animal skins.*
>
> *I know many people think I should feel remorse for what I've done. I guess this is the customary time where I'm supposed to grovel and beg for mercy. I assure you if that's how I felt I would. But, I am not sorry for anything I have done. Nor am I frightened by this court's authority. Because any system of law that values the rights of the oppressor over the down trodden is an unjust system.*
>
> *And though this court has real and actual power, I question its morality.*
>
> *I doubt the court is interested in the precautions that I took to not harm any person or by-stander and even less concerned with the miserable lives that sheep, cows and mink had to endure, unto death, so that a Colorado business could profit from their confinement, enslavement, and murder. Obviously, the owners and employees of the sheepskin factory do not care either or they would not be involved in such a sinister and macabre blood trade. So, I will not waste my breath where it will only fall on deaf ears.*
>
> *That's why I turned to illegal direct action to begin with, because you do not care. No matter how much we Animal Rights activists talk or reason with you, you do not care. Well, Mr. Livaditis (owner of the Sheepskin Factory), I don't care about you.*
>
> *There is no common ground between people like you and me. I want you to know that no matter what this court*

sentences me to today, you have won nothing!

Prison is no great hardship to me. In a society that values money over life, I consider it an honor to be a prisoner of war, the war against inter-species slavery and objectification! I also want you to know that I will never willingly pay you one dollar, not one! I hope your business fails and you choke to death on every penny you profit from Animal murder! I hope you choke on it and burn in hell!

To my supporters, I wish to say thank you for standing behind me and showing this court and these Animal exploiters that we support our own and that we as a movement are not going to apologize for having a sense of urgency. We are not going to put the interests of commerce over sentience! And we will never stop educating, agitating and confronting those responsible for the death of our Mother Earth and her Animal Nations.

My Vegan sisters and brothers our lives are not our own. Selfishness is the way of gluttons, perverts and purveyors of injustice. It has been said all it takes for evil to conquer is for good people to do nothing. Conversely, all it takes to stop the enslavement, use, abuse and murder of other than human Animals is the resolve to fight on their behalf! Do what you can, do what you must, be Vegan warriors and true Animal defenders and never compromise with their murderers and profiteers.

The Animal Liberation Front is the answer.

Seldom has there been such a personally powerful and internationally effective movement in human history. You cannot join the A.L.F. but you can become the A.L.F. And it was the proudest and most powerful thing I have ever done. When you leave this courtroom today don't be dismayed by my incarceration. All the ferocity and love in my heart still lives on. Every time someone liberates an Animal and smashes their cage, it lives on! Every time an activist refuses to bow down to laws that protect murder, it lives on! And it lives on every time the night sky lights up ablaze with the ruins of another Animal exploiters' business!

That's all Your Honor, I am ready to go to prison. "

Walter also pleaded guilty to the Tiburon foie gras restaurant arson and the Tandy Leather Factory arson and took one count under the Animal Enterprise Terrorism Act. He received a total of 12 years and 3 months in federal prison and is scheduled to be released on April 14, 2021.

Walter has written extensively about his early days working on a pig-kill floor and building slaughterhouses. He recounted to me an agonizing scene he witnessed one day. One of the pigs that was hung to be murdered escaped. The terrified individual ran helplessly, sliding across the blood-drenched floor to no avail. His co-workers were laughing as they cornered the pig and beat him or her mercilessly to death. He watched horrified. I believe it is at that moment that everything clicked for him.

Years later, at one of the slaughterhouses to which I gained access, a family-run, *humane* operation, I was allowed to film and report on their kill operation under the guise of being a journalist. I watched as the cows were led down the chute. I watched them try to back away only to be stunned, provoking them to walk to their deaths. I was not allowed to view the actual blow to the head which happened behind a wall. But as one cow was electrically shocked to walk down the ramp that led behind the wall, our eyes met. I was helpless. It was 5 am and I was alone with four big men that looked like they just walked out of the *Texas Chainsaw Massacre*. When the wall was raised, the cow that had looked at me to save him was on the floor writhing in seizures and choking. And then it stopped. I filmed his death. I published the film. That was one of the videos that vanished when my first YouTube account was deleted. But I became complicit in that individual's death that day in a very intimate manner. At that moment, despite the consensus that I had accomplished some great feat by getting the video out, everything clicked for me. I was guilty. I had blood on my hands.

So, I could only begin to understand the burden that Walter carried. The deepest regret he ever expressed to me was in building those slaughterhouses years before. While these may be the experiences that drive us, he spent many years educating the public about veganism, working with other activists, doing conventional forms of activism, and volunteering at animal sanctuaries where he found peace. And I think we both reached the same conclusion, in our own time frames, that mainstream moderation allows the status quo to continue unabated. He took matters into his own hands and showed us what's possible.

In January of 2012, Walter was transferred to the Communications Management Unit (CMU) at the Federal Penitentiary in Marion, Illinois. The CMU is a prison within a prison where communications are scrutinized and the inmates are severely restricted. It was constructed to warehouse *terrorists*; that is, political prisoners of Muslim descent and animal & environmental activists. Were the men in this unit not Muslim, they likely would never have been ensnared. And had Walter burned down a car wash rather than businesses that profit from animal death, he would have received the same sentence as any ordinary arsonist. He would have been afforded a big prison yard, a gym, college classes or training to learn a trade, and all the other amenities. But because he is an actor of conscience, Walter was housed in this exceedingly-harsh and punitive unit.

He began studying Arabic with the men in CMU and once recited a prayer for me on the phone. I was a little mesmerized by his intonation and inflection. Had I not known any better, I would have thought this was his native tongue. In one of our last conversations, I told Walter that we needed to get together in 2021 when he was finally released. Because of the frivolous nature of my charges, I jokingly said "I should be out of jail by then too." We both laughed. In early 2012, our contact was terminated by the

Bureau of Prisons citing "… such communication is detrimental to the security, good order, or discipline of the facility, or might facilitate criminal activity." I still read his work and was pleased to see a recent essay that suggests our respective attitudes toward abortion appear to have reconciled:

> *"Abortion, birth control, homosexuality, sterilization, and non-reproductive sexual activity really should be championed as responsible, conscious and evolved decisions, lifestyles and choices. and not stigmatized or discriminated against by religious wing nuts that think one little flesh-eating bastard is more important than the Earth and all life upon her!"*

In early 2016, Walter was granted permission to receive letters from me, but he may not respond. I suspect the overlords are allowing this one-sided communication simply to keep track of me. But that's okay. I hide from no one and apologize for nothing. And whether privately or publicly, my words don't change. So, I am happy to write Walter nearly every month to let him know he is in my thoughts. Occasionally he will publish an article through his website that will address issues I raise in my letters. I know he's okay and he's never acquiesced to the powers that be. And that's all that matters.

When he was operating as an underground operative, the Lone Wolf would end his anonymous communiques with six words that every activist needs to adopt, not as a slogan on a T-shirt, but, in how we all respond to nonhuman genocide:

"Animal Liberation whatever it may take."

Civil disobedience is not our problem.
Our problem is civil obedience.
-Howard Zinn

Escalation

As 2012 began, I was consumed in my work. I long had a vision of weaving a cohesive network of global activists and was always on the phone strategizing with colleagues from Florida to Europe. From Jacksonville to Miami, we had only just begun to work as a coherent unit. It was obvious that the Detroit prosecution was meant to distract and discourage me.

After my arrest, NIO Florida gained greater support globally. Another bonus was that Donal O'Leary's notoriety in my community skyrocketed to infamy. From behind bars, I was adamant that I wanted both Steve's and my posts to stay up on NIO. I was already in jail for taking a stand. All abusers seek to perpetuate their crimes in anonymity and peace. We should allow them none. Steve enthusiastically agreed and kept the posts up on NIO; I was surprised to learn, however, that, while I was locked up, he had permanently deleted his original Freddy Kruger comment to delete his IP, his cyber fingerprint. It was common knowledge that Steve was the author; we both posted it to our respective Facebook profiles where he openly accepted praise for his ideas. Investigative journalist Will Potter appeared to remain clueless though. He wrote an article about my case referring to the author of the Freddy Kruger letter as "one of her more dimwitted followers."[38] I thought that might have been the impetus for Steve beginning to distance himself from the writing while simultaneously leading the Facebook efforts to intensify the scrutiny already focused on Donal O'Leary.

One of Steve's associates created an image of O'Leary with his address and phone number under his face. The artist was Rhonda Brabbin, a woman who calls herself *Alafair Lee Robicheaux* on Facebook. Everyone in my community has either had to start using their real name or have their profile deleted. An entire new social media forum called *Ello* was created because many individuals in the LGBTQ community were being shut down on Facebook for using their drag names. I always wondered how Rhonda's alias remained immune inside the Facebook bureaucracy. Steve made the image his profile picture encouraging others to follow. It is not an exaggeration to estimate that hundreds of supporters made the image their profile picture, many with the tag *in solidarity with Camille* or *prosecute me too*. The contempt for this single vivisector was palpable, condemnation resounding across oceans continents; conversely, as hatred for this one man reached a fever pitch so did my support as I faced him one on one.

He was getting death threats, his family was being threatened, packages were allegedly sent to his home. There was never any public confirmation of the latter; sometimes Facebook people would say things just to impress me. I never put much weight in these claims. In court, I would ultimately be held responsible for the death threats. If Donal O'Leary was a baker and I re-circulated his publicly-available personal information, he would have gotten orders for cupcakes. But I re-published the readily-available personal information of someone who tortures animals to death, so he got death threats. My role is constant and pure. I am simply a messenger, a journalist, an information hub. The subject is the only variable. But they were holding me responsible for the

38 This article was subsequently edited and the phrasing now reads "a commenter." Will Potter, "Camille Marino Arrested – Are Animal Rights Activists a 'Hate Group,'" Green is the New Red (February 14, 2012) http://www.greenisthenewred.com/blog/camille-marino-arrested-negotiation-is-over/5680/

reaction the subject elicited. My response would be to focus all of that outrage right at his doorsteps.

Lisa Grossman kept pumping out NIO Florida posts while I was locked up. Now, getting the records back into my possession was my priority. I was in the news a lot and the reports were about my charges, not animal abuse. The welfare complaint Michael Budkie promised to file was nonexistent. And while my side of the fence was playing tug-of-war with the documents I went to court to secure, the federal complaint fell by the wayside as did my ability to leverage it in the press. And I grossly underestimated the media's role. Imprisoned journalist Mumia Abu-Jamal observes that "The media, itself an arm of mega-corporate power, feeds the fear industry, so that people are primed like pumps to support wars on rumor, innuendo, legends, and lies."[39] Indeed, their commitment to vilify me while validating and normalizing legalized industrial abuse was almost tangible. Thanks to social media, however, whenever corporate media published an article about me being an unhinged fanatic, it allowed my community a platform to open up a serious public discussion about animal experimentation and exploitation. There were even discussions about the discussions.[40]

I managed to get half of the records back from Lisa and allowed her to *analyze* the balance. Thankfully I had several movement physicians, scientists, vets and a UF lab insider who were very generous in explaining to me exactly what the veterinary records said. While I was in control, everything that was published was factually-solid and damning. But the control issues were becoming troublesome. I had a nagging feeling that several of my associates were more comfortable when I was in jail. The monkeys were suffering brutal existences in the labs and my only goal was to make life as uncomfortable as I could for their tormentors and get those victims out safely. Animal experimentation is a business.

39 MUMIA DFDR: 2/3/10 A Year In: More Same Than Change (https://www.youtube.com/watch?v=kvGKzs9oO9M)

40 Animal Liberation Front, "Discussion: The Arrest of Camille Marino, Compassion, the Sadism of Vivisection," (February 15, 2012) http://www.animalliberationfront.com/Practical/Shop--ToDo/Activism/EisenbudOnCamillesArrest.htm

Escalation

When the business is no longer profitable, when the detriment of continuing is too great, the business shuts down. Plain and simple. That had to remain my only focus.

Against this backdrop, I still had to contend with my legal issues. John Royal was professional, but I was disconcerted by the respect he extended to O'Leary. He also failed to respond to several of my emails. When I discussed my reservations with Steve, he shared with me a confidence. Belinda Morris was one of my supporters in Canada who secured John Royal's services while I was incarcerated. Steve told me that John took my case because he and Belinda were having cybersex on Skype. Now it made sense to me. John was ignoring my emails because he was more interested in Belinda. I sent him an email asking him if this was so. He never responded.

While I was in lock up, Gary Yourofsky told Jennifer and Alice that he would refer me to his friend, a vegan criminal lawyer who represented him on several counts of civil disobedience in Michigan. When Jennifer relayed this offer to my support team it was rejected. I only learned of Gary's offer from Jennifer after I was home. I sent him an email. He gave me Matt Savich's information. I sent John Royal an email firing him and I retained Matt. I wasn't pleased that my support team was making critical decisions without even consulting me. While I was in jail, Steve and I still spoke several times a day. I couldn't understand why he would place so much trust in a veritable sycophant and dismiss an offer from Gary Yourofsky, his longtime friend and a veteran activist.

In hindsight, I don't believe that Belinda Morris ever flirted with John Royal or did anything sexually inappropriate. John must have thought I was some kind of lunatic when I sent him the email questioning him about such. By being on my support team, Belinda found an opportunity to get close to Steve. I believe that putting these thoughts in my head was a tool for Steve to pit us against one another. I can picture him laughing in front of his computer when he read his blind copy of the email I sent to John Royal. He had no reason to try to position us as adversaries; I didn't even consider her an activist; but this is a tool he uses to manipulate the people around him. (I wonder what role he played in instigating the rivalry between Jason Miller and me.) I couldn't understand why Steve put this woman in charge of my support. We had nothing in common, but Steve enjoyed her adulation I guess.

Around the world, activists rallied around me; they donated to my legal fund, held events and fundraisers, wrote articles, wrote blogs, defended me and gave the animals a voice in the comments section of newspapers and industry sites all over the web. But the core group that made up my support team existed only online; outside of the realm of my colleagues in the real world. Steve had spoken to Belinda by email for a while before I was ever arrested. My only knowledge of their friendship was based on her emails to him that he would forward to me. They ridiculed Gary Francione and his associates and discussed any color of minutia in exhausting detail. Steve reveled in having recruited a new groupie to entertain his obsession with the Rutgers law professor, but he complained to me more than once that Belinda would never send him a picture of herself.

Rhonda Brabbin (hereinafter referred to by her Facebook alias, Alafair) was also among the core group and it was obvious she was supporting me to please Steve. When she wrote to me, we had nothing to talk about. She once told me that she had borderline personality disorder. I can only assume that Steve told her I was bipolar and this was a misguided attempt to find common ground. I found her very unmotivated; she was just there, but not necessarily for any reason. When I needed her to do a support task, the response was dead air. Steve would have to direct her and the job would then get done. There was also a woman in the UK named Ann Parkes and a few others who made up my support network. Without question, their zealousness in taking up my cause was a means for each of them to please Steve; but Ann, in particular, spent hours and days rallying people to the cause. I believe she was there as a loyal supporter and friend. She also donated a lot of money to my legal fund. I trust that her loyalty to both Steve and me was genuine.

137

Escalation

There were two other people on my team who were my friends from Florida. Ron Roberts and I would get together in South Florida from time to time, go to protests, go out to eat, or just spend some time together. The other person was Chris Lagergren. At a fundraiser for Walter Bond that we held in 2010, Walter called me from jail at a pre-arranged time; Chris held the bullhorn to my phone while everyone gathered to hear Walter's address. Someone took a picture of us at the center of the gathering while Walter spoke. Chris and I used that image for both our cover photos on Facebook for a while. So, with both Chris and Steve involved, and Ron on the periphery, I was confident that everyone was working in my best interest.

I still had tremendous reservations and internal conflict about the individuals Steve had assembled, however. It deeply disturbed me that I had become their cause rather than Animal Liberation. My support group never left Facebook. All they did before me was post atrocity after atrocity on Facebook, extend some obligatory angry statuses, and move on to the next post. Alafair, in particular, is almost obsessive in her frenzied social media posting. After they were assembled around me, all they did was post about me. Along with Steve, they began calling themselves *the inner circle*. Ann was the supporter in whom I placed a great deal of trust. She had my records of financial supporters to the legal fund and would even send out the thank you notes at one point. She would regularly browbeat people into contributing by saying that "this is the most important case in animal rights history." It was embarrassing. But she was extraordinary in freeing up my time so that I could focus on the animals.

Steve knew how I felt about the inner circle. He told me that they had "no other form of activism" and so they made me their cause. He told me to just accept the help and keep my feelings to myself. They created *Support Camille* t-shirts, *Negotiation Is Over* t-shirts, a *Standing by Camille* Facebook page, a dedicated support site, they created graphics and fundraisers. Ann rallied people every day. I made her an administrator of NIO on Facebook and gave her access to my sites but I remained very conflicted. I hated that these people functioned largely like cultists. I told

Steve that I wanted to write an article that used a lot of impressive language but said absolutely nothing. I was pretty sure I would get effusive reviews for my *incisive* perception. He laughed. I also told him that we should go on Facebook one day and announce that we decided that outlawing bestiality was speciesist and we should wait to see how long it took for this group to start dating their dogs. I despised this total allegiance and absence of critical thought in people. They were cultists seeking a messiah. Steve cultivated such followers and enjoyed their adulation.

They say the things we hate in others are only reflections of the things we can't face in ourselves. At the time I couldn't see that I was a cultist. I would have scoffed at the mere suggestion that Steve Best was my messiah. I vehemently believed he was my best friend. Steve despised Gary Francione for the cult-like following he enjoyed. I'm pretty sure he saw in his nemesis everything he wasn't. Interestingly, for all of the chest-pounding, constant critiquing, and public outrage he directed at Francione, the only time the law professor seriously challenged him to a public debate on Skype, Steve wouldn't do it. He told me that Gary wanted to record it and that no matter what happened he would spin it for his followers so that Steve looked foolish. "Gary's a very smart man" he would say privately. I thought that running from the challenge after all the bluster looked foolish. It was cowardly. But I never voiced that. When people called him a coward, I simply went into attack mode to defend and protect him.

Now I had Matt Savich to defend and protect me. He was vegan. He was from New York. We shared ideology. We shared an understanding. And he despised vivisectors as much as I. When I wrote him, he responded. Now that I felt more comfortable about my Michigan case, I turned my attention back to the animals. We crunched out the stories of more UF victims.

On December 2, 1998, ten macaques were shipped to the University of Florida from the Caribbean Primate Research Center at the University of Puerto Rico. One of those monkeys was a 3-year old male called 95-D, later named Harry by his new captors.[41] After being tortured inside his cage in a windowless bunker for 11 years, his principle abuser, a researcher named Dennis Brooks, ordered his murder. On September 1, 2009, his broken body was promptly incinerated.

Our source inside their lab explained the decision:

> *"...he was killed because the study ended. Housing and maintaining animals is expensive, especially monkeys. There was no funding for further research, so Harry needed to be eliminated.* **They don't like to release animals to sanctuaries because of the exposure.** *[Emphasis added.] They don't want the public to know that they do in any of these studies and a sanctuary may not be as discreet about the sources.*

> *"Harry went immediately to the animal facility's incineration room where he was later burned with all the other animals that are regularly burned several times a week. It would be nice if they went to introductory biology labs on campus for dissection (at least SOMETHING else could have been gained from their lives) but again, that lifts the veil of secrecy."*

The University of Florida was determined to stop me from releasing their records. And as furiously as they went after me, I returned the favor. In April of 2012 we demonstrated weekly and maintained a consistent presence at the vivisectors' homes and churches. Along with a small group of protesters, we always had an equal or greater number of police escorts. We had the documents, we had the pictures taken by the vivisectors themselves, and we had ample access to computers and copy machines. When we weren't online rallying the world against UF, we were in the streets handing out fliers, putting them in mailboxes, and on windshields. When parents and prospective students visited UF in the coming months, we would greet them

---

41 NIO Florida, "Harry: Tortured for 11 Years Until Funding Ran Out," Eleventh Hours for Animals (March 28, 2012) http://universityofflorida.us/harry-the-miserable-life-and-death-of-another-victim-of-the-university-of-florida/

with our *welcome* favors. Where there were football games, alumni events, restaurants or crowds of people anywhere in Gainesville, we were there with fliers and a monologue. Lisa was vital to this aspect of our campaign. She was like the expert party planner, finding venues and events for us to infiltrate. She was also our decorator, making signs and favors. I had no aptitude for, nor interest in, these things. Our partnership functioned well when we could rise above the personality clashes.

All the attention that was focused on me in the Animal Liberation community provided me with the means to launch an effective mirror effort against the Detroit *researcher*. I envisioned parallel campaigns. I wanted an initiative to take shape on the campus of Wayne State with the same energy and single-minded dedication as NIO Florida. Since Donal O'Leary had stepped up to help the University of Florida escape the spotlight, it seemed to me that he deserved that spotlight to fall directly on him; that is, if he wasn't enjoying our attention enough already. NIO Detroit was born.

I already had a plane ticket to be in Michigan in early May when my hearing was continued. Steve and I discussed the options at length. We both firmly believed that we needed to take the fight to abusers' doorsteps. During this time, I had put a logo up on NIO of Steve's image with one of his quotes, "when the law is wrong the right thing to do is break it." I saw an opportunity to manifest everything we both preached in a meaningful way as well as to get the NIO Detroit campaign off the ground. I decided that this was a perfect time to stage an act of civil disobedience on the campus of Wayne State. Both David Jentsch's and Donal O'Leary's restraining orders banned me from the UCLA and Wayne State campuses, respectively. There was a lot of internal debate about the most effective manner in which to stage this action. I simply wanted to chain myself to the doors of the campus library, making sure no one could enter or exit. I had no intention of repeating the failed action in Ohio. Steve urged me to find O'Leary's office and chain myself to his desk. He said we needed to confront abusers. I fully agreed with confrontation and escalation, but I thought it would be dumb as fuck to get myself 10 years' worth of stalking charges for a media stunt. Ron was always more moderate and practical than I. He was very persuasive that I should attend the protest, but stage a benign action right off campus where I would not violate the restraining order.

The salient part of this action was to defy the trespass order and, in fact, show up because of it. I told Ron that staging my action off campus would defeat the purpose. I told Steve that I had no intention of entering the science building or finding O'Leary. But I also told him that this was his opportunity to practice what he preached. I asked him to come to Wayne State with me and lock down or at least pick up a bull horn and rally our comrades. His response was stunning: "you want me to spend money on a ticket?" "Yes, I want you to spend money. It doesn't look right for you to always preach about breaking laws if you won't do it yourself." His lip service was wearing thin. Activists spend our money, our freedom, and every resource we have to serve the animals. And we consider it a privilege to do so.

Before I put anything in place, I discussed everything with Matt. He advised that I would probably have to do 30 days in WCJ for trespassing. The next step was to harness the outrage among our small group of Detroit activists and direct it into a protest in May. This group had been assembled around me by the inner circle, but Ron was amazing at identifying and motivating the few real activists among them. This gave me a comfort level about insinuating myself into my Michigan support group. I needed to organize them for a simple protest. As long as we had bodies present I would consider it a win. Only Alice who came down from Canada would know of the real plan. We would do the press releases, she would do the media interviews, and she would galvanize and lead our troops after I was arrested.

I had grown accustomed to the rigorous airport security checks and was very concerned that, with charges already pending, I could easily have been pulled off the plane and arrested before I ever left Florida. Relieved, I texted Ron when I made it to Michigan and was waiting for the shuttle to take me to the hotel. I called Steve. We were all excited. Alice and I met at our hotel. I was surprised when Ann Parkes called my cell from England.

It was the first time I'd ever heard her voice. She had a lovely British accent and was effusive in telling me how courageous I was, asking me to be careful, and wishing me luck. I thanked her. I had gotten used to this type of adulation but I never understood it. This was a simple protest and essentially a media stunt. If my actions warranted such praise, I could only surmise that there wasn't a whole lot of anything else going on.

Alice and I went to explore the campus taking care not to be spotted. Had I been identified and arrested for trespassing, our plans would have been for naught. Both of us having experience in choosing an effective spot to stage an action, we agreed that the library was the optimal location. Alice wanted to lock down with me but we needed a spokesperson and the group needed a leader. With just the two of us, we had to maximize our limited resources. She brought anti-vivisection signs and we created one with the Facebook photo of Donal O'Leary along with his name and contact information. There were heartbreaking images of the dogs that are burned and mutilated inside labs. We bought some chains. Then we went to have a drink.

The next morning, Alice and I sent out our press releases about an hour before the scheduled lock down. We walked onto the campus and sat outside the library. It probably is not an unusual sight to see students assembling to protest, but we could not allow campus security to identify me. I went inside to find a bathroom to waste a few minutes. Our protesters weren't there yet, but the campus police were paying a little too much attention to us. They passed. It was now or never. We quickly locked me to the library doors. I taped my mouth shut to symbolize the repression. Alice assembled our signs. I held one that screamed Banned. At my feet was the centerpiece that Alice created. It said "Publish information about the butcher, baker, and candlestick maker... only the butcher has a problem with it."

Media started to arrive. The first protesters began to trickle in. Students gathered. Alice was an eloquent spokesperson, explaining why we were there and the crimes of which O'Leary was guilty. In under 5 minutes the campus police were back. One of them took out his walkie talkie, pointed at me and said "it's her." Within seconds, three police vehicles surrounded me. They cut my chain and replaced it with handcuffs. I was taken to the Wayne State University Police Department.

*Auschwitz begins wherever
someone looks at a slaughterhouse
and thinks: they're only animals.
-Theodor W. Adorno*

7 Mile

I was seated at a table in the WSU police department. A small-framed, pale, severe-faced, white woman with big-red hair came in and sat across from me. She was probably in her 30s and went out of her way to be professional, but arrogance and contempt exuded from her being. I felt sorry for her partner or spouse. She turned on her tape recorder, introduced herself as a Wayne State University detective, clearly Jeff Moran's counterpart, and asked me why I was "targeting" Donal O'Leary. I chuckled, smiled, and said "My lawyer's name is Matt Savich." She picked up her toys and left.

I waited until two affable Detroit police officers finally showed up, cuffed me, and led me to their cruiser. The male reminded me of Carl Winslow, the father from the old sitcom, *Family Matters,* who was always being pestered by Steve Urkel. We laughed that they had to take a break from actual crime to come get me. They told me not to worry. I would be out in a few hours. We pulled into the 7 Mile police station, not to be confused with the next precinct area from the Eminem movie, *8 Mile*. They booked me in and took my mugshots. I was horrified when I saw my profile image. I had no idea I needed a face lift! I kept my clothes, but they took all my possessions including shoe laces, jewelry and even my reading glasses. They gave me a little 2" x 4" bar of state-issued soap, the standard little state-issued deodorant, and something I'd never seen before. It was a three-inch cardboard lollipop stick with a about a half a square inch of foam on the end of it. I learned that was a toothbrush!

The female officer and I chatted. She told me that when I got out she would like her daughter to start working with me. She thought it would build her character and keep her off the streets. I was put in the first holding cell on the block. There was one row with either 3 or 4 cells on each side. Through the bars we faced the men in the cells across from us. There was no privacy at all. At any given moment there were between 1 and 8 women in my cell. The toilet was behind a three-foot long wall that was probably four feet high. If you sat on the bowl, your legs stuck out. And when you stood up with your pants down, you were looking directly at the male inmates as well as officers walking by. There was a concrete bench that extended around the interior cell wall. It was loud. The light was always on. It was hot. It was uncomfortable. There was a big loud fan blowing at the end of the cell corridor. But I was only going to be there for a few hours.

The officers gave us a sandwich and some water. I wasn't hungry. I'd eat when I got out. I waited and waited. That night I took the sandwich and ate the bread. I gave away the hard baloney. I fell asleep momentarily in my clothes on the concrete block with the lights glaring in my face. Without any sheets, I found myself curling up unconsciously to shield myself. I woke up and sat there waiting until morning. One of the women in my cell rarely stopped crying. She was a driver and the officer who searched her found an unlicensed gun. That was an automatic 2 years and she was going to lose her taxi. We waited, talking occasionally to pass time. During the day, I got one of the phones in the cell to work and finally got through to Steve. But it was useless. We couldn't hear one another. I asked the guards what was taking so long. They told me they're probably just waiting for my formal trespassing charge to be filed and then they can let me out.

Two days passed. I learned that the FBI had taken possession of my cell phone. It wasn't encrypted.

Three days passed.

On the fourth day, it was obvious something was going on. *Carl Winslow* started talking to me differently. Instead of saying "don't worry about it; you'll be out in a few hours," he was now saying "you'll be okay." There was something ominous about it. It was clear to me that once again, the local police were simply detaining me while some higher authority pulled the strings.

On the fifth day, I was finally called out with the inmates who had come in the day before and taken to my video arraignment. Matt was in the courtroom. He had brought his daughter and her friend with him. They had all been out of town at one of her soccer meets when he got the call from the district attorney. During those five days, at least 5 universities including the University of Florida and Wayne State, and I'm unclear about how many jurisdictions, had participated in the conferences that culminated in my final charges. They went through every law on the books. At my arraignment the magistrate read my official offenses:

- I was charged with misdemeanor trespassing, 30 days.

- I was charged with an aggravated stalking felony for trespassing in violation of a restraining order, 5 years.

- And I am the only person in the state of Michigan ever to be charged with something they found on the books called posting a message, another 5-year felony. The state contended that Section 750.411 applied to Steve's Freddy Kruger letter in that (1) it could incite two or more individuals to commit violence and (b) was meant to terrorize O'Leary.

My bail was set at $25,000. Matt argued for a reduction in bond on the grounds that I had never been in trouble in my life. The judge snapped at him: "well she's certainly doing a bang-up job of it now!"

147

I exited the video room and returned to the main police desk in a state of shock. All I could utter was "10 years." My mind was flashing to myself getting out of prison at almost 60 years old. *Carl* looked at me reassuringly and said "don't worry, you're not going to do 10 years." I was transported back to Wayne County Jail. This time I welcomed changing into my puke-green uniform just to get out of my dirty clothes and brush my teeth with a real three-inch toothbrush. I was also anxious to have access to a working prison phone.

The cost of being prosecuted was becoming evident. I already owed John Royal $5,000. In order to retain Matt on the felony charges I had to come up with another $10,000 in addition to the $5,000 for the civil case I already owed. He signed on and allowed me to pay in installments. I had no clue how I was going to come up with another $2,500 to put down the 10% of my bail needed to bond out this time. And I was looking at travel expenses between Florida and Michigan as well as lodging for an extended period of time.

I was in jail for another 3 days while the $2,500 was raised. A supporter in Detroit named Linda Denton who was to become a friend came to pay my bond. The jail informed her that everyone who has any communication "with her" is getting reported to the FBI. "Are you sure you want to put your name down on Marino's bond?" Refusing to be intimidated, Linda signed. My belongings were returned to me. My cell phone had been cloned by the feds and returned. A colleague met me again and we went back to her house in Adrian. I left to return home the next day, scheduled to come back to Detroit for my pre-trial hearing the following month.

Ron never said "I told you so." But he had.

When you tear out a man's tongue,
you are not proving him a liar,
you're only telling the world that
you fear what he might say.
-George R. R. Martin

The NIO Laws

At the University of Florida's behest, Governor Rick Scott signed a bill in April of 2012 that would effectively allow them to prosecute me as a stalker for republishing the publicly-available personal information of their vivisectors. The law was to go into effect on October 1. The Gainesville Sun reported on the legislation that had been purchased by the university[42]:

> *"A half-dozen University of Florida employees have been harassed or threatened as a result of their home addresses and other contact information being posted on an animal-rights website, according to university officials, who hope that changes to the state's stalking law will help address these kind of threats.*
>
> *"Animal rights activist Camille Marino of Wildwood founded the group Negotiation is Over and has used*

42 Nathan Crabbe, "UF researchers being harassed, threatened by activists," The Gainesville Sun (May 1, 2012) http://www.gainesville.com/news/20120501/uf-researchers-being-harassed-threatened-by-activists

149

its website in a campaign against researchers who she claims experiment on animals. Marino was arrested at a Gainesville protest in February and extradited to Michigan for violating a court order to remove from the website the personal information of a researcher from that state.

"Information on the researcher has been taken down, and Marino has returned to Florida as she awaits a June hearing in the case, but information on the UF researchers remains online. UF Police Chief Linda Stump said those researchers have received death threats and other harassment by email and phone calls at all hours.

"'I think they certainly take them seriously,' Stump said of the threats. 'We're going to pursue everything we can under the law to seek legal remedies, and I think the new law coming into effect will help individuals that receive this type of harassment.'

"The law, signed last week by Gov. Rick Scott and taking effect Oct. 1, expands the stalking statute to include electronically delivered threats. It establishes cyberstalking as a third-degree felony and allows injunctions of up to 10 years to be issued. The changes are directed at domestic violence and exempt protests, but broaden the definition of what is considered a threat.

"Marino said she is simply posting publicly available personal information about researchers online and isn't responsible for threats to them. But she said that any means are justified in stopping research that she equates to 'murdering, terrorizing and abusing' animals."

I responded to my community through my website[43]:

---

43 NIO Florida, "New law criminalizes NIO's anti-vivisection campaign tactics at the University of Florida," Eleventh Hour for Animals (May 12, 2012) http://universityofflorida.us/new-law-criminlizes-nios-anti-vivisection-campaign-tactics-at-the-university-of-florida/

> *"Florida law has just been redefined to prohibit me from posting public domain information about vivisectors on NIO. Clearly, this is yet another assault on our First Amendment freedoms and demands a concerted response from this community. I just received UF's most recent vet records through December 31, 2011 and will begin publishing in the coming weeks. However, since I am in no position to take on any more legal battles at the moment, I am asking all of my comrades to close ranks and disseminate the info about my vivisectors throughout our extended networks. And, well, if it's harassment and intimidation they're worried about, that is not our problem. Perhaps they should find a less violent, bloody, and parasitic profession! -Camille "*

Wayne State University would follow suit in the coming months. In November, WSU was in court claiming that their public information should be exempted from public records requests. They asserted that my use of their public information might endanger their vivisectors.[44] Apparently, universities seem to agree that public information must be withheld from the public when it is used effectively. As one would expect, welfarists agreed with their vivisector counterparts.

---

44 Elizabeth Warmerdam, "College Alarmed by Animal Rights 'Extremists,'" Courthouse News Service (November 27, 2012) https://www.courthousenews.com/2012/11/27/52559.htm

I was now resolved to do everything
in my power to defeat the system.
-Oskar Schindler

Pretrial Hearing

Steve had my community up in arms before they ever unlocked my cell, rallying people now to contribute to my legal fund and take a stand against the state. None of my arrests or charges had fazed me. From my very first statement Gabby published, I referred to this whole thing as a "minor inconvenience." That wasn't bravado. It was an honest assessment of my own situation against a backdrop of unimaginable suffering visited upon nonhuman animals on an incomprehensible scale. After the initial disbelief wore off, my main concern was how I was going to manage a focused campaign in Gainesville going forward.

I called Michael Budkie and asked him if and when he planned to file the welfare complaint. Although I understood that he agreed with the vivisectors in opposing my tactics, it never occurred to me that he was actually working against me. He told me he wanted all of the records I had won in court before he would file anything. It became clear to me he would do nothing to further my efforts for the animals. This had always been about Budkie exploiting my victory to his advantage, not exploiting my victory to hold UF accountable. How sad that this man viewed me as his competitor. He was no different than Lisa except that he had been around for a couple of decades and had cultivated a lot of followers and enjoyed mainstream credibility. I came to understand that Michael Budkie was an integral part of an animal rights patriarchy that seeks to moderate the movement, acting as arbiters of which activists and which tactics will be *allowed* and supported. The welfare complaint was not going to be filed with the USDA. I decided I would learn how to do it myself and simply add this to my personal arsenal of acquired skills. But I had too much on my plate to take on anything else at the moment. It would have to wait.

As far as getting the mirror campaign off the ground, Ron had warned me when I was in jail that Ann Parkes was out of control. I had vested in her a certain amount of authority and it went to her head. He told me that she was insulting and alienating on-the-ground activists in Detroit. I told him I trusted her judgment. I wasn't seeing what he was seeing. I wasn't even paying attention. Where Ron was bringing activists in, Ann was playing online lord and master. She virtually single-handedly destroyed NIO Detroit. Of the few core people who remained, all but one were scared away by all the controversy swirling around me. It turned out to be a total bust.

When I was released from jail and began to see for myself how Ann was conducting herself online, it began to come into focus. She was part of *the inner circle*. She had absolute authority. I began to gently step in and resume control of my own groups and campaigns. With a core of apathy permeating my community, I will take one real-world activist over 10 online blowhards any day of the week. Ann resented me welcoming back Detroit activists with whom she had issues. *She* confronted *me* about going over her head and now my patience was fully exhausted. I was far more concerned about salvaging a campaign than I was about egos and Facebook drama. I let her remain on my fundraising team and took back control of any and all activism-related initiatives. While I wanted to dispense with the inner circle entirely, I was in no position to do so.

I turned my attention back to UF and the next set of records still haunt me. On May 26, 2012, we introduced the world to Bucky[45]:

> *"Bucky is a capuchin monkey who has remained a captive of Raymond J. Bergeron since 1999. As the records demonstrate, Bucky's existence is now one of nightmarish deprivation, self-mutilation, misery and pain. Blood is repeatedly found in his cage, he is self-mutilating, vocalizing, and his hair pulling leaves bald spots. He is agitated and aggressive, exhibiting stereotypical pacing, biting of bars, tail holding, as well as scratching around his face and eyes. As of December 31, 2011, it appears that Bucky was still actively being driven insane.*
>
> *"Among the injuries documented are a gash on his left big toe, his left inner thigh was excoriated and bleeding was noted, moist wounds were observed on both knees with significant swelling, and his tail was also found lacerated. The most severe injury Bucky sustained thus far was a deep cut on his leg and knee which required surgery, after which he would open his wounds. Another laceration by his left eye is documented as either another self-mutilation or as being sustained from lab equipment, which would indicate neglect."*

Our UF whistleblower observed:

> *"I'm sure all those injuries were due to thrashing about in his cage – exhibiting rage and hostility. These guys are in prison..."*

Prolonged intense confinement drives animals insane, humans and nonhumans alike. Whenever a fur farm is penetrated, it is common to see raccoons or foxes spinning hopelessly in their cages. This is a function of them literally going out of their minds. Whenever a lab is penetrated, we see animals self-mutilating.

45 NIO Florida, "Bucky's 'strictly regulated' hellish existence inside the University of Florida," Eleventh Hour for Animals (May 26, 2012) http://universityofflorida.us/buckys-strictly-regulated-hellish-existence-inside-the-university-of-florida/

Are they trying to kill themselves and end their nightmares? Or are they exhibiting the same behavior we see in humans who are driven mad in isolation cells: cutting themselves, smearing feces on the walls, overflowing toilets. Are the animals in so much pain that cutting themselves provides some sort of release? Whatever the answer, Bucky was exhibiting all the hallmarks of physical distress and madness. I had to get him out before they killed him.

It's repeatedly documented that UF will not release animals that are so deteriorated, even though they are of no use to them for their experiments. They don't go to sanctuaries. They go to the incinerator. We began doing protests to Free Bucky. We showed up at their church and at Bergeron's house. I did several interviews but the Gainesville Sun refused to report on Bucky. They would only report on my aggravated stalking charges. Simultaneously, every statement I'd ever made advocating capital punishment for serial animal killers was homogenized into a thesis of madness.[46] I was intent on diverting the attention back to Bucky and began organizing a Weekend of Outrage. But I needed to be back in Michigan so it would have to wait until I returned. In early June I flew out for my first pretrial hearing.

O'Leary showed up flanked by the red-haired detective, his private counsel, Wayne State University counsel, the prosecutor, and the police to *protect him from me*. Matt and I took our seats at the defense table. Matt's first tactic was inspired. He moved to have all of O'Leary's counsel removed from the courtroom arguing that they might be called as witnesses in the future. The prosecutor objected. The lawyers went back and forth for a few moments. The judge ultimately removed them from the courtroom. The trial continued. Matt and I were both nearly cited for contempt that day.

Donal O'Leary took the stand, was sworn in, and the prosecutor guided him as he read the Freddy Kruger letter to the court in its entirety. That day, June 12, 2012, prosecutor Ryan Lukiewski told the court "and if I may state for the record, just in case it

46 Anna North, "The Scary Animal Rights Activist Thinks Researchers Should Die," *Jezebel* (March 8, 2012) MARINO v. UNIVERSITY OF FLORIDA | FindLaw

doesn't come out through testimony, the article is actually written by Steven Best; he's a professor of philosophy and it's his." The whole world knew Steve authored the post in question. He'd taken credit for it on his own Facebook page. Because I allowed it to be published on my website, however, the state contended that I had adopted his words. I was the one they needed to neutralize and this was simply a vehicle to do it. Steve had a right to express himself creatively and I had a right to allow him a forum. Simply because the state alleged that the letter was intended to incite people to violence did not make it so.

I was admonished twice. Once for glaring at O'Leary while he performed on the stand and the second time, far more sternly, for chuckling while he read the Freddy Kruger letter. I was relieved that I didn't actually burst out laughing. Then the vivisector went on to discuss Steve's video "Every motherfucker who hurts animals is gonna feel the fear." He swore to the court that Steve directly threatened him by name in that video. That was utter nonsense. Steve recorded that video at a presentation in Italy two years earlier, before anyone even knew Donal O'Leary's name. He further testified about the death threats he received, how he had to install security cameras on his home, how I repeatedly threatened him, and how threatened he felt by me chaining myself to the campus library. On cross-examination, Matt was able to demonstrate that O'Leary was lying through his teeth, but the judge couldn't have cared less.

The court admonished Matt several times. O'Leary took exception to Matt referring to him as a "vivisectionist" (Matt's preferred terminology). The vivisectionist contended that being called a vivisectionist was derogatory. My lawyer successfully argued that vivisectionist/vivisector is a clinical term that simply means one who carves up live animals. Then O'Leary took exception to Matt referring to him as "mister" instead of "doctor." The judge ordered him to show O'Leary respect and deference and address him as doctor. Matt refused. He said he had no respect for him and argued that O'Leary was not a doctor. The judge then threatened him with a contempt charge. So, Matt simply avoided addressing O'Leary by name for the balance of the proceeding. I was very proud of my lawyer on that day.

Having gone on for a full 8 hours, a second part of my pretrial hearing was scheduled for July 13. I did not want to fly home and come back again. I was out of money and was having tremendous difficulty coming up with payments for Matt. Fortunately, I always had my best friend there no matter what. I called Steve from the hotel and recounted what transpired in the courtroom that day. One condition of my bond was that I could not mention Donal O'Leary on my site so Steve and I had been publishing my case updates on his site; I would just link to them from NIO. In that way I never mentioned the degenerate's name but everyone could follow the link to Steve Best, PhD and get all the details.

Before he published an update about my pretrial, we discussed everything at length. Steve had a way of making me laugh until I cried. And this was one of those times. He thought it hilarious that his name was mentioned in my hearing more than mine. I think it made him feel important. We both knew it was insidious that they were trying to shut me up and shut my site down by claiming the Freddy Kruger letter was a threat. It was a snuff fantasy. A creative writing exercise. Nothing more. And if we allowed the court to construe that letter as a threat, then they would have to prosecute every horror movie writer as threatening the public as well. It was absurd. Steve asked me if I needed him to testify in July. "At this point it would only hurt you and it wouldn't help me." I told him it wouldn't be necessary until I went to trial. He said "just let me know."

I was never concerned about posting a message. I seemed to have been alone in that opinion. I kept hearing that it met the definition of a legal threat. But even if that was so, there was no way it could have been construed as having been intended to incite 2 or more people to violence, a condition that which had to be met for the charge to stick. With Steve testifying on my behalf, I was confident we would prevail. The aggravated stalking charge was a little more troublesome. When I did the civil disobedience, I did not know that multiple violations of a restraining order can automatically be prosecuted as aggravated stalking. I had already accumulated three or four misdemeanor contempt charges for refusing to remove public information from NIO. Steve ultimately removed everything to protect me after I was charged with the felonies.

When I got home, I edited the article Steve authored about my hearing, added relevant details, and wrote up a summary on NIO with a link to the full story on his site. Having concluded the first part of my pretrial, I was free for the next month to turn my complete attention to Bucky. I needed to get that monkey freed before I went away. I didn't have the time for the sustained and consistent effort needed but I couldn't live with the knowledge of what they were doing inside the University of Florida. I would never back down until those animals knew peace.

All living beings, things that move, are equally important, whether they are human beings, dogs, birds, fish, trees, ants, weeds, rivers, wind or rain. -John Africa

Early-Morning Raid

or every swing I took at the University of Florida, I was now getting two or three hard body slams in return. All the shocks I had absorbed thus far were starting to accumulate. The bad publicity never affected me much because I had my own media network in place. In fact, I considered the contempt for my ideas high praise. I did, however, have an aversion to being labeled a stalker. Combined with the constant financial stress, making court dates 1200 miles away, defending myself against outrageous charges in an unjust system, being repeatedly locked up was taking a toll physically. I was tired. I found myself drinking more. My house began to mirror what was going on inside. It was filthy. Everything was spinning out of control.

Steve was always there to encourage me when I had a weak moment, telling me I would get through this. We turned to one another often; one notable time he was on a speaking tour in central America. In Costa Rica, his hostess was offended by his behavior and asked him to leave her home. I stayed up all night text chatting with him to make sure he was okay. I was the only person in the world he trusted at these desperate moments and it was comforting to know that he was the one person in the world who was there for me as well. If we weren't on the phone, we were on Skype. One morning he Skyped me when I had just gotten out of the shower. I answered the video call with a towel draped over my wet hair. He snapped my picture and teased me calling me "towel head." It was a really bad picture. In kind, I snapped him a couple of times snorting Ritalin. We thought that was funny too. He would pose for me with straws up his nose hovering over a pile of drugs. These days we were on Skype together a lot, him snorting and me drinking. One night we watched a movie on Netflix, the Baader Meinhoff Complex, while we were on the phone. It told the true story of a far-left group of German revolutionaries. We timed it to hit start at the same time so it that it played simultaneously for both of us. It was an inspiring film, but I couldn't stay awake. I fell asleep hard on the phone and he teased me that I snored like a truck driver. I loved Steve. He was my rock. And he always made me laugh.

With the constraints I was under, I was very concerned about how I was going to effectively raise Bucky's visibility and create the detriment to UF's image that would compel them to release him. Clearly, negotiating with these mercenaries proved futile. Those who came before me tried desperately to negotiate sanctuary for Louis. The net result was that he was murdered and incinerated and no one ever knew his name until I came along. I would not let history repeat itself. A week after I got home, I announced a *Weekend of Outrage* to take place in one month, from Friday, July 6 to Sunday, July 8. Then I would fly back to Detroit on the 11th. This weekend would be dedicated to freeing Bucky and I called in every ounce of goodwill I had in my community. I paid for two hotel rooms in Gainesville and invited people to come in from all over to make a stand.

While I rallied support for Bucky, Ann and Steve continued to rally support for me. Steve called me one day and was frantic. He was afraid and hysterical. When he calmed down, he explained to me that he was fighting with Alicia. He demanded she donate money to my legal fund. She refused. He punched her. She punched him back. He threw her to the floor and kicked her repeatedly. Her baby was in the room crying. She screamed so loudly he was afraid his neighbors would hear her and call the police. He put his hands around her throat and squeezed tightly to silence her. He thought he almost killed her. He eventually released his grip but told me he left big black and blue marks around her neck. He let her leave but was afraid that she was going to report him. Steve was terrified that her brother would see the marks and finally kill him. We learned later that he had broken three of her ribs.

We talked day and night. I urged him to get sober and get control of himself. This was not a rational response and he could easily have killed her. He was killing himself. One morning he overdosed, passed out, and couldn't stand up for about an hour. Steve was seeking counseling and would forward to me many of the communications between him and his therapist to whom he was lying. I wrestled with myself. I wanted to intervene and tell his therapist the truth about the destructive escalation in his behavior. I told him that he was damaging himself neurologically. It would really hurt me when he would make fun of my disabilities and he knew it. I didn't recognize the emotional abuse and how he would chip away at my self-esteem. I would usually laugh it off. He knew very well that my issues were a direct result of my overdose in 1993. Did he really want to end up in a hospital in a coma paralyzed? Did he want to be in prison for life for murder? Alicia never reported him but that beating was far worse than any of the others. I was worried for her. I was worried for him. I was worried for me. Mostly I was worried for the animals.

Lisa and I didn't protest much in June. We were too busy organizing the Weekend of Outrage and orchestrating online actions to plead with alumni to withhold donations and pressure UF to release Bucky.

At 5 am on Tuesday, June 19, I threw my clothes in the washing machine. I'd normally have been out of the house already but I didn't have the strength to go to the gym that morning. I put on a pair of old shorts and sat down to work. Around 6 am there was a loud bang at the door. Max and Jazz started barking. I went to the door and cracked it to see my carport full of police officers. I scanned the scene. My house was surrounded by uniforms. There was a camera pointing at me videotaping from the driveway. There were 10 police cruisers and unmarked cars lining the street. I asked the officer who was leading the raid to give me a second to put my dogs on the porch. I was terrified that they would shoot them if they got in the way. He let me secure the dogs.

I came back to the door and they swarmed my house. I was mortified that I was being videotaped in those shorts. Other than that, this was just another day in an increasingly surreal existence. Florida Department of Law Enforcement (FDLE) Special Agent Jeffrey Vash stood in my kitchen and read the search warrant for what seemed like an interminable amount of time. All I asked was to go out to the laundry room to get a pair of pants out of the dryer. He said no. I couldn't leave. He didn't want me to make any phone calls and have 20 protesters congregate outside the house while they were raiding me. They seized my cell phone and charger already. What was I going to do, send a smoke signal? He finally relented and a female officer accompanied me to the laundry room so I could get dressed. Then they let me make one phone call to a lawyer. I called Matt in Michigan to tell him I was being raided in Florida. Not a whole lot he could do. He told me I needed to consult with a lawyer in my state.

Back in the house, I went outside to sit on the lanai with my dogs. Special Agent Vash joined me. He wanted to know why I did what I did. I asked him if he was alive in the Antebellum South if he would have fought against slavery or enforced it? In humored disbelief he asked me if I was seriously comparing animal experimentation to slavery. "Yes, I absolutely am." Then I thought about it and qualified my position. "What they're doing inside the University of Florida bears a more striking resemblance to Nazi Germany and Josef Mengele." He couldn't believe I would compare animal experimentation to the Jewish Holocaust. I couldn't believe anyone could deny it. We basically hit an impasse and neither of us would concede a millimeter of an inch. While we were out there, every computer, laptop, cell

162

phone, thumb drive, CD, DVD, and iPod were carried out of the house. They took old cell phones, old lap tops, the router, Mike's old cell phone, cameras and webcams. They took every piece of paper they could find, phone numbers, recipes, notes. A procession of uniforms carried everything out of my house and loaded it into their cars while the neighbors watched.

My 87-year old next-door neighbor, Agnes, was probably the one person there who understood what was going on. Since she had given me the letter that was anonymously sent to my neighbors, we had become friends. She thought of me as a daughter. It was nice having a maternal-type person with whom to talk. She would come over and we would sit in my driveway when she wanted to sneak a cigarette without her husband seeing. And we talked a lot about veganism, UF, and the animals. She believed in my fight and supported me, but she worried about me at the same time.

Everything I had known about encrypting my computers was running through my mind. I always meant to do it but just never got around to it. In truth, I could never get it through my thick head that anyone would care what was on my drives. Vash wanted the password to get into the laptop on which I had been working. We both knew that they would have everything on that drive within hours. But I wasn't about to give it to him. After about an hour, I asked him if I was under arrest. He said I wasn't. I told him I was leaving with my dogs while they finished ransacking my house. He let me go. I drove over to my father-in-law's, logged onto his computer and changed all of my web-based passwords. I put up a status on Facebook alerting my community to the raid. I wanted to document what was going on. I borrowed Mike's cell phone and did a quick drive-by to snap a picture or two. I assumed that if they had seen me they would have seized that device as well.

Unable to shut me down with their multiple arrests and a grueling extradition, I was learning that the powers that be could do anything they wanted with absolutely no proof and even less justification. Steve wrote the story demonstrating that this raid was orchestrated to substantiate charges under the yet-to-be-enacted NIO Laws:[47]

> *"Florida Department of Law Enforcement (FDLE)*
> *agents stormed the residence of Camille Marino seeking*
> *evidence to substantiate felony indictments under*
> *Florida State Statutes 817.568(4) and 817.568(5)(a):*
> *'Criminal Use of Personal Identification Information [of*
> *vivisectors].' Ten police vehicles, marked and unmarked,*
> *lined her street and over 20 uniformed officers swarmed*
> *her residence."*

The Constitution no longer appeared to apply to me. As I had been doing since February, I used this latest legal assault to rally activists to escalate their actions:

> *"They can never intimidate or harass me out of fighting*
> *for what is right against a corrupt system. Let's try*
> *to see through what they're doing to me. It's all a*
> *smokescreen behind which they seek to keep the animals*
> *enslaved in silence and anonymity. We must never*
> *let that happen. Support me by waging war for them.*
> *Escalate. Never retreat. Never relent."[48]*

I kept hearing that no one in my community had ever seen the state descend upon one activist in such a concerted and consistent manner. My support team went back into high gear, Ann observing that they couldn't stop me so they decided to make sure I didn't have the tools I needed to get my work done. She sent me $300 so I could buy a laptop and get back to work. This woman was not one of the mindless sycophants. She was my friend.

Although everything I do is out in the open, there was some material on my hard drive that concerned me. I had downloaded a detailed manual on how to make timed electrical bombs to republish on NIO. I wasn't even nearly done in Michigan and it appeared they were clearly working to ensnare me at home as

47 Dr. Steven Best, "Florida Law Enforcement Storms Activist's Home," Animal Liberation Front (June 19, 2012) http:// www.animalliberationfront.com/ALFront/AgainstALF/ FloridaCopsStormActivist.htm
48 Ibid.

well. I needed advice. I consulted a lawyer in south Florida who was recommended by my colleagues with Smash HLS. When I told him my name, he said "I'm not licensed to practice in your part of the state." I would have respected him more if he would have come right out and refused to represent me. But personalities aside, this situation was getting out of hand. I was apparently so notorious that lawyers wouldn't even touch me.

I called the National Lawyers Guild (NLG) hotline. They referred me to their Regional Vice President in Florida, Anne O'Berry. I took a deep breath before I called. What if she hung up on me too? I was instantly relieved when we began to speak. Anne knew exactly who I was and seemed unimpressed with my notoriety. She was also vegan and clearly sophisticated about the atmosphere in which activists are demonized and discredited by the media. She was thorough and generous with her time. I was humbled that this important woman was taking the time to really try to help me. Anne put together a list of competent and experienced attorneys with whom I could consult. I was very relieved. She also extended an offer to let her know if she could help as we went along. Little did I know that she was to become one of my closest friends and confidantes.

The first attorney I went to see had his office in south Florida and had a stellar reputation for defending Muslims caught up in the net of hysteria. He was of Middle Eastern descent himself and we spoke at length. Should I ever need to revisit him in the future, I am choosing not to make public the content of our discussions. While I was down there, Gabby and I met for lunch. Although we would speak frequently on the phone, we only saw one another a few times a year. We were like sisters. We understood one another and connected on a very personal level in addition to our shared tactics as activists. Occasionally, Gabby would call me from work if someone was attacking her online. I was happy to defend her. We both understood that defending oneself makes one look weak. It is always better to have an advocate plead your case. I had no doubt she would defend me as vehemently as well should I ever need her. We published our pictures on Facebook having lunch that afternoon.

165

I also met with another criminal lawyer in Gainesville who had a history of defending victims caught up in University of Florida legal issues. The unprecedented assault on me was widely understood by seasoned activists as an evolution of the police state in which we work. Many people contacted me or wanted to associate with me because of my minor celebrity. Very few offered any assistance. Of those who did, I was extremely wary of their motivations. One vegan Animal Liberation attorney who contacted me was David Tenenbaum. The first thing I did was send an encrypted email to a mutual associate whose name came up in our conversation. My colleague assured me that David was one of us and so my fears were immediately allayed. In fact, like Anne O'Berry, David was to become another dear friend and confidante. He is the person who secured the records from inside UF proving that they arranged and financed my extradition out of Florida. He would be there to help get me through some very tough times that lay ahead.

A few days later on Saturday, June 23, 2012, I was driving to get a fresco bean burrito at Taco Bell when I saw a little black dog trying to run down the street. He was so weak he kept falling. And there were three derelict-looking men chasing him. I stopped my car in the middle of the street and attracted enough attention to cause the men to cease their pursuit. A few other people helped me chase down the terrified little dog. He finally ran under a dilapidated trailer that was strewn with broken glass where he collapsed. I gently pulled him out. I had Max and Jazz with me so I called Mike to help. When I got him in my car, I gave him some dog treats. He practically inhaled them. The emaciated pit bull had been unspeakably abused and starved. He had cuts, wounds, and scars from the top of his head to the bottoms of his legs. He was dirty. He was scared. His infected wounds gave off a pungent odor. He had clearly been used as a bait dog. These are the animals that dog fighters will throw to the fighting pit bulls to tear apart. When family pets are stolen from their yards or when dogs and cats are given away to strangers on Craig's List, there is a high probability that they will be used for bait.

We took the little black pit bull to a vet. She wanted $2,000 to do tests. I didn't have it. She told me that the dog needed to be euthanized. I wouldn't do it. She told me I was being emotional and selfish instead of thinking about what was best for him. He was too badly injured and sick and, in her eyes, clearly expendable. Tuning her out, I took the little dog home with me. While Mike, Max, and Jazz lived in the house, the injured dog and I lived on the screened-in porch for three or four days and nights. I fed him every 3 hours. I slept with him. When he was strong enough I would walk him to the corner. He learned to trust me. We took him to our vet on Monday and got him antibiotics. Within a week he was starting to gain weight back and his bloody wounds were beginning to heal. I named him Brutus. The first time I took Brutus inside the house, I sat on the couch and he sat on the floor mesmerized by the television. I don't think he was ever inside before and he definitely had never seen a TV. His reaction made me smile. It made me cry. It made me love him even more and want to protect him forever. Brutus became my heart. Brutus was home.

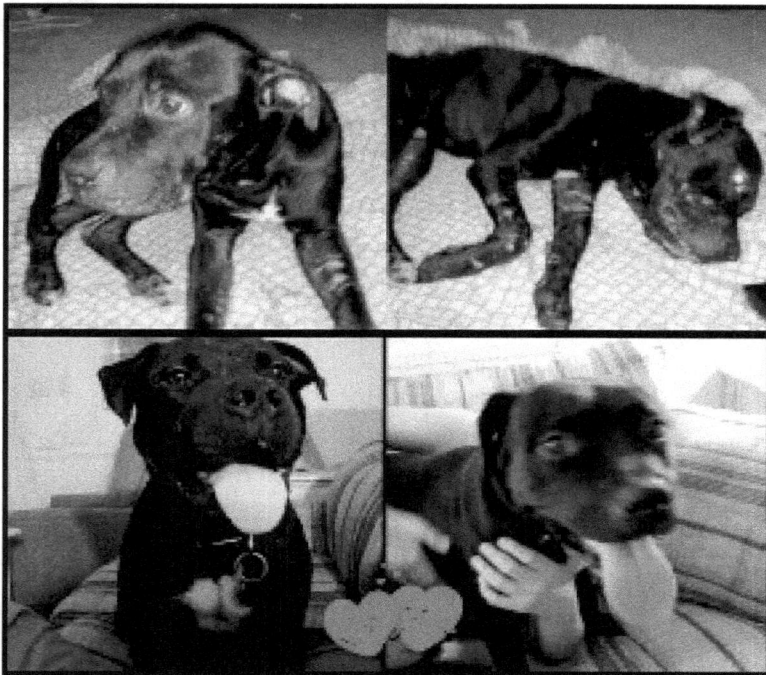

The ultimate tragedy is not
the oppression and cruelty by
the bad people but the silence
over that by the good people.
-Martin Luther King, Jr.

Weekend of Outrage

The simple fact that we had to call in resources from out of town to make a stand for Bucky speaks to the sad state of activism in Gainesville. It never even entered my mind at that time that Michael Budkie had begun working behind the scenes to begin freezing me out; working to damage my efforts in my own community. While we finally had a protest group coming together after the lawsuit, my repeated arrests scared those people away. There are well-meaning vegans who expend their energy on potlucks and human oppression, but there is no discernible commitment to the animals. The best they have had historically are SAEN's annual welfare-violation protests. I remained focused on building a solid base of activists, however, and on Friday, July 6, we started congregating at our designated hotel. Several of my friends drove up from South Florida to support us. We had activists drive down from Georgia, one came from Israel, and Lisa and I picked up several people each on our respective drives to the campus. Early in the campaign, perhaps the greatest impediment was apathy and it was tiresome having to continually encourage activists to engage. But that night we came from all directions.

I spent another $200 on poster boards, blowing up pictures of the vivisectors, and, mostly, blowing up images of the actual monkeys in the labs. It was heartbreaking. They say a picture is worth a thousand words. The pictures of these maimed, burned, and dead monkeys were chilling and priceless. It was evident why I needed to battle it out in court to extract this damning evidence. It is also the reason the university needed to keep me tied up out of the state. An artist named Jimmy made up about 20 signs, enough to equip every protester with visual artillery. While he did that, I visited businesses, restaurants, and other populated locations to disseminate fliers and invite people to the next day's protests.

At 8 pm that evening, the first three carloads of activists staged an impromptu demo outside Bucky's vivisector's home. I was tickled to arrive and see the infamous Raymond Joseph Bergeron sealed up inside his home, guarded by 24-hour police protection that would remain for the entire weekend. We were all trespassed from his property, our identification and license plates recorded, and we went back to our hotel for the evening. If taxpayers only knew they were financing around-the-clock police protection from dissent! As far as I'm concerned, anytime we can turn a vivisector's home into his own private cage, it's a minor victory for his victims.

Over the next two days, we protested at five vivisectors' homes and our loudspeaker and fliers ensured that their neighbors learned about their crimes against nature. We returned to Bergeron's home and stood on the perimeter of his property with our *Free Bucky* signs while my friend from Israel read out a litany of his abuses over the bullhorn. At church services on Sunday morning, about 20 of us protested outside and spoke to people as they arrived to worship. Three of us infiltrated the congregation and replaced the psalms inside their bibles with fliers about Bucky. We pleaded with them to write, call, and pressure the university to free this tormented little being. Many of the good Christians cursed us out.

If we couldn't break Bergeron's windows and drag him outside into the daylight, I was very happy that we had about 2 dozen highly-motivated, like-minded comrades assembled to make sure he got the exposure he so desperately needed. I promised myself that as soon as I got back from Detroit I would be back, even if I had to do it by myself, and I wouldn't relent until I won Bucky release.

As a strategic tool, I sometimes disseminated misinformation to encourage abusers to incur extra financial burdens. When our demos wrapped up, my published update reported that three activists remained in Gainesville and would be surveilling Bergeron for the balance of the week. I was certain he was walking around with 24-hour protection and looking over his shoulder everywhere he went for the next few days.

I have a lot of friends back in New York who are bikers, several of whom were associated with the motorcycle group, the *69ers*. Back in 2010, I had a couple of my friends join my Facebook initiative against David Jentsch. We had him believing that they were riding out to California to disrupt his pro-vivisection rally. Steve jumped on board. We published provocative announcements that Dr. Steve Best would be leading the bikers to meet Jentsch at UCLA. David Jentsch and his vivisecting cohorts spent over $10,000 in extra security that year. Misinformation can be employed very effectively sometimes as long as your opposition never knows whether you're going to actually show up or whether you're eating popcorn in a movie theater.

On Thursday, I flew back out to Michigan to appear for the second part of my pretrial examination.

Where justice is denied, where poverty is enforced, where ignorance prevails, and where any one class is made to feel that society is an organized conspiracy to oppress, rob and degrade them, neither persons nor property will be safe. -Frederick Douglass

Friday the 13th

I always loved Friday the 13th. It was a lucky day for me. So, I knew my hearing was going to go well. Matt and I sat at the defense table and Donal O'Leary came in flanked by his usual bloodthirsty entourage. Before the proceedings began, Prosecutor Lukiewski yielded the floor to someone I'd never seen. My lawyer was at a loss as well. They had brought in a special prosecutor and, rather than being present for my pretrial proceeding, we learned we were unknowing participants in a bail revocation hearing. Matt and I looked at each other. I had done absolutely nothing that could be construed as contacting O'Leary. Further, by this time I had removed the vivisector's information from NIO entirely; the data was now hosted by various colleagues. NIO only linked to innocuous articles about my case on Steve's site.

Friday the 13th

They were alleging that I had threatened Donal O'Leary. This was absurd. Then they produced screenshots of Steve Best's site. The last article he had written about my case, the article that I had formatted in its final version and hyperlinked from NIO, now had an image in it of Donal O'Leary being murdered! I was speechless. Alafair had created this picture and Steve must have thought it would be amusing to insert in my update. Did he really think this was a big joke? At that moment Steve Best seemed to me like an overgrown child in a playpen. My inner circle indeed! WTF! Matt was livid. I feared he would drop me as a client. I had no defense. I remained silent. We were railroaded by a convergence of forces.

Judge Lynisse Bryant-Weekes was no fan of mine to begin with and was clearly angry now. Rolling her eyes as she did through the entire proceeding, this stellar jurist declared that I have repeatedly demonstrated that I have no respect for their law. My bond was revoked and, parroting the prosecutor's words, she declared me a "danger to society." I was arrested in the courtroom and remanded back into custody on a $500,000 bond. She was indignant about this poor dog-murdering piece of shit having to contend with such harassment. O'Leary smiled at me with a deviant grin. He resembled John Wayne Gacy. I smiled back at him unfazed and winked, imagining his head being blown off. I knew there was no way I could come up with 10% of that number. We all did. That was the point of a half-million-dollar bond. So now I was confident I was going to be out of circulation for a while.

I called Steve repeatedly from jail. He wouldn't answer. This had never happened before and I was concerned for him more than for me. I wasn't even angry. I knew his cat, Willis, was sick and he was taking it badly. I hoped he was okay. Very few people knew the real reason my bond was revoked. I didn't want my community blaming Steve because I knew he hadn't done this to cause me harm. He just didn't think a lot of the time and obviously thought this was a big game on some level. But the consensus among my close friends was resounding: "is he a moron?" ... "this is your friend?" ... and from Matt, for the first time, "I knew the first time you mentioned his name that it was going to be trouble."

It looked like I was finally going to have time to write a book while I sat in jail.

Changes and progress very rarely are gifts from above. They come out of struggles from below.
-Noam Chomsky

Danger to Society

Elizabeth Tobier had led a number of NIO New York initiatives over the past several years. We met when she became the person primarily responsible for Walter Bond's support. She graciously stepped up to become my right arm as well while I was incarcerated. Not even remotely associated with *the inner circle*, she was one of the most reliable and trustworthy friends I would have during this period. With plenty of time on my hands I began keeping a journal that I envisioned publishing when I was free. I thought the title *Danger to Society* was appropriate and ironic under the circumstances. Every few days I would send Elizabeth pages of my pencil-scribbled writing and she typed it up. Without her loyalty and dedication, much of what was to transpire over the next month would have been lost.

Elizabeth would also send me all the articles that were published about me, keep me in the loop about events in the Animal Liberation universe, and she basically became my eyes and ears. I began to depend on her more and more as it became apparent to me that others with whom I worked appeared to be very selective in the information they would share with me. This journal as well as the journal I kept after sentencing would eventually be published in a highly-sanitized version in 2014. Two weeks later it would be pulled from print. While personally hurtful, this is as it should be. The censored version was little more than my manifesto, relevant to a very small, like-minded audience.

I republished a second edition of Danger to Society in 2018 so that it could stand alone as a one-month record of my incarceration where my struggle remained pure. It is a day to day account of my thoughts and experiences inside the high crimes unit of Wayne County Jail. In order to link the first part of this memoir to the second, however, it is necessary to note that I was troubled that, during this period, Steve stopped taking my calls. I knew that Willis was sick and, while I was initially concerned about him, I was very hurt. He had been my closest confidante and I felt very much abandoned and alone.

In coming weeks, my bond would be reduced to $35,000, but not before I refused to take a plea. I was going to trial in November and was confident that the one thing in the world on which I could count was that my best friend had my back. In a three-minute phone call on August 12, 2012, I told Steve I was going to trial and needed him to testify. His response was a decisive "NO." That was it. While I had been incarcerated because of an image he inserted into one of our updates, he had washed his hands of me. Further, in my last few days in jail, I began getting messages from Ann Parkes and others, related to me through several of my friends, that I had a lot of nerve trying to "throw Steve under a bus;" that I was a "coward;" and that they were waiting and watching.

The inner circle had now closed ranks around Steve Best against me. I had no idea what had happened, I did not understand what anyone was talking about. I was angry. I was hurt. I just wanted my best friend back. The final entry is re-published below in the interest of continuity.

August 12, 2012

I'm not sure if I'm going to include this entry in my book or not. I'm not sure I want to share it with the world. I've been betrayed. I cannot get angry in here; there's no outlet. My best friend -- the person I trust the most in the universe, the person who's been laughing with me since the first email was sent, the person for whose rhetoric I'm facing the posting a message felony -- told me he changed his mind and decided not to testify. No explanation. No discussion. After being blown off all month. Just a simple "No." I wanted to believe that he wasn't taking my calls because he was grieving. But I knew deep down that something had changed.

Is he just scared? Bored? Was this all planned? My head is going to explode.

I've gained a lot of strength and confidence over the past five months. I've always known that there is nothing fake or duplicitous about me and that I have never uttered a single word I would not stand behind 100%. I consider the struggle for Animal Liberation a war – not in some academic or theoretical sense. It is the reality in which the animals die and, therefore, it is the reality in which I live. Above all, integrity within myself and unwavering loyalty to the animals and my friends are constants in my universe. And I guess it's my own fault for expecting the same in return.

This is how I measure others. I take people at face value and I expect words and actions to be congruent. And, once again, the fault lies within myself for not wanting to admit things that I recognized in others a long time ago. So much of the most insane rhetoric that was ever published under my name on NIO was a group effort. I never had a problem insulating others. I would do anything in my power to protect my friends. That is not true of others.

So many things are running through my head. A fucking 3-minute phone call and that's it? He's got nothing more to say? Yep, it's definitely a good thing I'm restrained; I know I need to calm down and think rationally. And I definitely wouldn't be so reasonable about this if I was home tonight.

While I'm sitting in a cell, a campaign has already begun to pit activists and supporters against me. How do I know that? It's almost impossible to talk to anyone on the outside without hearing what a disloyal fraud I am. I was only in court 2 days ago. We only had our 3-minute call less than 48 hours ago. And three people already are warning me that *I* better not betray *him*? How I'm throwing him under the bus? WTF is that about? I'm sitting in a god-damned cell for his stupidity, facing a felony for his rhetoric. And never once have I uttered his name anywhere. Never even considered it. I've never betrayed anyone nor have I ever betrayed my own integrity, and this situation is cutting to the core of my being. And all of these people running interference – my *friends* – have no clue what they're talking about.

I don't understand how anyone can try to turn my supporters and friends against me while I'm locked in a cell; how he seeks to divide activists and make them choose sides rather than speak to me directly. So the only manner in which I can legitimately and, hopefully, objectively treat this topic is to try and gain something from it and move on. I did not realize how vulnerable, weak, and susceptible I allowed myself to become. And I'm not sure how I can use this because, barring never trusting anyone again in my life, I'm sure I will open myself up to being betrayed again.

But I'm crushed tonight. Despite what was glaringly obvious, I wanted to believe we were all equally committed. All I can say is that words mean nothing unless they're coming from those who've earned the right to speak them. Nonetheless, I still love and miss my best friend. I just want to go back to having fun together. My head hurts.

It's okay. I'll do my time. And if I have to stand alone, I'll stand proudly. The animals deserve nothing less and I regret nothing but trusting a coward. I guess untested loyalty is meaningless.

PART TWO

Do not trust to the cheering, for those very persons would shout as much if you and I were going to be hanged. -Oliver Cromwell

Facebook Wars

I finally got out of jail on August 15. They locked a GPS on my ankle and explained the conditions of my house arrest. The GPS would be tracked 24 hours a day so they would know where I was. I would have to sit in place for an hour and charge it every 12 hours. If I let the battery die, a warrant would immediately be issued for my arrest. I could not go outside the supervised parameters. While I was on house arrest in Florida, my only restriction was that I couldn't get within 100 feet of O'Leary's house in Michigan or the Wayne State University campus. And I would have to check in with the sheriff once a week by phone. For all intents and purposes, except for the fact that I couldn't go swimming with that restraint attached to me, house arrest would not affect my work in Gainesville.

While I was technically free to come and go as I pleased, the reality was far different. The vivisection complex was incensed that I was once again out of jail and the prosecutor began being inundated with calls from universities on both coasts, as well as Wayne State University, to revoke my bond and throw me back in jail, even though I was in full compliance with my bond conditions. Additionally, the University of Florida was pressuring Ryan Lukiewski, the prosecutor in Michigan, to violate me if I went through with any protests or home demos in front of Bergeron's house. They wanted the Detroit authorities to essentially ban me from everything relating to the University of Florida. While my campaign was not a violation of any of my bond conditions, UF suddenly found an unexpected ally within my community that was working furiously to secure their same agenda: my silence. A collaborator was about to rear his ugly head.

I wish I could say that I stayed as thoughtful, composed, and focused with respect to Steve's betrayal as I had been while I was behind bars. But I can't. The first thing I did when I left county was buy a bottle of wine on my way back to my hotel. And all the anger and rage that I had suppressed for the last week suddenly came roaring to the surface. I tried to call Steve. He wouldn't answer. I began to text him. I knew that he used silence as a weapon; he routinely did this to Alicia and would boast as she would invariably get neurotic, sending flurries of emails. He would share them with me like showing off a trophy he had earned. I also knew that he scared easily and that he would call when he realized I was not going to be ignored. I knew that if we could only speak we could resolve everything. I did not understand what was happening or why he way lying about me, telling people I was a *fraud*. But I was pissed.

While I no longer have the original texts, the tirade couched in my own brand of diplomacy went something like this:

> *"I'm out, Motherfucker. Now what?"*

> *"You think it's going to be that easy to destroy my reputation with lies? Fuck you! If you want a war, you got it."*

> *"Do you really think it's wise to act like a punk while I'm writing a book about being a political prisoner?"*

> *"The whole world is gonna know what a fucking coward*

and fraud you are. Try me!"

And then my cell phone rang. I momentarily thought I had succeeded in prompting a call back, but I was relieved it was my friend Chris Lagergren calling from Florida. I needed a friend to help me think this through and figure out what was going on.

"Hey Chris, how are you?"

"Not good."

Concerned for him, I said "Why, what's going on?"

To which he responded, "Why are you threatening my friend?"

I was silent. I couldn't process what he had just said. Then in an instant, I understood. While I had been in jail, Steve had ceased having any use for me. He had replaced me with *the inner circle* and, in this case, with Belinda Morris. Chris didn't even know Steve a month ago. They had never spoken, other than online communications concerning my support. And however it had happened, Chris now chose to align himself with Belinda, his online girlfriend, and Steve against me.

I tried to talk to him and explain my side but it was futile. He kept telling me "you have to take responsibility for your actions." I had no clue what that meant because I had never shirked responsibility for anything, especially since my first arrest. Then I became just a little indignant about explaining myself to this individual who had no clue what was going on between Steve and me. I didn't even know what was going on between Steve and me. I hung up and kept drinking. And I kept sending Steve emails and texts. And he remained silent.

I flew back home the next day. When we hit the tarmac at Orlando International Airport, I turned on my cell phone as we prepared to exit the aircraft. My notifications were lighting up – Facebook, missed calls, voicemails. I listened to a few frantic voicemails from friends. Everyone was telling me the same thing: Steve and *the inner circle* had taken all of my angry and not-entirely-rational texts and emails and were posting them all over the web. Gabby texted me "CALL ME ASAP!" She told me what was going on. Before my feet had even touched the ground in Florida after having been locked up for a month solely because of Steven Best's stupidity, he was all over the web calling me a "scorned woman" with a "fatal attraction." I had sobered up since the night before and I refused to take this matter public at first. I typed a status update on Facebook:

> *"Thanks to all of my friends and supporters for your concern. But please don't allow yourselves to be distracted from the animals by drama. I'm free. And I'm fine. Steve is just having a bad day and will come to his senses soon. As for me, my fight is with vivisectors and animal abusers, not other activists. In solidarity."*

I meant it. I had no intention of battling it out with him publicly. I sent him a few more emails telling him that he could easily be the hero in this situation. If he would simply testify as we had agreed, he would neutralize the state's case and secure a win for us against the vivisection complex. The Freddy Kruger letter was a creative writing exercise. He knew it. I knew it. They knew it. And it was never meant to incite two or more people to violence, a condition that had to be met for the charge to stick. He had actually once offered a reward on his blog if someone would kill a certain hunter. His department chair, John Symons, had called him into his office at the University of Texas, El Paso and reprimanded him "I woke up this morning to find out one of my professors is soliciting murder on the internet!" Steve deleted the post. But *that* was intended to incite violence. Not the Freddy Kruger post.

Steve didn't respond. I told him I could easily subpoena him, although I would never have done anything in cooperation with the state. I just wanted to scare him. I was confused. I was hurt. I was devastated. I wanted my best friend back. Being betrayed and thrown away didn't feel good. I knew if we could talk we would fix this. Being disposed of by the person I was closest to in the universe was far more traumatic than the prospect of prison.

In one of my most painful emails I told him "this hurts more than being abandoned by my father." I meant it. I think seeing that email go public was maybe the most devastating. I had only met my father a handful of times. And while Steve remained silent, suddenly my private emails to him were all over the internet being bandied about like baseball bats bashing me over the head as I became weaker and weaker. They were saying hurtful things like "no wonder your mother hated you," they were going on and on about me being a fraud and "gangbanging cops," and it was now all over the internet that I was never in a motorcycle accident but that I overdosed on heroin. How could I counter these half-truths and lies?

Because I had mentioned that I could subpoena him, I was now a "snitch." Because I couldn't control myself, the flurry of emails demonstrated my "fatal attraction." I began going back and forth, apologizing for threatening him then lashing out when he refused to respond. And that was the *evidence* of my being bi-polar. They posted my apologies to demonstrate that poor Steve Best was the victim of his psychotic stalker. I wrote Steve repeatedly begging him to call off his minions and to stop playing this out in a public forum. Silence. I then wrote things like "motherfucker, you're gonna pay."

I knew exactly what was happening. The same way I had always stepped in front of Steve to *defend him* by attacking Gary Francione, Karen Dawn, Roger Yates, or any host of activists by whom Steve felt intimidated or threatened, the cult was now standing in front of him insulating him from me – the only person in the universe who truly knew what a pathetic fraudulent man he was. Everything he said, all the militant rhetoric, everything was a lie. I understood exactly how he was orchestrating my public lynching. And I understood the blind loyalty of the cultists that now surrounded him who had no use for facts or truth. The sole function of the cult was to protect their leader and neutralize me. But I still couldn't admit that I had been a cultist too, although I did understand that I had been summarily ex-communicated and was now being ostracized. And I couldn't demonstrate his complicity because he was hiding like Oz behind the curtain.

Facebook Wars

I had the entire vivisection complex converging on me, with Florida and Michigan both determined to put me in prison, and now my former friends and allies were shooting me in the back and laying me at the enemy's doorstep. This was clear to me. But there were other things going on too, some of which I couldn't understand. People were calling me a "fraud;" what had I been fraudulent about? Many people who tried to talk to me kept telling me that I had to "take responsibility;" take responsibility for what? The bullying went viral. People I didn't know and to whom I had never even spoken were now saying that they had seen the emails and had *proof* that I was a liar and a fraud. I was simply some psychotic woman with a fatal attraction.

Alafair Robicheaux was relentless in rallying my supporters against me with the evidence of my being a *scorned woman* who couldn't accept that Steve didn't want me. Ann Parkes who had access to all of my financial donors, was now spending day and night writing to all of them one by one telling them I was a thief and a liar. Ann, in particular, must have felt betrayed. She had been loyal to me. And whatever lies Steve filled her head with must have hurt. I understood this but didn't know how to make anyone see what he was doing. I didn't have a penny and now people started writing to me telling me that I didn't send them a thank you note and demanding their money back. Thank you notes? I was locked up with no way of knowing who sent what. Ann was supposed to have sent out thank you notes. It was like all of a sudden, those who had put me up on a pedestal were now not only knocking me off of it, but taking a truck and running it back and forth over my body to make sure I was dead.

Then a colleague who was allowed into the secret discussions of the inner circle forwarded to me the proof that Steve was orchestrating my lynching. Following is only a small excerpt from one single 79-page private discussion on Facebook. It included roughly 50 different activists who would then take the information and disseminate it exponentially. I've added emphasis in bold type to some of Susan Duke's comments. Other than that, these comments were copied out of that private message stream and pasted here exactly as they appeared. This excerpt is from only one of about a dozen such discussions of which I am aware:

Ann Parkes
Please share with TRUSTED friends should you wish to, but only via pm. This woman should NOT EVER be sent their hard earned money!! EVER!!

From: Camille Marino [mailto:camille@negotiation-isover.com] Sent: Wednesday, November 24, 2010 7:33 AM To: xxxxxx@xxxx.com Subject: $$$$$$$

I'm having a weak moment...

I need money. I need to move. I need a car and computer. I want high. And just to maintain nio on the new servers is going to cost $600+ a year.

My being active depends on my being independent, having transportation, and money to finance campaigns.

We could start accepting donations.

We're good at what we do and I bet we could generate a decent income if we tried.

And, seriously, NIO is you and me so it could be our own little personal dollar faucet.

Imagine....

Steve must have been furiously rummaging through every email I had ever sent him looking for ammunition. And he apparently found this one I had sent him over a year before I had ever been arrested. An unfortunate choice of words, perhaps, but innocuous and irrelevant nonetheless. And the fact that Ann had blocked out Steve's email address demonstrated how far they were willing to go to do his bidding:

Dawn Woody
Unbelievable

Ann Parkes
I've just started one message thread - going to start another later on. Only THIS PARTICULAR EMAIL will

be shared for now.. But there is much more that cannot be shared atm. The dam is going to burst wide open very soon!!

Dawn Woody
Her own personal dollar faucet...IM SPEECHLESS

Noelene Evans
As Dawn said......."our own little personal dollar faucet".....Unbelievable!

Dawn Woody
This woman needs to be exposed for what she is....THE SOONER THE BETTER

Ann Parkes
There is far, far more Noelene. In the meantime, I'm concerned that no-one throws more money at this bitch from hell!

Noelene Evans
It's disgraceful that she is carrying on like this. Thanks for the info Ann. Let me know when it is OK to inform others. Xx

Jennifer Connor
Shared with some aussie donors to her faucet fund... They will be livid, but hold their tongues.

Dawn Woody
Just when you think it cant get any worse....BOOM...

Eleish Harvey
i am speechless...she is an utter bastard... the sooner she is exposed the better... damn her to hell.

Dawn Woody
Couldnt agree more Eleish. Love you sp

Eleish Harvey
love you too sp. Xxxx

Ann Parkes
Noelene - Feel free to inbox others with this information,

Noelene Evans
Thank you Ann. I'm off home now. Will do later when I am back online. TC xx

Beverley Holden
I have heard this before, that she is a fraud, don`t ya get sick of it al !!!!

Lianne Bailey
Absolutely disgusting, I am appalled that she could do this!! :(
x

Ann Parkes
Totally sick of it. And she is determined to continue; donations are still being requested, emails are still being sent and threats are still being made. She is determined to destroy certain people in this movement, and says she is now "omnipotent." PLEASE ENSURE PEOPLE KNOW AT LEAST ENOUGH NOT TO GIVE MONEY TO THIS PERSON! GIVE TO ANIMAL SHELTERS.

Jennifer Connor
This has been going on far too long Ann..She is a devious devil with other ppls money and not a thought for the animals..Criminal...this is criminal..To think how much money she received from us..because we believed..I could break her neck..truly I could. xx

She lies without flinching and ppl believe her rubbish..I did for heaven sake..She must be stopped.

Eleish Harvey
ann, you rightly said that you should of been told what she was like ages ago.. the best thing we did was to stop donating to her... and supporting her... the tax people need to be told, because i doubt she has declared all the money that has been donated...this has made me so

*sick...the animals who are still suffering because of her...
and what breaks my heart... no justice for... queenie....
how dare she still have queenie's picture up on sbc.... all
the monkeys still prisoners... because of..HER... I HATE
HER.....HATE HER...HATE HER....*

Eleish Harvey
*jen, i hate her, i realy do. and we will get justice for
queenie and all the innocent babies who she has help to
kill... the monkeys who should be enjoying their freedom
are probably dead because of her.. suffering every day...
because of her... jen i am crying here for them.... psycho
is too full of her own self importance... once in a while
she will post what she is doing concerning the animals..
like asking for files on where the monkeys are.... the
other 99% of the time is her being a total vindictive
bitch..and harrassing people.... and being responsible
for the deaths of the babies in the labs... the same
animals she ... claims... to be fighting for.... she needs
to be..DESTROYED... i will never..ever..forgive her, for
what she has done...never...... :'(*

And then Susan Duke chimed in to confirm that Steve Best
was providing the ammunition, directing its dissemination, and
preparing for more "fireworks" to light up the cyber sky:

Susan Duke
***Everything Ann says is true! As she says and also Dr.
Best suggests, please pass this along as a pm to people
to get the word out. I've been talking to Dr. Best over
the last week via email and the fireworks are just
getting started. He joked that CM may be a good case
study for me in the future. ;)***

*In my opinion, all of us who gave our money, time,
heart, and trust to NIO and CM are owed an explanation
as to how all this shit started!! As a psychology scholar,
I'm dying to know! The worst as Ann stated is that she
interfered with the release of animals! Ann, are you the*

188

only one who can add someone to this thread? If so, I can copy and paste

Susan Duke
I believe that Steve will be releasing more info./emails in due time. His advice to me was to delete her cronies as well as her hitman, Jo Du....please trust him on this. The fireworks are just getting started. ;)

And on and on and on it went, the hatred and malice being fanned with every new person to enter the fray, most of whom I did not know. I understood now why people from Germany to the states were threatening to break my bones if they ever saw me in person. I understood the threatening emails. I understood why I was being called a fraud. I understood how they were using the email to serve their own agenda, but I had no clue what anyone meant about animals dying because of me. The last monkey that UF refused to release was Louis. He was murdered and incinerated on Michael Budkie's watch although I had never said that publicly.

Gabby told me "I am a very well-respected activist" and couldn't tarnish herself defending me. Jennifer and Alice came to my defense. They knew exactly what was happening and tried to stand by me, especially Jennifer. They stood with me and took on everyone who was spreading lies and trying to destroy me. But then people started attacking Jennifer for her support. It became a full-time job to be my friend. Worse by far was my own inability to center myself. I was drinking non-stop now. All I remember doing for three months was drinking from the time I woke up in the morning, sending Steve more damaging emails, begging him to stop the attacks, flailing around trying to defend myself online, and passing out. I would be on the phone with Alice and Jennifer every night. Jennifer pleaded with me to stop contacting him. "He's a sadist and he's enjoying this." … "You have to stop. He's using everything you say against you." Alice and I never spoke again. Jennifer had to walk away because she couldn't stand to watch me self-destruct. And I couldn't stop. Here is a sampling of the emails I sent to my former friend:

"I need your help. I'm drinking and I have little ability to control my anger. You cannot just tune me out after everything I've done for you and everything we shared and go on your merry way without so much as an apology. I deserve more than that from you and I need closure. But Steve, I told you before, I'm not wrapped too tightly and you don't know who you're dealing with."

and

"...instead of dealing with me directly you are seriously getting your friends to fight your battles? no one can mitigate your damage except you and the clock is ticking. I want an apology or you are going to regret having betrayed me."

and

"i just tried to call you at the number you gave me the other day. but apparently you changed it again... i'm not laughing... I SWEAR!!!!! I KNOW how militant you are. look, steve, this is over as far as i'm concerned. fighting with you is like shooting fish in a barrel. please! give me a break and let me get back to the vivisectors. if not, you get your lawyers lol and i'll depend on myself. whatever. all I want is a simple apology – written out in detail to be simultaneously posted on your site and mine. whadda ya say, dude? let's stop before a tourniquet won't be enough to stop your bleeding."

My most loyal friends in Florida were Joshua Durden and Ron Roberts who stood by me through everything and defended me to anyone and everyone. They knew that Chris Lagergren had sold me out, although none of us could figure out why. (In 2012, we believed the FBI was unsuccessful in trying to get to me by infiltrating Smash HLS. I now believe the large sum of money offered by the feds would certainly explain why Chris Lagergren went from friend to Judas in 33 days.) They stood by me even though the assaults were constant and relentless. Where the inner circle had spent 20 hours a day playing games online and had moved to spending 20 hours a day working on my support team to ingratiate themselves with Steve, they were all now spending 20 hours a day doing absolutely nothing else but taunting me to destroy my reputation and eradicate me for Steve. The taunts were in my texts, in my emails, on my home phone, on my cell phone, on Facebook messages, and all over Facebook as more and more people joined in my public lynching. Gabby and I spoke privately once or twice but she never defended me publicly a single time as I had regularly done for her in the past. Activists say that it is our silence that allows atrocities to happen. And this was no different. Those I thought were friends turned out to be politicians who would allow me to go down in flames rather than come to my aid. Joshua, especially, was very vocal about identifying those among us who no longer saw any benefit in associating with me. He called out Gabby and most of Smash as traitors and false friends. I was unwilling to see the truth yet. But he was right. Joshua was so disillusioned by all the hypocrisy and self-serving personalities that he eventually left the movement.

There were many who cashed in on the currency of their association with me when I was in the headlines every day. Most of them faded away when I needed friends the most. It hurt tremendously. At my weakest, I grabbed for some solace wherever I could find it. People who had been friends on Facebook for years would write me private messages of encouragement. When I would begin to open up, they would take my messages, post them publicly and laugh at me. I take people at their word. I trust people. I can't get it through my thick head that they are duplicitous and selfish. I was all alone. And now bashing me was clearly providing both sport and entertainment for many.

And Steve remained silent.

> *"I'm so fucking in love with you I can't control myself. It's got nothing to do with the fact that you betrayed me, shut your phone, turned my friends and supporters against me, and sold me out at the most vulnerable point in my life, right douchebag? No, I'm fucking scorned*

because you and your three-inch limp cock are so irresistible! Motherfucker, you're gonna pay!"

The cult would make fake profiles and were now accusing me of everything from being a prostitute, a drug addict, a sociopath, being bi-polar, a coward, and, of course a scorned woman. I knew exactly from where these things were coming. My most private secrets were now public. It was all over the internet that I was never in a motorcycle accident but that I had overdosed. They were calling me trailer trash for living in a manufactured home in a beautiful development. All of my secrets I shared with Steve were now public. Alafair went on a campaign to get my Facebook page deleted and succeeded. I will never know how. I put up a new page but my 5000 friends and supporters were gone. Many of my colleagues around the globe came back and stood with me. But I no longer had the reach I once did. Their networks expanded exponentially discrediting, mocking, and taunting me. And I had no means of effectively defending myself. Their agenda seemed to be to put me in prison with no money, no support, and no friends where I would finally be silent. They took down my support site. They tried to hack NIO but couldn't. They lamented publicly that since NIO was hosted in Iceland, sadly, there was nothing they could do to take it offline.

And I drank and drank and drank. I sent emails. I flailed around. I posted ominous Pink Floyd videos on my profile as I descended deeper into my own despair. It was impossible for those who really stuck by me to do anything to help me. But the simple fact that they didn't desert me is a gift I will never be able to repay. The vivisectors who were prosecuting me were watching this sideshow in ecstasy. The fur industry, the agri-terrorists, everyone who had tried to eliminate me watched with glee. They were never able to faze me. It took those that were closest to me to do that and they were intent on eliminating me altogether. Where they were once advocating for me, Ann was now teaming up with the vivisectors. While I was being prosecuted on behalf of Donal O'Leary, Ann Parkes was now visiting David Jentsch's blog to publicly tell Donal O'Leary and the rest of the ecstatic vivisectors:

> *"My dear comrade, Dr. Steve Best, has given me all the evidence we need to put this heroin-addicted prostitute in prison for good. See my Facebook page for her private emails."*[49]

Every day I would drive to the liquor store and envision myself driving into a truck. I just wanted to make it stop. I wasn't even showering for days. One night I drove to the gas station to get a bottle of wine. There was a police cruiser sitting outside in the parking lot. I have a GPS ankle monitor, I'm out on a $35,000 Michigan bond, facing 2 felonies and 10 years in prison, and I had already been drinking. I didn't want to drive past the cops. It seemed like a good idea to drive drunk through a car wash that was closed so I could come out the other end of the parking lot. My right mirror hit something driving through and got torn off my car. I exited the car wash and the cruiser exited the parking lot right behind me. I'm driving down the road holding the steering wheel for dear life, watching the cruiser in the rear-view mirror and imagining the headlines the next day. I think I must have driven in the straightest line I ever have because after a mile, the cruiser turned around and I was on the road alone. I was in disbelief that I had not been arrested. I didn't realize it at the time, but I was in the middle of a full-scale nervous breakdown.

I wrote to several colleagues that I didn't know well, but for whom I had a lot of respect. They knew Steve. And they were veterans. I wrote to Ryan Shapiro. He is an MIT professor and has a long history in the movement. I asked him how I could make Steve stop. In retrospect, I'm not sure anyone understood what was going on or what I meant by "make Steve stop." It was his cult out there doing his bidding. People saw me losing my mind. They saw the appearance Steve was cultivating of being dignified and silent. But he had been writing everyone he knew since I had been behind bars and I had no clue what he was telling them, only that he was on a mission to pit the movement against

49 Speaking of Research, "Prof. Steven Best gets a taste of his own medicine… and doesn't like it," (October 23, 2012) https://speakingofresearch.com/2012/10/23/prof-steven-best-gets-a-taste-of-his-own-medicine-and-doesnt-like-it/

me. Other than these private communications, many of which were relayed to me, he remained invisible. A lot of people didn't like me and hated my tactics. That was fine. Now people were bullying and bashing me nonstop and I didn't know why, only that Steve was orchestrating it.

Ryan Shapiro was not one of them. He was among the serious few who saw how unbelievably damaging this public spectacle was to the movement and the animals. But no one could see through my eyes and I am not the type of person to write people to plead my case and damage Steve. I wasn't trying to create sides, my side against his side, I just wanted help. Ryan is also the person who has a number of lawsuits against the FBI. He uses the Freedom of Information Act to secure the FBI files of many animal rights activists including me. He wrote me back and was so compassionate and reasonable. He called me one night. I was mortified. I remember nothing of what was said. All I remember is trying with every ounce of energy in my body to form coherent sentences and stop slurring. I failed. We never spoke again.

One night I texted Jerry Vlasak, the founder of the North American Animal Liberation Press Office. Since this organization publishes anonymous communiques from underground activists, he takes security issues very seriously. The simple fact that Jerry would entertained me on this unsecured mode of communication speaks to the fact that he wanted this drama on steroids to go away. It was an embarrassment to all of us. I remember telling him "it really hurts. He's sticking the knife in my back and twisting it." Jerry tried to reason with me. He said, "I know it hurts. But you have to take responsibility." And there it was again. Why was everyone telling me to "take responsibility." Then I passed out.

I needed to know why everyone kept telling me this. But no one would explain. I wrote to Steve three separate times pretending to be three different people, lending him some support and asking him how things were going with that "lunatic Marino." He would play the victim and, again, I couldn't control myself. Before I could bait him enough to get my questions answered, I would explode and just berate him for being a pathetic liar.

Years before, I had created a fan page for him on Facebook on which I made him an administrator with me. I had deleted him as an admin and put up a status as if it were him speaking saying "I am the king of Facebook warriors" (*Facebook warriors* are those who do nothing but pound keys). Now he contacted me to ask me to please remove the status and give him back control of the page. I was so glad that we were speaking that I happily removed the status, made him an admin again, and took myself off the page. But he only wanted things from me now. He wanted me to remove things from my profile that I had said about him. It was suddenly clear that our whole friendship was just about what I could do for him. And when I became a liability, he replaced me.

I couldn't feel my own hurt. It was too great for me to deal with. I was far more comfortable with anger. If he wanted to use all of my private emails to have his followers publicly embarrass me, then two can play at that. Joshua and I put up a dedicated web site of all Steve's personal emails to Tom Regan where he fancied himself going off to Africa and fighting elephant poachers, emails talking about women and high-profile activists, emails from his department chair where John Symons called him an "academic hack." That site stayed up 24 hours before I took it down. It was beneath me. I began privately forwarding to Alicia about the first 40 emails I could find about his trysts, the women he abused, his dating services, and the manner in which he denigrated her behind her back. She was crushed and broke up with him. He wrote to me to ask me if I could help him make things right with Alicia. I only wanted my friend back. I wasn't thinking anything through. I sent her an email telling her I had made everything up and apologized. He thanked me and stopped talking to me again. I was still allowing him to manipulate me.

I put the image of Steve back on my site as a logo. But now I adjusted his quote to read "When the law is wrong the right thing to do is break it... and then wet your pants and run like a coward."

I woke up one morning and had the bright idea that if I issued a public apology to Steve for calling him a drug addict, a liar, and a coward that he would do the same. I wanted the attacks to stop so badly that I would have done anything. So, I did. I published "A Public Apology to Dr. Steven Best." A lot of people told me they were glad I had taken this step and had chosen to move on. Steve's response was silence. No reciprocal apology. Instead I received a message from a mutual colleague that he was on his way to Europe for a speaking engagement and couldn't deal with me now. And that did it! It was all over now! I knew exactly what Dr. Steven Best was going to do in Europe. He was going to encourage direct action and, in fact, was going to be recording one of his speeches with a band where he repeats Martin Luther King, Jr.'s words "we will fill the jails with singing children!" WTF! You want to fill the jails with singing children so you could run away like a magnificent coward once they're behind bars? Maybe you want to help prosecute those children once they're restrained? Aw, hell no!

The insidious fraudulent facade of everything he wanted people to believe was empty. And I was livid. Whether or not we had ever been friends, whether or not he had ever betrayed me, whether or not he decided not to testify in my defense or allow me to take the fall for him was all irrelevant from a political standpoint. Simply publicizing my private information that the state could use against me was bad enough. But when he made my emails public while I was being prosecuted by vivisectors, when Ann Parkes posted information from "my dear comrade, Dr. Steve Best" on Speaking of Research and invited the vivisectors to visit her profile so they could finally put me in prison, he had sold out every animal and every activist who fights for their freedom. Steve Best and his cultists were now actively feeding information to the vivisectors, to the state, to help them prosecute me while I was a political prisoner. This is treachery. This is collaboration. This is an irredeemable sin. And he would never be allowed to play the part of the militant spokesperson ever again after he had betrayed the movement and every animal for whom we fight.

But in my drunken haze and against hundreds of attacks a day, the only thing I could do was put my hands over my head to fend off the relentless blows from all the schoolyard bullies. The worst part was how these people who do nothing in the real world yet have 1000s of Facebook followers would host parties on their profiles where they would ridicule me about things they knew nothing about. They would call me a jail bird. They called me a lot of things. But why were they saying that animals died because of me? Then they all laughed at how I was publicly unraveling. I returned to my fetal position on my couch. Then I would have a brilliant drunk idea and I would have to put it in an email and send it off. I think an appropriate subtitle for this book might be *"Don't Drink & Email."* I can see myself laughing like a lunatic in front of my computer:

> *"oh god, I am about to go for the kill. I can taste your blood and tears and it turns me on so fucking much daddy. lol it may take a minute though. there are real monkeys being tortured in a new concentration camp at yale. I know it defies your level of comprehension, but I have REAL work to do in the struggle for Animal Liberation and then i'll come back to romper room to play in the sandbox with you.. just wait for me... no more heads up... even though I enjoy this so. you'll know when the hammer drops on you. :)"*

Was it a threat? I guess so. And I completely intended to fulfill it by telling the truth and making the world understand what a liar he is. In subsequent emails I would apologize, I would tell him I loved him and he was my best friend, I would tell him I hated him, I would repeatedly ask him to stop the public campaign and handle this privately, I would tell him I would destroy him. And he remained silent and let the inner circle dispense with me for him. In September, Chris Lagergren called me at home and laughingly told me that I better stop contacting Steve or he was going to take legal action. This upset me. I couldn't imagine having more legal issues in yet another state. But against my unmitigated public lynching, I still think that my email tirade was an underwhelming response. Besides, he may be a liar and a fraud, but Steve was not about to go run to the state like the vivisectors to silence me. Chris was just trying to scare me.

Then Alicia sent me a message that she wanted to talk. I called her back. And out of everything and everyone in the universe, she was the one person who understood and knew exactly what was going on. Alicia finally left Steve and it was she who helped me regain my sanity. I was finally able to stop drinking and start talking. She and I had so much in common. As we spoke, we began to understand that we had completely misunderstood each other. We were never each other's competition. We both allowed Steve to pit us against one another. She confided in me that the abuse was not exclusive to her. He would regularly wish her to drive into a tree and kill her daughter. Alicia asked me why I always allowed Steve to treat me as a subordinate, "like a secretary." I couldn't answer. I didn't know why.

I also didn't know why if he called me up right then and there and wanted to be friends again, I would have been the happiest person in the world. And I guess that she didn't know why she would take his beatings and abuse and keep going back as well. We weren't that different after all. And the fact that she and I knew Steve like no one else also meant that she was the only other person in a position to understand how unbelievably manipulated all of his cultists were. Each of them would swear they knew Steve and that they knew the truth. Alicia and I both knew that the only *truth* they had was that which Steve found convenient to feed them. We both agreed that they had never even begun to see behind his mask.

Steve was incensed that Alicia and I had begun to talk and bond. And she was scared. Despite the fact that they had been seeing each other for years, she had never told him where she lived because she feared for her own and her daughter's safety. But she also knew that she was susceptible and didn't know if she could stand her ground when he contacted her. We were there for each other in a genuine way. We would text each other every day and talk on the phone to encourage one another to be strong and to make sure that we were both taking care of ourselves. We would not let him hurt us anymore. I would get through this. The worst part was behind me. And talking to Alicia allowed me to begin to reconnect with my own inner strength. I began to heal. I was very worried about her though. She sent me several texts discussing her broken ribs and asking me if she could still get a restraining order against him. I didn't know. I did know she was afraid and I was afraid for her. They say the most dangerous time in an abusive relationship is when the victim leaves.

But the animals are always imprisoned in the most abusive relationship of all. I would receive a package at home in early September that would jolt me back into reality and the real reason I fight. The package contained the highest compliment one can give me. With the permission of "The Team" in Madrid, I published the contents:

> *"We are writing from [deleted] that fights actively against speciesism and which also gives shelter to refugees from exploitation centers in Madrid, Spain. We heard about your story not long ago and that is why we are writing this letter. We would like to know how are you now and to let you know we are very happy you've got released.*
>
> *We would like to send you lots of courage since we consider that your detention has been an injustice and we believe that you should be free without any judgment or fine. Did they fine you? We now that things are not easy but it is very unfair what you were going through. We also would like to thank you for your strong belief and your fight for this better world without discrimination with which all animal right activists dream about.*
>
> *Our work at [deleted] is saving lifes. [sic] We safe [sic] the life of those who have been forgotten, those which nobody wants and which are no longer useful to obtain benefits from, and we give them a new life. You know, changing hell for heaven is in our hands. Our resources are not many, but our determination is great. Thus, not long ago we found in our way a new friend. A sheep, which just like many others, was meant to suffer hell. Now she, Camille, is resting at our home. She has*

several wounds which we are devotedly take care of, but she is recovering. Your story has inspired us to call her like you, and we hope that her story of liberation will give you courage and strength to go on.

We include some pictures so that you can meet Camille and we hope to hear from you soon.

From Madrid, all the inhabitants of [deleted] send you a big hug and we want you to know that we think of you every day."

My friends in Madrid gave me the strength and courage to go on when I needed it the most. And I remembered that we all must continue to encourage one another, not only to engage, but to continually escalate! "Camille" was liberated in Madrid. And her liberation gave me renewed strength to push forward.

*Lack of character always reveals
itself in the end.* -Unknown

A Domestic Violence Re-
straining Order

On October 15, 2012, The Dona Ana County Court in New Mexico issued a Temporary Domestic Violence Restraining Order. But it wasn't issued to Alicia Rodriguez against Steven Best for domestic abuse. It was issued to Steven Best against me! I was served in Florida by my friendly, local process server. We were on a first-name basis by this time. It stipulated that I could not contact Steve, could not *abuse* him, nor could I cause anyone else to abuse him.

It was based on a sworn statement from Steve in which he said that I am "a person who has stalked [him]." He presented all of my most irrational emails and further swore that I was "harassing and stalking me." He said I was "dangerous" because I had assumed others' identities to try and find out what he was doing to me. He said that Alicia was present for an instance of "domestic abuse" on October 14, 2012 at his home in Anthony, where I showed up at his house with "weapons." (On October 14, 2012, I was in Florida on house arrest with a GPS ankle monitor.) He also swore that "drugs were involved." I sent him 100s of emails and, where he initially used them to saturate cyberspace with great glee, he now presented them to the court and swore he *feared* me. Because I had removed his name from the Facebook page that I controlled, he swore that I "hacked" him. I allowed him and his third-party mercenaries to drive me out of my mind. And now he was prosecuting me for having a breakdown.

Then in his own words, while I was being prosecuted for the words he wrote about Donal O'Leary, his sworn complaint to the court read:

> *"she has a history of this. In fact, the [sic] Wayne State, [sic] University has her banned from there and a Professor has obtained an order of protection against her to stay away from his home and the University but she violated that and was arrested."*

This from the same man who encouraged me to go find O'Leary and lock myself down in his office! And now that it was convenient, he did some kind of hypocrite's contortion act -- shamelessly using my animal activism against me and aligning himself with a vivisector; with the vivisection complex! He continued "I am a Doctor Professor [sic] and can't have her slandering my name."

My response to this insidious instrument was to publish it. Let the world see what a liar and snitch he is. As far as all of my embarrassing emails that he included, well, I had no secrets anymore. He had made sure of that. They were posted all over the internet to embarrass me way before he submitted them to the courts and said he feared me. It was rather liberating to have no secrets and nothing left to hide. I told him to go fuck himself. He was using a restraining order to keep me silent so that he could rewrite history. And the only thing he was concerned about was "slandering my name" with the truth. He was trying to make it a criminal offense for me to use his name, clear my name, and set the record straight. No judge in their right mind would allow a prosecution for that. And he would never be allowed to rewrite history.

On October 26, there was a hearing in New Mexico on his temporary restraining order. I barely had enough money to get back to Detroit to go to trial in three weeks. I certainly wasn't in any position to fly out to New Mexico and start defending myself there and he knew it. The fact that he would join the vivisectors to prosecute me into silence speaks for itself.

Unchallenged, he went into court and testified under oath. The following is simply cut from court transcripts and pasted here with errors intact:

> *"I want to proceed to a full hearing and full sentencing... She is in flagrant violation of her PPO and I want to tell you her story...*

> *"This woman is certified insane, a lunatic and she is relentless in her persecution and harassment of me and the forms in which she takes to make my life a living hell are unlimited. Now, I'm a university professor. I live or die off my public reputation. I'm an internationally known speaker, writer, and activist. So, my name is my word, and I can't have someone out there in this world dispersing my name on Facebook, and on her well-trafficked blog with impunity.*

> *"Ms. Marino was in prison because Ms. Marino specializes in issuing threats against people. She has issued threats against David Jentsch, a UCLA vivisector and animal researchers at the University of Florida. In fact, at the University of Florida there is a mass PPO case against her involving over 100 people, this is the scale I'm talking about, and she is now being sentenced or will be sentenced in mid-November into Wayne County in Detroit for issuing explicit death threats against a medical researcher.*

> *"My principle concern, because she lives in Florida and I live here, is not that she is going to come and kill me. My principle concern is her cyber stalking and my reputation which she violates daily on Facebook and on her website."*

The court issued a 14-year Domestic Violence Protection Order which expires on October 26, 2026. And the hearing officer added:

> *"She is not to threaten you or stalk you and of course cyber stalking is a real concern but I think the reputation harming issues are things that you may need to take up in another court that has more authority. I mean I don't have any ability to find liable or slander, anything like that. All I can do is try and protect your safety, your physical safety from her."*

Alicia and I were still talking every day. The last phone conversations reiterated everything she had been telling me in texts; she was becoming increasingly fearful for herself and her daughter. And then in October the texts stopped.

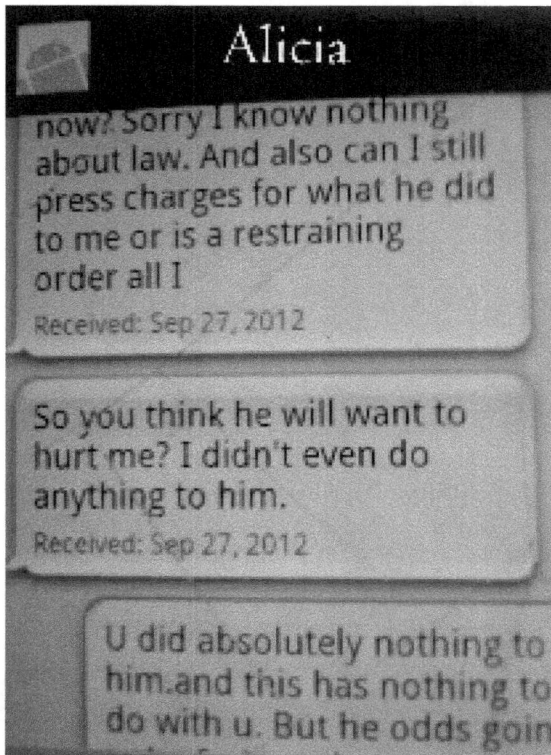

And her phone was dead when I called. I knew in my heart

that she had probably gone back to her abuser and changed her number. But I couldn't be sure. Steven Best now hated me. And as angry as he was when she wouldn't donate to my legal fund, he was even angrier and more unhinged now. That time he broke her ribs. What if she was seriously hurt? What if her baby was hurt? What if it was my fault?

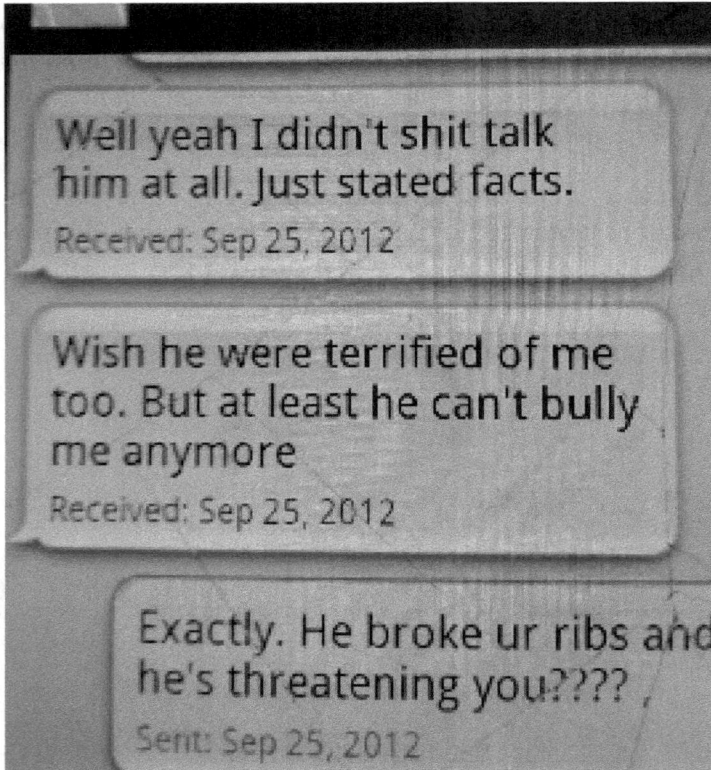

I had stopped drinking by now. I thought about this for more than 24 hours. I wanted nothing to do with this man anymore. He had betrayed everything in which he alleged to believe. He aligned himself with vivisectors and was now on record pleading their case. David Jentsch, Donal O'Leary, and every vivisector I had devoted myself to exposing at the University of Florida were now *medical researchers* as well as his colleagues, fellow *college professors*. He was a collaborator and courtroom documents would attest to that for posterity; many of my emails that Steve Best gave to Ann Parkes to publish on her profile as well as Dr.

A Domestic Violence Restraining Order

Steven Best's sworn testimony in a New Mexico court would be used by his new comrade, Donal O'Leary, in the coming month and become part of the official record of the State of Michigan v. Camille Marino. I was being prosecuted for Dr. Steven Best's violent rhetoric and, simultaneously, being prosecuted by him in the same case.

This man was a disgrace in my eyes and had ceased being of any relevance to me. But what if Alicia needed me? After wrestling with myself for two days, I finally broke down and called the Dona Ana Police Department. I gave them my name. I gave them my address. I gave them his address. And I told them I had no idea if there was anything wrong, but I hadn't heard from Alicia in several days. I asked them if they would do a safety check to make sure that if there is a baby in his house that it was okay.

The next night my cell rang while I was out shopping. It was Steve (violating his own restraining order again) asking me to remove something else from my website that I had written about him. I only wanted to be left alone at this point and tell the truth. I wanted my good reputation back. I had completely stopped emailing and texting him. I took down the article so he would just go away. My one-time mentor disgusted me. While we were on the phone there was a knock at my door. It was the police. He was having me arrested for *stalking* him because I asked the police to do a safety check. He was prosecuting me for violating his restraining order by checking on Alicia and her daughter, yet he was violating his own restraining order by calling me. I was on the phone with Steve Best while he was having me arrested.

How was I going to get to Michigan while I was in jail in Florida? Were they going to extradite me to New Mexico? I was flat broke. He had effectively killed my support and my legal fund was empty. I was put in isolation. I couldn't be in population with the ankle monitor and they couldn't remove it because it was out of another jurisdiction. Sumter County jail is tiny and isolation was grueling. There was a bare light bulb that stayed on 24 hours. I had no glasses so I couldn't even see the ID number on my wristband that I needed to enter into the phone to make calls. The guard loaned me her glasses. After three days, Mike was able to borrow $3,000 from his father to bail me out. I went home and should have never went back online.

Now they were laughing, as were the vivisectors, that I was finally arrested for stalking Dr. Best. People who have never done anything in their lives except post on Facebook for their insipid followers, people I don't even know but were taking tremendous pleasure in bullying me, were declaring victory at my demise. The vivisectors were blogging with glee that I had now been arrested for stalking Dr. Steven Best, their new best friend.

I couldn't breathe. I was out of jail three days before I went to the hospital and was admitted for another three days. They couldn't get my blood pressure down. I couldn't calm down. I just kept mumbling "I can't stop the attacks. They're everywhere." No one knew what I was talking about. They pumped me up on anti-anxiety medications. I would calm down, fall asleep, then wake up and we would do it all over again. I left the hospital that weekend with a prescription for Xanax. It was the only way they could get my blood pressure down.

A few days after being discharged from the hospital, I left for Detroit.

I feel like a man who has been asleep somewhat and under someone else's control. I feel that what I'm thinking and saying is now for myself. Before it was for and by the guidance of Elijah Muhammad. Now I think with my own mind, sir!
—Malcolm X

Posting a Message

On November 19, 2012, I pleaded guilty to trespassing for my civil disobedience and *posting a message*. Without Steve's testimony, I was unable to effectively challenge the state. And contrary to legal advice, I never invoked my former friend's name to plead for leniency; I took full responsibility for publishing the content of Dr. Best's *Freddy Kruger letter*. I was strongly urged to place the blame at the feet of the acknowledged author when I addressed the court to mitigate my own culpability, but I refused. Steve may have run to the state and become a tool in the repression apparatus, but that was a road he was going to walk alone. I would rather take the full weight of their wrath than apologize or equivocate. I would stand behind his words even though he would not. To do anything less would have been a betrayal of the animals.

Essentially, although the entirety of my statement consisted of uttering the word "yes" twice, I pleaded guilty to threats and intimidation at my allocution. All of my contempt charges for alleged repeated violations of O'Leary's PPO were dismissed and the aggravated stalking charge was dropped. I'm extremely proud of myself. I stood my ground when it mattered. But it's also ironic that the stalking charge about which I was so concerned was dismissed. And the ridiculous posting a message charge was the one that ultimately stuck. I would do six months in jail, be on probation for another 2 ½ years, and then I would be free and clear.

Matt and I decided that I should sign my bond over to him and that the $3,500 would be returned to him to cover my outstanding legal fees. Had I not signed it over, the courts would have taken it and likely awarded it to Donal O'Leary toward a $6,000+ civil restitution judgment he had previously been awarded. And since I had no other means of paying Matt, we asked the court to revoke my bond that day; I could begin serving my time pending sentencing and he could cash in the bond. At this point, jail was a welcome escape from the relentless hate campaign that ultimately broke me over the previous three months. I returned to Wayne County Jail a convicted felon.

On December 5, 2012, I was officially sentenced to three years of probation, the first six months to be served in Wayne County Jail. With credit for 59 days having already been served, I was to serve the 121-day balance. As part of the felony please agreement, I conceded to a 5-year restraining order on that day stipulating that I could not contact Donal O'Leary or mention his name online until December 5, 2017.

On December 10, 2012, I was transferred to the Dickerson Detention Facility in Wayne County where I would serve my sentence. It was a lot cleaner and more comfortable than WCJ. But if I had thought jail could be cold before, this was a nightmare. Michigan is unbearable in the winter. Inside our cells there was frost on the windows every single day until March arrived. With only one sheet and a non-vegan wool blanket, I would go to sleep shivering and wake up shivering. In the middle of the night I would wake up racked with pain from the cold. The only relief was warming up in the shower in the morning. I learned that even on those days when the water was cold, my body would warm up once I dried off. Dickerson Detention Center was like living inside a refrigerator. The guards regularly wore layers under their uniforms and coats. Aside from that, it was comfortable.

You can jail the revolutionary,
you can't jail the revolution.
-Fred Hampton

William Dickerson Deten-
tion Facility

January 5, 2013

The Dickerson Detention Facility is a concrete refrigerator with
no fresh air but it is a hotel by comparison to WCJ. We have
private cells with wooden doors and porcelain fixtures instead of
steel. I have a desk and a stool as well as my own light switch so
I can read or write whenever I want. A younger girl in here named
Nichole looks to me for guidance. I like to mentor her. She comes
in and cleans my cell when there are no guards around. Dust has
simply never been a priority for me. I also have my own window
which is one of the things I value most some days. There is a
population of 64 women although this is primarily a men's jail
with 900 male inmates. My cell is on the second tier and we are
locked down from 10 pm to 9 am. My cell was on the lower tier
the first few weeks I was here. With snow on the ground and little
to no heat, those cells are like deep freezers. The upper-tier cells
all have frost on the windows too, but they are so much warmer
by comparison. I never experienced the physical pain one feels
from being exposed to frigid temperatures for extended periods

of time.

There is far more diversion here. We have a gym in which to exercise, play volleyball, play cards, or just socialize. I'm also learning how to engage some of the inmates and have started holding informal re-education classes that subtly promote veganism and an anti-vivisection agenda. There is a carpeted TV area downstairs with plastic lounge chairs and foot rests. The upper meal area doubles as the movie area after the trustees clean up. They play about two movies every day, but I don't watch movies or TV. I find promoting activism and subverting the system from in here a far better use of my time.

I spend a lot of time walking laps or monotonously walking up and down the stairs, playing cards or volleyball, recruiting, trying to organize initiatives outside, reading, writing, thinking, or doing Sudoku puzzles. I have a tremendous amount of support from anonymous people in the court system as well as inside the jail and I am frequently allowed access to their computers. One of the officials with whom I associate was once arrested for liberating chickens; another has been alienated from family and friends because she is intractable on the issue of fur. Most guards as well as the other inmates appreciate my position. I'm one of the few people behind bars who says "I did it, I'm proud of it, and I'll do it again." Whatever the reason, my captors enjoy helping me while I'm in here. I guess I get a kick out of being on Facebook too. It is a lot healthier for me to focus on the animals and put out my statements and info without being inundated with the constant assaults and attacks. I am feeling like me again. I'm getting stronger every day.

While I have not changed my views about the efficacy of vegan outreach, I find it extraordinarily gratifying to have learned how to engage people in such a way that makes them want to adopt my ideology. I still think veganism is a moral imperative without consequence, but it is an imperative nonetheless. We have a microwave and far better commissary. I make the best vegan bean burritos which might explain why I have to exercise so much. And I'm getting vegetarian trays here, so I can eat about 80% of my food. The women are always wanting to try my burritos or peanut butter and jelly. I'm thinking of promoting a new slogan in here "Go veg, get peanut butter!" Whatever it takes.

My closest friend here, also named Camille, is here for aggravated stalking. Camille Perry and I are like sisters. When we were in WCJ together, someone stole one of her Nutty Buddies. We call it the "Nutty Buddy incident." She went around the pod and had these girls cowering under the tables until her snacks were returned. I just laughed. A devout Catholic, she now thinks vivisectors are evil and is interested in veganism both for health and ethical reasons. She's also my spades partner and we kick butt.

One of my other associates, Nikia, has been vegetarian for the past two weeks. In her case it's not for the peanut butter. She is disturbed by what we've discussed about factory farming and I believe in her case that this is the beginning of a profound change for her. I just hope that whatever seeds I am able to sow will continue to grow after I am no longer here to cultivate the crop. I am also locked up with two people closely associated with Providence Research Labs. One is a prostitute with a heroin addiction who has been disowned by her mother who, incidentally, is an administrator of their lab. I'm learning as much as I can about this prisoner. The information could provide useful leverage in the future should a campaign ever get off the ground out here. The other inmate is a weekender who maintains her job during the week. She's been able to give me the names of their vivisectors but I am unable thus far to isolate anything I can exploit. This woman, Beth, is already vegetarian and we think about some things in very similar terms.

Anyway, when Matt negotiated this deal for me, we were sure that I would be out in under six weeks. No one does their full time in Detroit and every non-violent offender who walks into Dickerson has their time cut at least in half within a week of arrival. After waiting over a month for them to "find my file," I was informed last week that I am ineligible to get an automatic time cut because of "what you did" and will do every day of my time. But no one will tell me exactly what it is that I did. Win my lawsuit against UF? Refuse to be silent about animal abuse? Not be apologetic and fall to my knees begging for mercy?

The truth is actually compelling. One of my supporters, a corporal who is not associated with my rock, got word to me about exactly what's going on. They classified me as a Level 5 offender, incarcerated for aggravated stalking. Level 5 means that I've had three felony convictions in the last five years and am considered violent. That allows them to bypass the time-cut criteria and keep me here legally. So what if this is my first offense in 48 years and the stalking charges were dropped?! One of those mere pesky details. And now that my reservation has been extended for two more months, I'm organizing a hunger strike as a demonstration of unity, resistance, and defiance from behind bars.

The call to other political prisoners only went out two days ago, but, so far, I'll be on a hunger strike starting on February 22 at Dickerson and Ebony Malcom will simultaneously stop eating in Wayne County Jail. Ebony and I were both on house arrest over the summer and we spent a lot of time on the phone. Now we're both back in jail and never have, nor ever will, yield to the corrupt system. As vegan as one can be in the Wayne County Jail system, she and I have genuinely merged our struggles and ideologies and I am proud to call her my friend. I have press releases to prepare and people to rally. I have no idea what, if anything, this demonstration will accomplish, but I'll never know unless I try. Resistors will understand and I am hopeful that we inspire some solidarity actions outside. But I've learned not to hold my breath. The fence-sitters will watch and wait for someone else to do something. The cyber groupies will cheer, condemn, or gossip online. And the animals will keep dying until we figure out how to end their captors' reigns of terror.

I will be released shortly thereafter on March 9th. I can't wait to roll around in the grass with Brutus, Max, and Jazz and curl up with Socks and Peanut. I also can't wait to get home and get NIO back online. The site was allegedly hacked shortly after I was locked up so I had it temporarily redirected to a mirror to remain vital. I am unclear about the technicalities surrounding this attack, but they weren't able to penetrate the security I have in place on my servers in Iceland. I am told that some of the images may have been infected and that people going to NIO are getting viruses. I suspect that one of my associates is just overreacting to some technical glitch, but I don't want to deal with it from in here. Even if I did, with all of my server credentials tucked away somewhere in Florida, it is virtually impossible to do anything with the site while I'm in a cell in Detroit..

So I get the domestic terrorist probation special: any violation in the next three years, even trespassing or jaywalking, and I go straight to prison for 18 months to five years. My judge was kind enough to hand write this little caveat into my court papers. This is unheard of for a non-violent, first-time offender and is generally reserved as the strictest form of parole for repeat violent offenders.

And as far as New Mexico goes, I cannot allow Steve's malicious restraining order to impede my work any further. My brother loaned me $5,000 to retain a lawyer out there. Neither of us knows when I'll be in a position to pay it back. I told my lawyer that I just want this nonsense to go away. The prosecutor doesn't want to be bothered. My lawyer doesn't want to be bothered. The only person pursuing this is Dr. Steven Paul Best. I will plead guilty to one misdemeanor count of violating his restraining order. I had to make sure Alicia and her daughter were safe; if calling the police to do a safety check is a violation, so be it. And the number of times he violated his own order is inconsequential. I don't even care. I just want to be done with Steve Best and the cancer he has chosen to become. I will not allow him to infect me anymore. So, it is agreed that I will plead to the misdemeanor and get six months of non-reporting probation. I'll sign it when I get out and be done with it. Interestingly, my lawyer told me that my former mentor threw fit when he learned the prosecutor wasn't going to prosecute me. I could not have foreseen who Steve would become. Maybe I simply chose not to see who he really was all along. As for me, I now understand that I had more support than I ever knew. Many people watched from afar in disbelief. I will clear my name when I am free.

On January 16, an 8-page article entitled *Arson, Cracked Testicles, and Internet Death Threats: How Animal Rights Extremists Are Learning From the People Who Murdered George Tiller*[50] *was published on the popular gossip site, gawker.com. I received a copy of it in the mail from Elizabeth about a week later. By now, reporters everywhere are attributing the "cracked testicles" rhetoric, Steve's words for which I was prosecuted, to me. But in this article, they created a picture with Jentsch's car on fire in the background underneath which there was a picture of me from the back in handcuffs being arrested at my last civil disobedience. On the left-hand side was my mugshot from February 4, 2012 and to the right was Walter Bond's mugshot after he was taken into custody by the ATF. In the middle, between us, was the quote "One day we're going to come up behind you and slit your throat."*

Neither Walter nor I ever uttered that sentence. But it was a great quote and an extremely creative graphic. So now it didn't matter whether Steve Best authored some words or if they just pulled other words out of thin air; if it served their purpose, all kinds of things were credited to me. This article went on to connect me to everything from forcing Jentsch to move by publishing his address to ordering his car blown up which happened before I ever even knew his name. No matter, the article did offer a good deal of actual quotes from Jordan Heller's and my extensive interviews and, mixed in with the tall tales, were actual facts. This single article made me a celebrity inside Dickerson.

February 22, 2013
Our hunger strike began at 12:01 am this morning and we

---

50 Jordan Heller, "Arson, Cracked Testicles, and Internet Death Threats: How Animal Rights Extremists Are Learning from the People Who Murdered George Tiller," gawker.com (January 16, 2013) http://gawker.com/5976473/arson-cracked-testicles-and-internet-death-threats-how-animal-rights-extremists-are-learning-from-the-people-who-murdered-george-tiller

expected a handful of people to gather outside Dickerson and at WCJ at 1 pm to support Ebony; Nikia was released last week and was scheduled to be here with friends promoting veganism; and an anonymous Dickerson employee arranged to have her son and his friend show up to stand in unity with the resistors; blacks, whites, animal liberationists, vegans, and other community activists – standing united in solidarity. This is a prime example of alliances arising generically with a common goal.

Someone in the jail notified all the local news stations including FOX, ABC and CBS. So, of course, there is a major blizzard outside and it looks like everything fell apart. My sources told me the news would be blacked out in the jail tonight and, like clockwork, the TVs all shut off at 5 pm and came back on at 7 pm. I have no idea what happened outside or if we got any coverage. I have no direct contact with Ebony because I don't know anyone who can patch us in on a three-way conversation. It gets complicated trying to talk directly between jails and prisons – it's also prohibited – but it can be done.

We're on a strict diet of water and some orange juice here and there for the next seven days. I am also getting some supplemental herbal teas from a sympathetic corrections officer that I'll share with my fellow resistors. Inside the jail, we came down for lunch, sat down, then the guards allowed Nichole to read a statement that I prepared before everyone began to eat. She spoke the following words and then those of us on strike gave away our trays and left the meal area:

> *"At 12:01 am this morning, several prisoners throughout this county began a 7-day fast for unity behind bars.*
>
> *Many oppressed minorities and victims of society who have not had the benefit of a good education or proper opportunities for true freedom are coming together to declare our rights. While this city is bankrupt, people are losing their homes and jobs, and living in extreme poverty, billions of our tax dollars are flowing right*

over our heads into universities that gratuitously torture animals for profit. Marino is here for simply exposing this corruption and to keep her silent.

While we fast, we have many supporters around the world who are tired of being silenced. It is time for all of us – black, white, Asian, Mexican, able-bodied and differently-abled, abused women, inmates and officers – to come together in peace and unity. Our common enemy is not each other but the system that draws the lines between our groups to keep us separated and enslaved, both people and animals alike.

For the next week, it is our hope and prayer that we can all come together as sisters and reclaim our power and to continue to go forward in unity after this fast; not just for today or this week, but forever."

Then the press release went out from outside:

"FOR IMMEDIATE RELEASE:
Dickerson Detention Facility & Wayne County Jail

Michigan, U.S.A

February 22, 2013

For our various actions in defense of the animals, the earth, or oppressed minorities, we are behind bars while the criminals who run this country are free to torture animals, rape the planet and jail dissenters with impunity. We are the prisoners of conscience and the state needs to silence us. They lock us in these cells to isolate us from the apathetic and complacent masses to allow their corruption to flourish unimpeded. But we will never be silenced. From behind bars, we will unite our respective struggles, we will recruit and multiply, and from the bowels of their system, our armies will rise.

In a demonstration of solidarity, defiance and organized resistance, several prisoners began a 7-day hunger strike at 12:01 a.m. this morning that will end at 11:59 p.m. on February 28. We are inviting our friends, supporters and resisters everywhere to do what your conscience dictates and take actions in solidarity with us against oppressors and in defense of the earth and the animals all week long while we fast. If we want to get a glimpse of what a cohesive resistance movement could look like, now is the time to stop using words and start taking coherent action.

The Hunger Strikers:

Camille Marino *(#2012027580) is the founder of Negotiation Is Over! (NIO) and a Vegan Animal Liberation activist. After repeated arrests last year for exposing vivisectors, spending most of 2012 in jail, and enduring an FDLE raid on her home, she is currently serving 6 months at the Dickerson Detention Facility in Hamtramck, Michigan, where she continues to radicalize the inmates.*

Ebony Malcom *(#2012017262) is a Black Sovereign and aspiring vegan. In a singularly blatant and corrupt fashion, her constitutional rights have been trampled and are being held in abeyance, due to her politics. Rather than beg or plead with the oppressors for mercy, she has chosen to sit in jail indefinitely and petition the court of appeals. She is incarcerated in Wayne County Jail in Detroit, Michigan, where she continues to radicalize the inmates.*

Nichole Hollingsworth *(#2010025850) is a federal prisoner being held at Dickerson while awaiting transfer to federal prison. While she was victimized by the system, abused and manipulated by a corrupt older authority figure, and has made some mistakes; she is now vegan and committed to Animal Liberation. She is working to make vegan meals available in jail (and prison) on religious grounds. She is also becoming* *astute at weaving the vegan Animal Liberation message into the Christian ministry as a vehicle to reach and recruit the masses behind bars.*

Carol Gilbert *(#2013000776) is now a paraplegic who fights for the rights of the disabled. Prior to her accident, 12 years in prison made her an active prison abolitionist. She joins this hunger strike to shed light on the needs of disabled prisoners who, like the animals in the vivisectors' labs, are abused, neglected, intimidated and forgotten.*

Several recently-released prisoners from Dickerson, as well as local activists, are expected to gather outside the facility at 1:00 p.m. for a brief demonstration of unprecedented unity among different groups, to show resistance against all oppression, and promote the vegan agenda. Racism and sexism were constructs of the white power patriarchy to keep different oppressed groups marginalized. We must erase all of the imaginary lines that have served to fractionalize us and reclaim our power.

Animal Liberation will be achieved when the detriments of animal abuse outweigh the benefits. Founded in 2009, NIO strives to be an instrument of defiance, disruption, disobedience, subversion, creative & aggressive grassroots action, and a catalyst for revolutionary change."

February 24, 2013

I wish I could say that my level of enthusiasm is constant and remains unaffected by my peers, but I can't. On the first day of the hunger strike, I watched from the upper tier as one of our resisters stocked up on junk food from commissary below. I was thoroughly disheartened by Carol's defection. But that made the bond between the remaining three of us that much stronger. And by last night, three more prisoners had joined us but I am not at liberty to identify them by name: one is a victim of domestic abuse in jail for protecting herself; one is a black activist who has taught me as much about Tupac Shakur as I've taught her about Fred Hampton; and the third person is a recovering heroin addict who wants to make a positive contribution to the world. She has begun to trade her unhealthy habits for discipline, focus, and a cause greater than herself – fighting for the animals. I am hopeful that she will bring our message with her to the rehab when she transfers next week.

I've had a somewhat colorful life which includes a fast track to investment banking stardom, law school, and a history of drug abuse followed by an overdose in which I almost died. It took me over a year to learn to walk again and, by the time I was able to will myself back to health, my former life as a money-obsessed workaholic seemed so artificial. I'm beginning to understand that I have a tremendous store of experience that allows me to connect with a wide array of people on many different levels. I am finding that I am able to bring people around by letting them in and connecting with them where their heart lives. I thought that my greatest challenge would be to connect Animal Liberation with all of the other human struggles in a credible manner. But it appears that I'm overcoming my paralyzing fear of public speaking out of necessity and connecting the dots to subvert the vivisection complex comes naturally. I've been told by more than one individual and on several occasions that I have *disciples* in here. I prefer to believe that I provoke people to think and, hopefully, inspire them to action. The animals don't need disciples, they need relief. But, again, whatever it takes...

February 25, 2013

Socks died from cancer last night. She went to sleep on the couch with Max and Jazz and never woke up. I can't help feeling guilty for having left her when she needed me. My heart is broken. The balance of the hunger strike is dedicated to her.

Rest in peace, Socks. I'm sorry I couldn't be there with you.

February 27, 2013

I WON MY APPEAL YESTERDAY! The location of the University of Florida's labs (and university labs as a whole) was ruled public record. The Smashing Pumpkins song keeps playing in my head:

> *"Today is the greatest*
> *Day I've never known*
> *Can't wait for tomorrow*
> *I might not have that long*
> *I'll tear my heart out*
> *Before I get out"*

I want to jump out of my skin I'm so happy. Everyone is. Some of my keepers in here printed a few of the news articles that are online. They're circulating all over. It has given me more credibility in the jail to talk about exactly how universities steal money from the people to torture animals and how desperate they are to keep their secrets.

Three judges unanimously decided that the redactions in the records I won on December 30, 2011 were illegal. I dictated a request for the location of the primates which was filed with UF within hours of the decision. I hope every university campaign follows suit and keeps pushing forward before statutes are re-written across the country. I will be released from jail in Michigan in 10 days and will be back home in Florida in less than two weeks. It appears I've just about come full circle. There are few things more vindicating than declaring victory against your enemy when they have you locked in a concrete box. But that's just my ego talking. The only relevant fact here is that we just shattered yet one more wall behind which vivisectors terrorize their victims in peace and anonymity. Their crimes cannot withstand the light of day and I remain convinced that exposure is the single-most damaging weapon activists possess.

I don't know whether our hunger strike is inspiring any action in the outside world or if anyone even noticed, but we've made some amazing steps forward in here. We brought more people into this informal coalition which now boasts key alliances within the jail as well as with retired school teachers, activists, and inmates across the board. And I've clearly constructed a persuasive thesis that identifies the vivisection industry in universities as our common enemy. I'm most proud of Nicole who introduced Vegan Christianity into the jailhouse culture. As an atheist myself, I have no use for religion outside. But behind bars, the God opiate is pervasive and I'm confident that this new form of activism will follow her to federal prison.

As of this date, all of my outstanding legal issues have been resolved and I am free to return home when I'm released on March 9. But I'm fully aware that as I evolve and continue to fight back with everything I'm made of, the enemies will continue to come at me even harder. Torturing the innocent to death is how they make their money. My job is to stop them. Neither of us is likely to give up easily.

March 4, 2013
It's probably about 7 am and it is the most clear, crisp, bright beautiful morning outside. It's Monday. I guess they'll unlock my cell in another couple of hours. Then I get released in five days. I'm out of here Saturday. I'm feeling really good this morning. I've had such an amazing couple of months getting something of a movement started behind bars. This Saturday, a colleague will pick me up and maybe we'll get together with some of my new friends out here; hopefully at least Camille Perry. She got out about a month ago.

When we were in WCJ, she had come in on an aggravated stalking case. Someone took out a bogus PPO on her and then had her violated. Camille was in a convenience store; her *victim* followed her in and then called the cops. Personal Protection Orders and the resulting stalking felonies are highly problematic across the board. If Perry was going back to jail, she was going to earn it. When her accuser left the stand after testifying, Camille jumped her in the courtroom, beat her down, and after she was restrained by the bailiffs, she turned to the judge and said, "Guilty, Your Honor." We bonded. She calls us "sisters from another mother." I think Camille Perry will make an excellent Animal Liberation activist.

Nicole, the inmate who believed she got a revelation from God during our hunger strike/fast and started the Vegan Christianity movement in here is now also the first inmate of whom I am aware to ever be granted a vegan tray on Christian grounds in this county jail system. That was days ago. Then, yesterday, Pastor Charles Richardson, Jr. preached her Vegan Christianity essay at the Galilee Gospel Center in Detroit to a mainstream congregation. This could potentially be one of the biggest breakthroughs for the animals yet.

On the anti-vivisection front, I can't wait to get back to Florida and hit the streets with my repackaged message, using some of the strategies I've developed in here to bring people in. My only concern is Animal Liberation and I couldn't care less what anyone needs to hear to achieve the objective: God, taxes, ethics, resistance. They're all just a means to an end. I saw the *Gawker* article again today. Someone got a guard to make copies so I could autograph them before I'm released. I had some fun in here.

Later...
It's 2 pm. We lock down every day at this time until 4 pm when we eat dinner. I kicked my exercise regimen up a notch to get back in the routine for when I get out. Exercised on the big stairs for 30 minutes as soon as they let me out at 9 am and did 45 minutes on the little stairs after lunch. Then I took one of the coldest showers I've taken since I got locked up. You don't get to regulate your water in jail; just push a button and hope it's bearable. The one thing I really miss besides my four-legged children is waking up and hitting the gym with metal pumping through my iPod. Next Tuesday I'll wake up at home, be in the gym by 5:30, in the pool by 6:30, out in the field with the dogs by 7:30 and then I'll make my first quart of juice in months. I think I need a 5-day juice fast to detox my body.

I have to go see my probation officer in Detroit on Monday before I fly home that night. I am so hoping they keep my probation here and just let me call in once a week like when I was on house arrest. I don't care what anyone says, Florida is a conservative red state and the laws there are petty and punitive. Besides, I like my probation officer out here and I like having supporters in the court system too. But, whatever the situation may be, I just need to be crystal clear about the restrictions on me – which are bound to be myriad more if I have to report in Florida – so I don't violate.

My activism is growing in a lot of different directions that will hopefully prove more effective and keep me out of the line of fire for a while. I feel tarnished by some of my past behavior and the poor choices I exercised in choosing associates. The public feud was embarrassing and so destructive. But I think everything was necessary. I'm not one of those people who believe everything happens for a reason. I believe a situation is only worth what you can get out of it. I've grown in ways I couldn't have foreseen and wouldn't trade this entire experience for anything. I know who

I am and of what I'm made. I know who my friends are. That's priceless.

When I got out of jail in August and was first dealing with being betrayed, I was wondering what I could learn from it. I've learned so much that words elude me. Perhaps all that needs to be said is that I learned to stand on my own as an activist. And living in a cage has only made me that much more determined to release the animals from theirs.

March 8, 2013

Getting released tomorrow. It snowed and looked pretty cold outside yesterday, but it's nice and bright this morning. The frost in here melted about a week ago. I am looking so forward to breathing some fresh air. With a newly-secured win and exciting things happening in my UF campaign, I refuse to lose my focus. Even with toxic people re-emerging and threatening to present considerable headaches, they can only disrupt my fight if I allow them to. I need to maintain my self-restraint and discipline when I get out and not engage.

For lack of a better phrase, I'm very much aware of a new sense of personal power. I looked in the mirror this morning with no makeup, hair that has not been properly groomed for months, an ill-fitting grubby uniform that I've been wearing for a week, and I still have 15 – 20 pounds to take off. And I looked into my own eyes and smiled. Despite the safety net of my appearance being stripped from me, or maybe because of it, I was able to create tremendous changes here: one of my guards is now vegan, a new vegan religious sect is emerging behind bars, I've cultivated and nurtured a handful of Animal Liberation activists who have now been released, and I've formed relationships with a handful of individuals within the system. I look forward to continuing these friendships. I'm proud of myself.

A passage from a book I'm reading, Way of the Peaceful Warrior by Dan Millman, resonates with me this morning:

> *"Moderation? It's mediocrity, fear, and confusion in disguise. It's neither doing nor not doing. It's the wobbling compromise that makes no one happy. Moderation is for the bland, the apologetic, for the fence-sitters of the world afraid to take a stand. It's for those afraid to laugh or cry, for those afraid to live or die."*

I'm sitting here in my room and I hear a disembodied voice in one of the cells start screaming. Apparently, someone in another cell was running the water and it was annoying the screaming inmate.

But then a bunch of people started playing with their water one by one and, the more the first woman screamed, the more the other numb-skulls tried to agitate her. I sat back laughing to myself at all the inanity surrounding me. And then it hit me like a lightning bolt: In dealing with Steve's merry band of numb-skulls, I was the crazy lady screaming in her cell. Nichole calls this a revelation. I think it's just what they call *wisdom*. At least I hope so.

I have nothing left to talk about. I choose to be quiet going forward and let my actions alone speak for me. The animals are dying in the real world. And that's where I need to be fighting too. Animal Liberation will be achieved when the detriments of animal abuse outweigh the benefits.

Animals, whom we have made our slaves, we do not like to consider our equal. -Charles Darwin

Probation

When I was released from jail on March 9, 2013 I issued a short statement that read, in part:

> *"My release is not a cause for celebration, but a signal that we all must re-double our efforts. While I am free from my concrete cage tonight, billions of animals around the world are still entombed in theirs. It's never been about me. I am only an instrument through which I hope to promote Animal Liberation. But I think my story speaks volumes about the climate in which we work."*

I put NIO back online and started going through all of the veterinarian records that had laid dormant while I was locked up. I learned that Bucky died while I was in jail. I was heartbroken. And then like a giant punch in the face, the online attacks started again. While I had been locked up, Mike's father bought one of his son's a home. And he bought Mike a little red sports car, a Crossfire, for his birthday. I had no use for a sports car. I had an Impala I used to chauffeur my dogs and get my signs, banners, and bullhorns to protests. But here it was all over the internet, the inner circle posting pictures of Mike's car all over Facebook –

proof of how I had used my legal fund donations to buy that car.

But they were posting something on my profile that I had never seen before that would prove devastating. They were sending it to all of my associates. And, now, for the first time, I understood why my attackers had been blaming me for monkeys dying, although the timing will never make sense to me. In November of 2012 before I went back to jail they said animals died because of me. Bucky wound up dying in his cage of heart failure in December of 2012, a month later. And back in November they were saying that I was banned from Primate Friends Sanctuary in Gainesville yet no one had ever mentioned it to me. The last time I had spoken to Kari Bagnell, the owner, about a year before, she had invited me to sleep over if I ever needed to when I protested. But now everything was beginning to come into focus. The information was presumably fed to the inner circle by Michael Budkie as part of an all-out effort to eradicate me.

In order to secure his restraining order in October 2012, Steve Best falsely testified that the University of Florida vivisectors had a case against me that consisted of "one hundred" personal protection orders. In fact, as this book goes to publication, other than being trespassed from their campus, there has never been any legal action taken by any vivisector in my state. Did this information come from Michael Budkie who was clearly being fed information about me directly from the vivisectors? Did he pass it on to Steve Best for maximum impact? The vivisectors, Dr. Steven Best, and Michael Budkie, (the founder of Stop Animal Experimentation Now) all collaborating with a single agenda: to neutralize me.

Michael Budkie never said a word to me directly; he only fed others information behind my back. It seems he and the inner circle shared the same playbook. He did, however, release a public statement after I was locked up, as if to put the final nail in my coffin. Without ever mentioning Louis or his failure to win release for that monkey two years earlier, without ever mentioning that vivisectors will never release their victims that are too deteriorated and broken, without ever mentioning that the vivisectors are killing animals every day of the week, he parroted all of the vivisectors' talking points about me; he allowed himself to be used as their tool. It must have seemed convenient since he had seen me as his competition from the beginning. Indeed, I had rattled many cages; I never expected so many collaborators to fall out. And now the inner circle was reposting his public statement all over Facebook to make sure I saw it.

After I was safely behind bars, Michael Budkie publicly wrote:

> *"Regarding this whole situation, I have remained silent for far too long. It is high time that everyone knows a few things about the damage that has been done to the overall situation in Gainesville, Florida. Some of you may be aware of a primate named Bucky, some may not. Bucky was a primate who lived and died inside the labs at UF, but he didn't have to. I know this because SAEN had provided the funding for an enclosure to be built at a primate sanctuary. Just as Bucky was about to be released, Camille Marino began using his name in campaigning and his release was cancelled. No one other than the sanctuary and SAEN (and UF of course) knew he was to be released. This took place during the summer of 2012. Bucky was chosen for release because he was a severe self-mutilator. As a result of the tactics used in the campaign against UF, not only was Bucky's release terminated but the entire primate retirement program (which had been going on for at least seven years) was halted. As a result, Bucky died in the labs at UF in December of 2012 due to heart failure. He never saw the sunlight or felt the grass as he could have. His freedom and the remainder of his life in a sanctuary was destroyed. This is something that should have come out in August of 2012 but I was trying to avoid being drug into the whole Steve/Camille conflict. It's high time everyone knows the truth."*

He went on and on for five more paragraphs claiming I never had a victory and that I was a danger to the animals. Then I saw a comment on his profile that cut me deeply. It never mentioned my name or made any reference to me whatsoever. It was from the Barbi Twins: "We only support Michael Budkie" and went on to speak of his commitment to the animals. Sia and I used to refer to me as "the third twin." Although I hadn't spoken to them since my arrests began, I considered them friends. That statement from my friends made it abundantly clear how much damage my reputation had sustained.

I broke down. Bucky never would feel the sunlight or the grass because of me. That was too much to handle. While I understood that Budkie waited for an opportune moment to jump in the melee like just another schoolyard bully to neutralize me, while, like Steve Best, also cultivating an appearance of remaining above it all, it didn't seem to matter. I killed Bucky. I tried with everything I had to get him out. I stayed up in jail crying about this poor little monkey that I failed. I had failed him worse than I knew.

I copied the posts and sent them to the three people I trusted most; Anne O'Berry and David Tenenbaum had both become very close by now. The third colleague was the only person who, despite the constant harassment and abuse from his old friend Steve Best and Steve's cultists, refused to choose a side against me in the war. Anne and David shared my utter despair. But they also were struck by how Budkie chose to jump in when I couldn't defend myself. My third colleague began helping me see things clearly. I wrote him an encrypted email and said "I need to know your honest opinion. Am I a danger to the animals?" And I sent a link to the scathing statement. He said something that never clicked for me: "Look, Budkie is a welfarist. You're a revolutionary. Big difference. You didn't kill Bucky. The vivisectors did." And he went on to help me think this through. After a couple of days, I got passed my own grief and began to see clearly again.

If Bucky had been in danger because of my actions, Michael Budkie could have picked up a phone and called me like he did to swoop in and get publicity when I won my first lawsuit. He could have sent me an email like he did so many times when he wanted me to send NIO activists to his demos in various parts of the country. I would only learn later that at those protests, Michael Budkie would actually tell my friends that I was dangerous and warn them to not associate with me. If he had knowledge that could have saved Bucky and failed to share it with me, then he alone had blood on his hands. He, of course, never mentioned his own failure to get Louis or any number of other animals out of bondage. In fact, while UF released a total of 4 primates over that 7-year period, Michael Budkie turned a blind eye to the 100s of other animals entering the labs and dying horrific deaths. He said nothing about the monkeys that were poisoned, mutilated, and tortured while he remained silent. He gave his tacit approval for murder while simultaneously applauding the vivisectors for releasing a token victim here and there. All the time he assisted them in perpetuating an illusion for the public that welfare laws protect animals from harm.

Michael Budkie had no problem communicating with me when he wanted an introduction to my UF insider. Michael Budkie showed himself to be another pathetic little man. And he could sit at the abusers' feet and beg for crumbs from their table. I wanted to stop them. Now I fully understood what Steve had told me years before about not trusting Budkie because he saw me as his competition. I was naive. I had no understanding of the politics of the movement in which I worked. I only saw animals that needed relief. I never even considered that activists would work against one another.

Who else could possibly jump into this mess? Even Lisa Grossman was grudgingly coming to my defense. She had seen firsthand how Michael Budkie tried to co-opt our campaign when I was first incarcerated. He wanted everything I won in court under his control. Then again, so did she. It was Michael Budkie who came to Gainesville to lecture about brain-mapping experiments happening in UF in 2010. When I went public and it was demonstrated that he was wrong, he disappeared and left me hanging. While there is no shortage of egos in this community, there certainly appears to be a critical shortage of integrity. I couldn't figure out whether the vivisectors or other *activists* were working harder to destroy me. They were all working together.

234

At approximately 1:30 pm on the afternoon of Thursday, April 18, two Sumter County Florida police officers came to my home and informed me that there was a "VOP [violation of probation] Warrant" for my arrest out of Michigan. While I was distracted getting Brutus out of the line of any potential fire and locking him outside on the porch, the officers entered my home without presenting a warrant and, definitely, without an invitation. They proceeded to walk around my home visually inspecting at least three different rooms. They did not cuff me or place me under arrest. After securing Brutus and making one phone call to inform someone that I was being arrested, I went outside as I did not appreciate their intrusive presence in my home.

Outside in the driveway, I was cuffed in front of my neighbors who had been alarmed by the two police cruisers in my driveway. After being handcuffed, I was informed that I was not under arrest yet, but merely being detained while they waited for confirmation of the alleged warrant. After about 25 minutes, I was informed that Michigan did not want to extradite me and so I was not under arrest after all. They uncuffed me and left. I took a deep breath, went straight to the gym, and then for a relaxing swim.

Neither my Detroit prosecutor, my Detroit lawyer, nor my Florida probation officer were aware of any probation violation or warrant being issued out of Wayne County in Michigan. Without all the facts being available, I was convinced that I was the subject of a continued campaign of police harassment orchestrated by the University of Florida. When all the facts became available, it was quite obvious that I was correct. The following morning, April 19, 2013, I was able to confirm through sources in Detroit that a VOP Warrant was indeed issued on Tuesday, April 15 at the behest of the University of Florida. UFPD Detective Jeff Moran subpoenaed Google for a dormant YouTube account that had not been used in almost a year. YouTube had deleted my NIO account in an ongoing censorship campaign and I didn't even remember this one existed.

But on that page appeared *Defiance is a Virtue,* a video recorded in May of 2012 as a fund-raising instrument. This one single video had repeatedly been deleted by Facebook, YouTube, and Vimeo. It may well have been one of the most censored videos online ever. I made one or two soundbites and Ron narrated the balance. It identified several vivisectors and their crimes against animals and was put together by a professional filmmaker. The 6-minute, 40-second video began with me speaking:

> *"The enemy expects us to cower in fear in their presence so we must go forward defiantly. Imagine a movement of activists that had zero fear and were mentally prepared to fight this war on our terms. They might be able to eliminate one or two of us, but they could never stop us all. Defiance is a virtue. Fearlessness is power"*

Then Ron eloquently discussed vivisectors, their atrocities and the innocent animals that had succumbed. He spoke of my victories and articulated the threat I posed to their continuing animal torture industry. As he spoke, images of the vivisectors, their homes, their addresses, their contact information, and their victims played. I had not even owned a copy of it nor had I even seen it since the FDLE seized my computers 11 months earlier. I was surprised when Moran found it, but also glad that video had survived the censorship campaign. I downloaded it to my hard drive and deleted it from YouTube.

The media's the most powerful entity on earth. They have the power to make the innocent guilty and to make the guilty innocent, and that's power. Because they control the minds of the masses.
-Malcolm X

Wire Fraud

I resolved to save some money and fly back out to Detroit to deal with the VOP on my terms. Meanwhile, Special Agent Jeffrey Vash contacted me and told me they had finished their investigation and were ready to return the evidence they had seized (i.e., my computers and electronics). I didn't want cops at my house again so I arranged to go pick up my things on May 22 at the Sheriff's Office in Gainesville. Mike drove me to help me carry everything.

Jeffrey Vash is nothing if not arrogant and smug. And that day was no different. He said that my public statement on NIO was correct: they had found nothing of evidentiary value to use against me. He reminded me, however, that I had instructions on how to make bombs on my drive as if to intimidate me. I wanted to get my things and leave. I had nothing much to say to him.

237

Then he told me "you need to wait." I looked at Mike and said "he's arresting me" and told him who needed to be called. Vash laughed. He shrugged his shoulders and smugly said "I'm going home tonight," the implication being that I wasn't and we both knew it. Then the phone suddenly rang. As if choreographed, he stood up, took out his cuffs, and told me to put my hands behind my back. I was under arrest for being an out-of-state fugitive because of the VOP. While I was cuffed, I asked Mike to slip $100 into my pocket so I would have money for phones and commissary. Vash told him to take it back, that "they won't let her keep it." Mike began to take it back and I snapped, "Why are you listening to him? This is the enemy." Mike put the money back in my pocket and went home without me.

I was booked back into jail in Florida to await extradition to Michigan once again. This was really starting to get old. And just when I thought there could be nothing worse than another extradition ahead of me, I began getting reports from my friends the next day about the articles in the newspapers. The Gainesville Sun was reporting that I was arrested for WIRE FRAUD.![51] WTF!

Naturally, Steve's groupies were all over the article claiming vindication. And Elizabeth and Ron and several other friends were trying to defend me once again. Apparently, there is no charge in Florida comparable to the ridiculous Posting a Message felony out of Michigan. When they had to assign to me a criminal offense for which I would be under supervision in Florida, the closest thing they could find was wire fraud. When Michigan issued a warrant for a VOP for a video that remained online, in order for them to execute it, they recorded that I had committed wire fraud. I guess it would have made less sense from their perspective to record that they were arresting me because Jeff Moran found a YouTube video from a year ago online.

How do you even begin to undo the personal damage? How would I ever recover from all of the relentless attacks from every imaginable direction? And now I had the van to look

51 Jeff Schweers, "Animal activist back in custody," The Gainesville Sun (May 23, 2013) http://www.gainesville.com/news/20130523/animal-activist-is-back-in-custody

forward to on top of everything. To say I sat in jail distraught this time is an understatement. But I never shed a single tear. One of the undercover videos PETA had recently released was so heartbreaking that I could only watch a few seconds of it. I forced myself to read the article about what I was looking at. In the video, there was a little monkey strapped down on a steel table. He was shaking, bleeding, and dying. But he didn't die. The military was subjecting this poor little soul to chemical warfare experiments. These ghoulish excuses for humans were just standing around taking notes and examining the damage they had inflicted on this helpless baby. And just when he would finally begin to recover a little bit after three or four weeks, they would attack him again and again. His heart finally gave out and he died. I would never begin to compare the attacks on me to what these mercenary monsters did to this innocent victim, but there was a distinct parallel. I was now being allowed no time to recover whether it was the vivisectors, Steve Best, Michael Budkie, Jeff Moran, the media, or any number of cyberbullies converging on me. People began telling me that if I didn't stop fighting that I was going to be found dead in my bed one day. Hadn't Fred Hampton been executed while he slept?

Many people say it is insane to resist the system but, actually, it is insane not to. -Mumia Abu-Jamal

Extradition No. Two

When I was arrested this time on May 22, I remained in jail for 12 days before enduring my second extradition. But to my utter joy, this time I was transported in a bus. I was able to stand periodically and I actually liked Chris, the sergeant in charge on this trip. I was the only woman on a bus with about 30 men and it afforded me a little bit of leeway. Chris didn't bind my hands together; rather the cuffs hung from my left wrist. I had my own two-person cage to myself and, after dreading being stuffed into that mobile tomb again, I was almost elated to be in my own big cage. I could move, stand, and look out the window. Instead of living on French fries from McDonald's like on my first extradition, Chris got me my own loaf of Wonder Bread and jars of peanut butter and jelly so I didn't have to deal with the fast-food stops three times a day.

There were no stops at filthy jailhouse bathrooms with shotguns trained on us. The restrooms were on the bus and were cleaned daily. Chris was funny. We talked and laughed a lot. And I joked with the prisoners who were sitting behind my cage. They laughed and said "no one is going to put you in prison in Detroit for a video!" "Detroit has real crime. They don't care." Yet here

I was being extradited again. I just smiled. I didn't even try to explain anymore. Who could possibly understand what they were doing to me? Compared to all my anxiety about being sealed up alive again in a van, it felt like I was on a party bus this time.

I had a lot of time to think about welfare issues. I am grateful for the privilege of having been allowed a glimpse of what it might be like to look out through the eyes of the entombed animal, but it was extremely difficult for me to negotiate. I defy anyone to argue that a bigger cage and the ability to extend one's limbs are inconsequential to the imprisoned animal. I react in utter revulsion at the theorists who denigrate welfare issues from an academic pedestal. In my eyes, they have no right. I sincerely hope that where welfare reforms are initiated along the way, that they afford the nonhuman slaves a greater ability to tolerate their confinement.

But in reality, all welfare reform does is allow people to participate in a holocaust and simultaneously feel good about themselves. Paradoxically, welfare legislation ensures that greater numbers of animals will die. And, mostly, they cannot be enforced. We can't even film inside factory farms or labs without being prosecuted. Every single time one of us does penetrate the perimeter, we find the most unspeakable atrocities are commonplace, with or without governing welfare regulations.

The reality of which we can never lose sight is that we either war against a holocaust or moderate our approach and become complicit in it. Welfare reforms are not enacted for the benefit of the animals. They are written and passed by abusers to legalize torture. Nonetheless, I can never again be objective about this issue. I can only envision myself in my cage and hope that my actions on behalf of the entombed animal are consistent with the actions I would want others to take for me.

A revolutionary career does not lead to banquets and honorary titles, interesting research and professorial wages. It leads to misery, disgrace, ingratitude, prison and a voyage into the unknown, illuminated by only an almost superhuman belief.
-Max Horkheimer

Banned from the Internet

When I was taken from Wayne County Jail to appear at my probation violation hearing, the lengths to which they were prepared to go to silence me became crystal clear. When Matt entered the booth adjacent to my underground mausoleum-like cell to consult before I was brought into court, he was relieved that my probation officer was going to recommend that the judge let me go home with a warning. She had never wanted to violate me but it was out of her hands. On the other side of the court would be the prosecutor who was going to move to put me in prison for five years unless I agreed to take Negotiation Is Over offline and plead guilty to a technical violation for the video that remained online.

I was considering going to prison but was told, "If you go away for five years NIO is going to come down anyway." I would have my honor, and the animals would lose everything. Further, there was something I shared only with a handful of trusted colleagues. When I first got out of jail in March and met my probation officer, she told me that as long as all of my fees were paid, she was going to move to discharge me from probation on December 5, 2013 – two years early. If I could just hold on a few more months, it would be all over and I'd be out of the system. I would take the technical violation and take NIO down for now.

In the courtroom, I stood next to Matt while the judge lectured and admonished me for a solid hour. When the bailiffs brought me back to my cell, we were all exhausted. They told me they had never seen her jump on any prisoner in a similar manner. She basically went on ad nauseam about me terrorizing researchers and that if she heard my name again I was going straight to prison for at least five years. As if she were acting as some benevolent beacon of justice, a good 20 or 30 minutes must have been dedicated to telling me how she was saving me from being repeatedly raped and beaten if she sent me to Huron Valley. All I could think was that I have no fear of criminals and I had a lot of friends in the prison by this time. No inmate could ever rape or beat me in the manner the state had for almost two years now. Torture, rape, murder, and violence are the domain of the oppressors. I had to restrain myself, be silent, and wait for the judicial windbag to run out of air. After I pleaded guilty to a technical probation violation and agreed to take NIO offline, with one final baseball bat to the knees, she said "and you're off the internet. I don't even want you looking at a computer!" And there it was. The real reason for my entire experience thus far as a political prisoner:

Silence!

I was floored but betrayed no emotion. Aside from my work being blotted out, I had just personally been sentenced to do the balance of my probation effectively in exile from my community.

Banned from the Internet

My entire support system was online. One would never describe Wildwood, Florida as a haven of social consciousness. And I was just sentenced to solitary confinement in this ideological wilderness. My mind racing now, maybe I could become a fixture in Gainesville and simply talk face-to-face to one person at a time like was done in the days before computers. Maybe I could associate with other vegans once in a while at their potlucks. It was going to be a long few months.

I was allowed 10 days to delete myself from the internet and then sign off for the remainder of my probation. I so wanted to put up a final statement telling the world exactly what they were doing but I would never have made it out of Michigan. They would arrest me at the airport if not sooner. When I silently went online hours after my court appearance, imagine my surprise when Alafair was online celebrating my internet ban. Were they actually in direct contact with the vivisectors? How the fuck did they know what happened in the courtroom? The only people at my hearing were Matt, me, O'Leary, the prosecutors, and the judge. Someone in that chain apparently had a direct line to Dr. Steven Best, PhD. And it wasn't Matt or me.

I flew back to Florida and met with my second probation officer who would supervise me at home. Just when it couldn't get any worse, it did. Ms. Bradshaw advised me that the University of Florida had my supervision appended to dispense with my voice entirely. I could not speak about the University of Florida. I could participate in no activism whatsoever. If I had handed out *Go Vegan* fliers in front of a supermarket, I'd be sent to prison. It was now going to be an excruciatingly-long few months. I couldn't speak, I couldn't write, I couldn't work, I couldn't socialize.

Supervision included having my probation officer show up at my home unannounced at any hour of the day or night, looking in draws or under mattresses to find some device with an internet connection; no warrant is necessary while one is on probation. While most people would be concerned about hiding drugs or guns, I would make sure that I had a quick place to slip a laptop if I had been using one. Even if I had only been writing up a manuscript and was not connected to the internet, I would have been found in violation. The times when she would show up eventually became perfunctory. She was afraid of my dogs so she only walked through my home once.

To keep me busy, I had to report to her office once a month and take random drug tests. I was court-ordered to go to drug counseling as a result of the insidious online smear campaign in which I was relentlessly cast as a heroin addict and prostitute. Actually, when the Freddy Kruger letter was written, the author most definitely was on drugs. So what if I wasn't the author?! My counselor saw me three times before she officially signed off that I had no substance abuse or mental health issues.

It is impossible to function in today's world – from checking one's bank balance online, to watching Netflix, to streaming music when one exercises, to shopping, to socializing – without accessing the internet. And, given the intense scrutiny to which I was subjected, I had no doubt they had subpoenaed my cable/internet provider, Bright House, and were monitoring me. If I had heard someone make that statement two years earlier, I'd have thought they were suffering from paranoia. First things first. We took my name off of all of our accounts and put them under Mike's. Since I never saw a need for a woman to relinquish her name when she marries, he and I have different last names. Despite this precaution, when I was online it was rarely from my home.

I would generally log in from a remote location. And only among those I trusted implicitly, I began using a Facebook profile called *Robert Osbourne* to connect and funnel information to be published. When I needed to be on for an extended period of time, I would have someone book me into a local hotel overnight under their name. My work for the animals was never going to stop simply because they had taken my name from me.

Lisa Grossman and I started to talk again during this period. I couldn't get any more public records out of UF. If I had tried, they would have sent me to prison. NIO was offline, so I had no platform to disseminate the information anyway. I began using the name *Eleventh Hour for Animals* instead of NIO and Karen Kline became the front person to get our information out. Although she was in Michigan, she was able to run the universityofflorida.us website which we now also called Eleventh Hour for Animals. It took me a lot of convincing for Karen to patch things up with Lisa. Karen also knew firsthand how abusive and confrontational she was and simply didn't trust her. Adopting the rule that had guided me for the past several years, Karen put her personal concerns aside and brought Lisa back into the fold to amplify the animals' voices while I was muzzled.

Karen put her name on our new public records requests from UF. In the fall, she requested records for some monkeys, dogs, and horses, all of whom had been classified as Column E animals during the USDA's last lab inspection. Column E is an innocuous label that means these victims are enduring surgeries and various mutilations with absolutely no pain relief. They are either being subjected to deliberate pain experiments or simply having their pain medication withheld. My stomach literally turned when I logged onto the USDA's site and saw the numbers; hundreds of dogs, horses, guinea pigs and other animals being used for nothing except to explicitly cause them pain. I had started using Tor in addition to non-corporate proxy servers to mask my IP no matter where I was when I logged in. Everything I owned was now encrypted should it ever be seized again. Everything I did was as anonymous as possible.

For months, I would talk to Anne O'Berry and David Tenenbaum and all I could say is "they took my name." My friends saw the assault on my civil liberties up close and personal. Anne and David struggled with how we could challenge these unconstitutional sanctions, but when one is on probation they essentially cease enjoying those alleged protections. Anne was able to have wire fraud removed from my Florida probation records. The only other charge that even remotely resembled why I was in custody was misdemeanor stalking. I had a choice: would I rather be known as a con artist or a stalker? I chose the latter which now stands as a technical notation on my files.

Jeff Schweers, the Gainesville Sun reporter who wrote the wire fraud story, refused to retract the article or issue an apology. He refused to even add a notation that the information was incorrect. The position of this media outlet which functions as a propaganda arm for the University of Florida was that when the story was written, Schweers accurately reported on what the Florida Department of Law Enforcement's records reflected. Journalistic integrity, indeed! So what if they were wrong? So what if there will always be an article in circulation saying I was arrested for wire fraud? There's no room for truth or fairness when you're part of the industrial animal torture industry.

And just like they had done back in 2010, UF was now refusing to honor Karen Kline's legally-cited open records requests. They must have been thinking that it had just taken them 3 years to successfully neutralize me and they weren't happy about the campaign continuing anyway. I put Karen in touch with Marcy LaHart who officially filed suit on December 26, 2013. While we were waiting for the case to be docketed for a hearing date, they conceded out of court and turned over the records. We had won our third successful legal action against UF.

With all the free time I had on my hands, I learned how to write up welfare complaints and had no further use for Michael Budkie. I prepared the complaint for Louis which I would file in my name after the new year when I was free from probation. In the meantime, I wrote up a few more which repeatedly cited UF for negligence and fraud. Karen and Lisa would take turns filing these. Because we all pulled together for the animals, we were finally able to get the monkeys back in the papers.[52] The local motel came in very handy and every time the USDA would do the perfunctory lab inspection that the law requires when a federal complaint is filed, we'd file another one.

We started 2014 with a victory for the animals. That was sweet.

---

52 Shayna Posses, "Gainesville activists fight for monkeys' rights," The Independent Alligator (January 9, 2014) http://www.alligator.org/news/article_c13ffdfa-79b1-11e3-8eb3-001a4bcf887a.html

*It's better to have the courage of
conviction and silent resolve than
the nonexistent wherewithal of
cowards and flakes. -Walter Bond*

I'm Baaack!

I had paid all of my probation fees and, as agreed, on December 5, 2013, my Detroit PO submitted papers to the court to release me from supervision. On January 17, 2014, Judge Vonda Evans signed the documents officially terminating my probation. It was over. The UF campaign may have been diverted but not derailed. We had a strong unit of activists in place, all of us committed to Animal Liberation.

A few days later, I found a letter from the Michigan Department of Corrections in my mailbox. The first call I made was to David Tenenbaum. His phone almost always goes to voicemail so I was surprised when he actually answered. I tore open the letter while he was on the phone and the relief was palpable, not only on my end but on his too. It was really over. I was free. Then I called Anne O'Berry. We were all so excited. They were genuinely happy for me. Throughout my ordeal, Anne and David had become the two people to whom I turned most. Even though they're both attorneys, there was little they could do other than offer moral support as they watched the system crush me. Then

I called Matt. Even though I had the piece of paper in my hand, I almost needed permission from everyone on whom I had been leaning before I went to retrieve my computer from the house in which it had been hidden. Then I tore off my invisible restraints with a vengeance.

NIO went back online. I went back online. I logged onto Facebook and declared "I'm Baaacck!" There were two songs that I listened to repeatedly that helped get me through my probation. One was *Lift Me Up* by Five Finger Death Punch:

> *"I won't be broken*
> *I won't be tortured*
> *I won't be beaten down*
> *I have the answers*
> *I'll take the pressure*
> *I'll turn it all around"*

The other was *You're Going Down* by the Sick Puppies. And to all the "vivisectors, cowards, and traitors" on both sides of the fence who had converged upon me while the animals died, I posted a picture of a handing flipping everyone the bird with the words "fuck you" followed by a verse from the latter song:

> *"Define your meaning of fun*
> *To me it's when we're getting it done*
> *I feel the heat comin' off of the blacktop*
> *So get ready for another one*
> *Let's take a trip down memory lane*
> *The words circling in my brain*
> *You can treat this like another all the same*
> *But don't cry like a bitch when you feel the pain*
> *It's been a long time coming*
> *And the table's turned around*
> *'Cause one of us is going*
> *One of us is going down*
> *I'm not running,*
> *It's a little different now*
> *'Cause one of us is going down"*

249

I'm Baaack!

My energy was back. I was back. And the love and support from around the world was intoxicating. Hundreds of shares. Thousands of people welcoming me back and re-friending me. Where this new profile only had about 500 activists on it when I had been shut down, that night I nearly returned to my old numbers. I had almost 4000 friends and supporters back. The next morning, I called Lisa anxious to get a bonafide multi-faceted campaign back off the ground. I could tell by her voice that she was upset about something. I had forgotten about holding my breath when her emails used to come in. I never knew what I said or did that would set her off. And now that I was free for less than 24 hours, I was already tensing waiting for it. Whatever *it* was.

Lisa was beyond angry; she was seething. She was livid that I had enjoyed being welcomed back the night before. "You had thousands of people celebrating YOU! What about the animals? You could have used that publicity to fight for them. But no. It's all about YOU, YOU, YOU! You're so selfish!" When I had gone to sleep the previous night, I felt very guilty about being free while the animals were still in cages. I had cried myself to sleep. I shared that with no one. I know that guilt is an unproductive emotion so I put it aside. I had to be whole to fight effectively. Lisa couldn't control herself, bashing me over and over again. Even though her outburst was born of the same old jealousy, she had hit a very open wound. After everything I had just endured, I could now easily identify the few toxic people who remained around me. I wanted to protect and distance myself. Yet I knew I had to get the monkey campaign back on track. There were dogs and horses for whom I could now effectively speak as well. But that old sick feeling was creeping back.

My community was back. I had my name back. And the vivisectors were back too. In early February, I was served with a lawsuit filed by Worldwide Primates in South Florida against me and 33 other activists associated with Smash HLS. Worldwide Primates imprisons nonhuman primates, some are kidnapped as far away as Mauritius, and some are bred in captivity. All are used for cruel experiments, sold into laboratories, or their body fluids, blood, and tissues extracted from their bodies while they are alive to be sold for profit. The president, Matthew Block, is a convicted felon who spent 13 months in federal prison for the infamous *Bangkok Six* case. A shipment marked "live birds" was seized at a Thailand airport in the 90's. Inside were six orangutans that he was trying to illegally ship from Indonesia to Russia. The apes were packed into a crate with no food, water, or air. Their cries alerted airport workers. Only two of the orangutans would survive.

In addition to paying $30,000 in fines, Block became an informant and began helping the feds seize other illegal animals while he resumed his own slave trade. Law enforcement turned a blind eye to their confidential informant's sadism and, rather than prosecuting him, they now acted to protect him from conscience-driven protesters. This convicted felon, Matthew Block, was now orchestrating a malicious prosecution aimed at silencing all of us, even though my association with Smash HLS had been tangential at best. Just the same old tactics of running to the state to secure free speech injunctions against activists. It's a very disturbing strain of fascism that is increasingly being woven into the fabric of our culture.

I copied Anne and David on the paperwork and had also introduced Anne to my colleagues in South Florida. She was able to introduce a law firm into the equation, Hunton & Williams, that had some history. In addition to having defended another activist in the past that had been maliciously prosecuted by Matthew Block, they also specialized in Constitutional law. The firm took our case pro bono. Over the next year all of the charges would ultimately be discharged. One of the objectives of such frivolous actions by industrial abusers is to tie up activists in court for extended periods of time, damage their work for the animals, and break them financially. Whether or not their actions are successful is secondary.

South Florida is rapidly becoming ground zero for the primate trade industry, a literal modern-day slave trade; a global monster with tentacles stretching around the world. Gary Yourofsky is credited with converting as much as 10% of the entire Israeli population to veganism. In Israel, they actually have a link to his website, adaptt.org, on their vegan foods. When Israeli anti-vivisection activists were looking to network with their counterparts in Florida, they wrote Gary. Fortunately, he put them in touch with me. *The Monkey Struggle in Israel* had been campaigning for over a decade to shut down Mazor Farms, a notorious monkey-breeding facility in their country. As of January 1, 2015, Mazor would no longer be allowed under Israeli law to export monkeys out of the country into vivisection labs. At the same time, a third mysterious breeding facility popped up in South Florida. The big animal welfare organizations were signing petitions and holding town meetings. Jane Velez-Mitchell took up the cause and started to investigate the new facility.

Natalie Beach in Israel and I, both outsiders with many critics, would undertake connecting the dots between Mazor and the new facility in Hendry County. And we identified the men at the top of the global organization. Natalie and I were kindred spirits from the first time we spoke. I have met few people in this movement who are as genuine and dedicated as she; we connected as women and as activists immediately. We understood that those who abuse animals only have one agenda: profit. And they worked together around the world to achieve their objective. We shared a vision that activists also needed to come together globally and learn to work as a cohesive unit. We were also acutely aware of those in the movement who were driven by egos and actually sabotaged our efforts.

I know what it takes to remain committed to the struggle despite personal attacks and at great personal cost. These people on another continent shared my dedication. Mazor Farms had been breeding monkeys for decades and shipping them in containers that are stuffed in the cargo area of jets. Air France/KLM is one of the last airlines that participates in the global slave trade. The Monkey Struggle was relentless in their efforts. They identified the individuals who owned the farm, they protested regularly, and they penetrated the perimeters of Mazor on several occasions, gaining footage of their operation. Their objective was simple: shut down Mazor and get the monkeys to a sanctuary.

Finally, they could see the end in sight. Until the ban would go into effect on January 1, the only monkeys that could legally be exported into the states would have to go into vivisection labs for *medical research*. The Monkey Struggle uncovered documents that proved Mazor Farms was, indeed, shipping monkeys out of the country before the ban went into effect, but they were illegally sending them to holding facilities here. Between the secret monkey facilities being built in South Florida and the secret illegal shipments from Israel, it appeared that Mazor Farms was relocating its base of operations to Hendry County. The Monkey Struggle and NIO co-authored several articles and actions aimed at (1) stopping the illegal exports out of Israel and (2) drawing attention to exactly how the global trade operates. The Israeli activists successfully uncovered and stopped at least three shipments destined for the United States where the primates would have met certain horror. And with South Florida vivisection breeders now enjoying worldwide scrutiny and community outrage, we looked forward to continuing to connect the dots. In late 2014, a businessman named Ady Gil stepped in and purchased the remaining monkeys from Mazor to ensure they would live out their lives in peace in a sanctuary. At least that segment of the industry had been shut down. Now we looked toward focusing on the growing slavery hub in Florida.

After enduring blow after blow after blow for the past several years, after having endured some serious personal betrayals and devastation, I was reveling in being home. I was free. And the love I felt being welcomed back overwhelmed me. But every time I saw a police cruiser outside, I would tense up. I was clearly experiencing some kind of PTSD. And then I would get online and the safety and support of my community gave me strength. I needed to focus and get the University of Florida back into the media. I was equipped not only with the documentation of how the animals suffered inside their labs, but also with my personal story which demonstrated the lengths to which they would go to keep their insidious experiments secret. I began writing several articles such as *Criminalizing Dissent at the University of Florida*[53] to get my message to communities outside of animal advocates.

I finally was able to file the next records request in my own name and was pleasantly surprised to learn that there were 13 monkeys left in UF's labs, all of whom were scheduled to finish their currently-funded experiments in 2016. The last protocol would be completed in October of that year at which point, they would all be released to a sanctuary or re-assigned to new experiments. No new primates had been acquired. Everything I had endured was suddenly well worth the cost to me. The primate experimentation program had become too much of a liability for the university. For the first time since I began, I was unclear about my next step.

I wanted nothing more than to stop my campaign and allow the UF to quietly phase out this piece of their animal experimentation industry. I sought advice from the one veteran whose opinion I still valued. I was advised that if I took the pressure off now, they would simply resume their operation and the monkeys would continue to die. "These are vivisectors. You can't trust them." I ultimately agreed. I was free now and focused. We'd come this far and I wasn't going to retreat until I won that real victory for the animals. I wouldn't stop until the cages were opened, the lab was shut, and the monkeys were placed in a sanctuary. I went back into high gear.

I filed the federal complaint for negligence for Louis who lived with a broken hip in a cage inside the University of Florida for a full year. They gave him no pain relief whatsoever, refused to release him to a sanctuary, and they incinerated him one year to the day after their own veterinarian documented his injury. Louis lived in agony. I wanted his death to have some meaning. I filed a flurry of federal complaints for negligence and incompetence. In one instance, a monkey escaped. He ran in futility to find safety and relief. No one even knew he was gone. Someone accidentally found him in a stairway the next day where he had been trapped with no food and water. Other complaints were technical in

53 Camille Marino, "Criminalizing Dissent at the University of Florida," Dissident Voice (April 2, 2014) http://dissidentvoice.org/2014/04/criminalizing-dissent-at-the-university-of-florida/

nature. The University of Florida receives nearly half a billion dollars every year in taxpayer money to perform cruel and unnecessary experiments on animals. The instruments that guide these experiments are called protocols and they outline exactly what parameters must be met under the terms of the federal grants. In many cases, images, footage, or digital recordings were demanded in the protocols. UF refused to disclose these damning documents. We filed federal complaints alleging that the minimal requirements of the grants were not being met since they apparently did not exist. If they did exist and UF was simply withholding them, they would have been breaking the law.

Then we began to go public with the fact that the Michael J. Fox foundation was funding experiments on monkeys inside the university. I was extremely uncomfortable allowing Lisa to discuss science in our releases, but I was constantly trying to appease her. I had no inclination to argue over minutia. The night before we were to go public, I was up into the early morning hours preparing our articles and press releases.

One press release would address the Michael J. Fox Foundation, another was tailored for UF's alumni, and a press release needed to go out to the media. I allowed Lisa to exhaust herself making changes all night until she fell asleep. Then I finished preparing everything that needed to be done. The next morning the articles were published. I sent off another complaint to the USDA alleging negligence in the handling of the Michael J. Fox monkeys, I sent out the cyber action to the alumni, but I hit an email glitch when I was sending out the press releases. They kept bouncing back. Lisa was waiting for her copy. She emailed me. I told her to give me five minutes to take a break and blow my hair.

Her response was swift and decisive. My phone rang. "Blow your hair? Here we go again. You need to be on meds. I can't take your mood swings anymore. It's always about YOU, YOU, YOU! I'm done. Don't write to me again!" I was actually relieved. I would handle all the media by myself. I was just a little annoyed with myself. In one article that came out, *UF and Michael J. Fox's*

Foundation are torturing monkeys, activists say,[54] they quoted me as saying researchers were trying to determine whether "a drug called doxycycline will penetrate the blood/brain barrier in primates." I let her strong arm me into including that language and it would be a day or two before a movement physician would explain to me what that even meant. I couldn't care less about such irrelevant details. If vivisectors were experimenting on mentally-challenged humans, no one would be debating the scientific efficacy of their sadism. In fact, it's well established that these *researchers* would routinely conduct human experiments inside of prisons, asylums, and other institutions. The public never debated the efficacy of these atrocities in shutting them down. I will never give any deference to their research either as long as it is rests on the blood and torment of sentient beings.

I considered the rest of the article a victory. It didn't matter how much they tore my character apart. Without my kind of notoriety, one cannot get blurbs like this published in mainstream media:

> *"Against this back drop of admitted junk science, for which they cannot get funding elsewhere, and which has absolutely no therapeutic application for humans whatsoever, the Michael J. Fox Foundation wrote UF a blank check to go find and torture six innocent macaques. According to the plan, they would be turned into drug addicts by repeatedly being given ever-increasing doses of ketamine and other tranquilizing agents, they would be poisoned with doxycycline, they would have a sterotactic ring affixed to their little skulls, a virus cocktail would be injected into their brains, they would live with brain damage, injuries, and in torment, and, eventually, all six would be murdered before their eighth birthdays."*

Karen and I published pictures and information about the horses that were being abused for profit inside UF on our websites, NIO

54 Kyle Swenson, "UF and Michael J. Fox's Foundation Are Torturing Monkeys, Activist Says," Broward New Times (February 20, 2014) http://www.browardpalmbeach.com/news/uf-and-michael-j-foxs-foundation-are-torturing-monkeys-activist-says-6353444

and Eleventh Hour. The images of the horses suspended in midair and having their bones intentionally broken inside their labs elicited nothing short of outrage. We began to focus on horses and dogs to bring in new activists, those who would be sympathetic to one domesticated species or another but who could then be gently brought into an overall anti-vivisection agenda. And it worked. We had people signing on by the dozens, several from inside UF who had no idea what was happening there. Then we went public about them withholding records, this time the digital images of the horse experiments which were demanded by their own protocols, but which the university now said did not exist. Federal complaint aside, was I going to have to sue again?

With this renewed excitement and energy surrounding our campaign, I was able to recruit new activists in Gainesville. Lisa decided she wanted to compete with me out in the open rather than privately and would lead her own group for the monkeys where she lived in Jacksonville even though there were no monkeys or even any tertiary targets in Jacksonville. As long as she occupied herself and didn't interfere with my efforts, I thought her tantrum laughable.

After I went back online in late January, I began answering emails that sat in my inbox for months while I was offline. One was from Dr. Barry Friedman, a professor of political science at the University of North Georgia (UNG). He had known of the state's attacks on me through a mutual associate and had become one of my biggest supporters. In time he would also become a trusted friend. But at this time, while I no longer needed his advocacy on my behalf, I desperately needed his advocacy on behalf of the monkeys. Dr. Friedan became an outspoken opponent of vivisection and would boldly host our information about the monkey experiments at UF on his own page at UNG. He also initiated a letter-writing campaign designed to petition Congress to stop funding the atrocities at UF.

I was contacted by Susan Schindler on Facebook. Su was the producer of her son's radio show. Kevin ("Storm") Schindler was 13 and the youngest radio host in New Jersey. They were both vegan and we immediately clicked. They allowed me to speak on the *Kevin Storm Show* to discuss my odyssey over the past 2 years and, mostly, to get our information out about UF's animal torture industry. I began to organize protests. The few people who actually left their computers to come out and give a voice to the animals were the handful of people that had been there with me from the beginning. I also had a few new recruits as well that had been brought in from the social media onslaught.

And then it began.

Fake profiles were set up to stalk me. They called themselves *Tyler Newman* and *Susan Oleson*. I didn't want to believe that these were Steve's people. I already knew that he defended vivisectors in court; but I didn't want to believe that he would actually now work to promote their agenda against the animals. Without having the resources to subpoena Facebook or hire a detective I cannot prove what I know to be true. All I can say is that the only real profiles who commented on public posts on the fake profiles, and vice versa, were Alafair and other people who had jumped on the Steve Best and/or Michael Budkie bandwagon over the past two years. If these profiles and the next round of attacks were initiated by vivisectors I could have digested it more easily. But this was the work of traitors. Of collaborators. And there is no redemption for what they did next.

In order to dismantle all of my efforts and isolate me once and for all, Tyler Newman and Susan Oleson, each profile individually, began sending this private message to every single person with whom I associated on Facebook:

"Tyler Newman (04/03/2014 14:53)

Dear _____

It has come our attention that you are planning on attending a protest against the University of Florida (UF) sponsored by Camille Marino/Lisa Grossman. While we are certain that Lisa has the animals' best interests at heart, the same cannot be said for Ms.

Marino. Some of the relevant facts about Ms. Marino, which may help you to rethink your decision to support her, are provided below:

Ms. Marino's so-called "activism" goes beyond challenging the law, or even civil disobedience. As a case in point, the murdering of individuals or the abduction of children is NOT something condoned by even the Animal Liberation Front (ALF). In contrast, Ms. Marino has stated that: "If abusers are dead, they cease being abusers. I fully support justifiable homicide in the war for animal liberation." She even went so far as to write a story that promoted -- in the name of animal liberation – kidnapping a child! http://www. negotiationisover.net/2013/02/14/the-animal-warfare-act/

These threats showed that, amongst other things, Camille Marino is blatantly opposed to both ALF guidelines and any viable tactic that would not discredit the noble ethics of the entire movement. Her absolute disregard for innocent children is alarming to genuine animal activists, damaging to the movement, and is more the mark of a destructive sociopath than a credible animal activist. Additional evidence of her promotion of unethical and illegal actions can be found here:

http://www.splcenter.org/blog/2011/11/03/animal-rights-activist-if-you-spill-blood-your-blood-*should-be-spilled/*

http://gawker.com/5976473/arson-cracked-testicles-and-internet-death-threats-how-animal-rights-extremists-are-learning-from-the-people-who-murdered-george-tiller

http://www.splcenter.org/get-informed/intelligence-report/browse-all-issues/2012/spring/negotiation-is-over)

Camille Marino has a criminal record of stalking and threatening behavior. She has been the subject of Personal Protection Orders (PPO) in CA, FL and MI. She has acknowledged being diagnosed with mental illness on social media, where she continues to engage in vicious attacks on serious and dedicated animal rights activists in the US and abroad. Her involvement with the animal rights movement is highly questionable and has been shown to be little more than an outlet to purge her hateful and aggressive impulses; a vehicle for promoting her skewed agenda; and an opportune means of soliciting money -- not to benefit animals, but for her own self-serving purposes. 3) Many violations of legal requirements in laboratories have been vociferously and successfully challenged by organizations such as the Physicians Committee for Responsible Medicine (PCRM) and Stop Animal Experimentation Now (SAEN). However, Camille Marino effectively sabotaged these initiatives. Through her direct intimidation, threats and lawsuits, she single-handedly undid years of excellent work by those credible organizations, which focused on securing the release of laboratory animals -- including dogs from labs at Wayne State University (Detroit, MI), and primates from labs at the University of Florida (Gainesville, FL).

In fact, prior to the "activism" of Camille Marino, Negotiation is Over, and now Eleventh Hour for Animals, marmosets, squirrel monkeys, and cebus monkeys from the University of Florida were routinely allowed to retire to Jungle Friends Primate Sanctuary (http://www.junglefriends.org/). The retirement of these primates to Jungle Friends dates back to 2005, long before Camille Marino even knew primate research was being conducted at UF:

http://www.junglefriends.org/junglefriends/Lab_Capu-chin_Arrival_April_2005.pdf

http://www.junglefriends.org/monk_angel.shtml

http://www.junglefriends.org/monk_arnold.shtml

Not surprisingly, discussions between UF and Jungle Friends Primate Sanctuary broke down as a direct result of interference by Ms. Marino. Sadly, the transfer of primates from UF to Jungle Friends was halted, -- perhaps irrevocably. It is of interest to note that Jungle Friends

*has banned Camille Marino from ever setting foot on
their property.*

*In addition, Ms. Marino's interference has ensured that
legitimate animal advocacy organizations have had to
abandon their long-standing campaigns, and that the animal rights movement is being held up to public scorn and
ridicule.*

http://www.courthousenews.com/2012/11/27/52559.htm

*As animal advocates, we are asking that you reconsider
your decision to give this disturbed and fraudulent
woman any platform or credibility whatsoever. Camille
Marino does not represent the best of the movement,
but rather the worst -- she is one of a tiny minority of
fringe lunatics that actually damage the movement. In
closing, we regret that we cannot personally sign this
letter; please accept that this decision is based solely on
a justifiable fear of reprisal, and a potential compromise
of our ongoing legitimate projects. Thank you for your
time and understanding.*

Yours truly,

Very Concerned Animal Activists"

And yet these "very concerned animal activists" didn't feel
strongly enough to use their real names. Since Steve Best is the
only person who has ever gone on record, incorrectly testifying
that restraining orders had been issued against me in Florida
and that misinformation is again included here, it seemed clear
who directed this latest assault. Because some of the information
included came straight from Budkie, I concluded that the effort
to discredit and silence me -- to eradicate my presence in the
movement -- had returned with a new ferocity; *activists* were
using everything the state had compiled to further the abusers'
own agenda. Reading that letter now still gives me chills, not
for the attacks on me but, rather, for the sheer ease with which
anonymous people can betray the animals – act as collaborators.

My more sophisticated and veteran colleagues, all of whom have FBI files and have been accused of any number of free speech crimes were speechless. They forwarded to me the communications privately and cut ties completely with the collaborator cliques. But my new recruits ran for cover. They had little to no grounding in the movement, had absolutely no familiarity with the Green Scare, and were terrified of associating with me. The reason industrial abusers frame activists as terrorists is to discredit them and manufacture fear. And now my former colleagues' minions had taken the football passed to them by industrial abusers and were running with it at full speed – to silence me at the expense of the animals for whom I fight.

They wrote to anyone who published one of my articles. The more sophisticated outlets dismissed them. The animal rights venues severed ties with me and refused to publish my work again. They wrote to Dr. Barry Friedman asking him to withdraw his support. He supported my efforts even more. They wrote to Susan Schindler and Kevin Storm telling them not to allow me to speak on the radio. Very much a kindred spirit, Su's response was to give me more air time and use it to promote my appearances.

On April 24, 2014, colleagues at the Institute for Critical Animal Studies (ICAS) came out with their list of the top 5 worst universities for animals in the country. With no particular order assigned, the University of Florida made the list along with the University of California, Davis, the University of California, San Francisco, the University of Wisconsin, Madison and Oregon Health and Science University, Portland. This was a great boost in gaining support, credibility, and wider exposure in our community.

I was shocked when Lisa came out with Alafair publicly with a retort to this list entitled "LIES, LIES, LIES." They were now not only slamming me publicly, but they were actually saying that the University of Florida was not such a bad place for animals. Unbelievable! These people hated me so much that it didn't seem to matter to them how much damage they were doing to the animals. Lisa's toxicity was out of my life forever, but when the hell did she become friendly with my stalkers? Friendly, indeed. They were now publicly consoling one another for ever having worked with me. Again, WTF!?

My old friend-turned-traitor, Chris Lagergren, re-emerged in the fray. Having both been named in the Worldwide Primates suit, it was killing me that he was now enjoying pro bono representation thanks to me and my friendship with Anne. I slipped. I drank a bottle of something and went after him online for everything I was worth. He instigated my lynching. I called him out as a traitor and publicly asked Worldwide Primates why they were trying to sue us when they had a collaborator piece of shit who would be happy to help them destroy other activists. Fortunately, Facebook blocked me for12 hours which prevented me from doing any more damage. When I came to my senses, I realized that this was a road I could not go down again. In the midst of a renewed full-scale onslaught, the one person I would have to take care of and be able to count on was me. That meant I would have to be disciplined and sober.

I only got the Michael J. Fox cyber action off the ground during this period. It was critical that I was able to reach UF's alumni and benefactors with new information as it was published. But the collaborators successfully derailed that effort for the animals as well. I believe it was Alafair who hijacked my alumni actions and wrote to UF's alumni telling them that "Marino is a prostitute, a heroin addict, a petty criminal, and a terrorist." How do you fight this? Without going to the police myself and trying to have charges brought against my stalkers, I had no recourse. I'm the person the police had been trying to silence for three years. Could I really seek protection against collaborators in my own movement who were now helping them?

I'm Baaack!

Mark as ▾   Move Copy This message to ▾

elete Reply ▾ Forward ▾ Redirect View Thread Message Source Save as Print Headers ▾

Date: Sun, 29 Jun 2014 11:41:56 -0400 [08:41:56 AM PDT]

From: Angela Caparella <angela.caparella@gmail.com>

To: Hide Addresses questions@thrg.com, jgoldberg@ufalumni.ufl.edu, vhorton@ufalumni.ufl.edu, ryan.lorenson@gmail.com, communications@tampagatorclub.com, pr@tampagatorclub.com a

ubject: Harassment by Animal Rights Activists

Alternative parts for this section: 🖼

📄 📄 unnamed 1 KB ⬇

This message was written in a character set (UTF-8) other than your own.
If it is not displayed correctly, click here to open it in a new window.

The person responsible for you being harassed by animal rights activists is
Camille Marino. She is a former prostitute and heroin addict, petit thief,
and convicted felon. She may be reached by phone at 352-396-4767, by email
at eleventhhour@riseup.net or by snail mail at ████████████████
Wildwood, FL, 34785.

http://www.splcenter.org/get-informed/intelligence-report/browse-all-issues/.

https://www.youtube.com/watch?v=2TLR4M2yT-4

I knew these attacks were being orchestrated by Steve Best or Michael Budkie, both comfortable in their respective roles as Oz behind the curtain. If that account, angela.caparella@gmail.com, were to ever be subpoenaed, the house of cards would begin to crumble. I am willing to bet that Alafair is the author. But without resources to pursue that avenue, my only response was to begin to clear my name from all the lies the inner circle had been disseminating for 2 years. And I did so, at first, only to let these people know that if they didn't leave me alone it was going to get a lot worse for their leader. Then I became ferocious about getting the truth into the public domain. It was not 2012. I was not facing 10 years in prison and I was not in the middle of a nervous breakdown. I was extremely focused on my work and didn't appreciate the interference. But if they wouldn't relent, then I would go toe to toe with anyone, anywhere, anytime. I acquiesce to no one.

When I first got off probation, the North American Animal Liberation Press Office (NAALPO) agreed to publish my writings in a very sanitized version not discussing Steve Best or the feud at all. I just wanted *Danger to Society* to be released and was far more concerned about what UF does to the animals rather than what anyone did to me. Against this backdrop, Steve Best called his friend in the press office and cursed him out for having any association with me; I think was colleague was annoyed by the abuse but wasn't swayed. Then someone named Jerry Friedman contacted my publisher to browbeat him into not to publishing my book. I had no clue who Jerry Friedman was or why he was trying to get my book shelved to no avail. And then the irrelevant sycophants began pestering NAALPO to disassociate with me. Except for what he forwarded to me, I doubt my publisher even responded.

Then my pages started to be hacked. Alafair would start a campaign on Facebook to have me deleted from that site. They circulated a petition. I didn't realize it at the time, but the inner circle must have been livid about my returning with all of my support intact and my initiatives back on track. I don't know how she was able to do it, but she would post that they needed to take down my profile and the next morning it would be deleted; it would simply be gone. The link didn't go to a disabled page like it normally would when Facebook disables a profile. The link would simply go to dead air. Then they would put up a new profile with my name and image and post things to completely isolate me like telling people to remove themselves from my mailing lists because they had been hacked. By this time, my friends and colleagues who had stuck with me very clearly saw the new wave of attacks to which I was being subjected and ignored the inner circle. Many, many more Facebook users, not necessarily activists, jumped into the schoolyard-bullying sessions everyday simply for entertainment.

Everyday there would be new posts, people laughing at me for being a joke, for being a coward, and for not taking responsibility for my actions. I didn't care about these individuals, but the things they were saying disturbed me. One day I told someone on my profile that I was proud to have gone through everything with my integrity intact. Some nitwit put up a post that said "Marino said she acted with integrity? Her? Did I blink and miss something?" And then they all jumped in to tear me up. And every one of these people, many I did not know and to whom I had never spoken, all claimed to have the *proof*. But none ever offered any. No matter. Stalking and bullying me had simply become an enjoyable sport for many while the animals died silently in UF's labs.

The serious issue for me with being repeatedly hacked is that I cannot do my work in a vacuum. And each time my profile disappeared, I was cut off from 1000s of colleagues. I started using the Robert Osbourne profile to get my work out. I commented using that profile in my NIO Facebook group. Watching everything that happened in my groups, literally stalking me, Alafair publicly identified Robert Osbourne as me and the next morning it was gone. I put up a new profile about five times. They would stay up for a couple of days to a couple of weeks. Then she would somehow get them deleted.

A friend, Virginia Ray, called herself *Green Consciousness* on Facebook. Alafair incorrectly identified her as one of my fake profiles and her profile disappeared overnight. I had another person who was a former sexual interest of Steve's with a vendetta. She was a psychologist who had determined that Steve was a narcissist and sociopath. She was less a supporter of me than a hater of him. But Alafair incorrectly identified this individual who called herself *Flower Blossom* as being me and, one after the other, five of her profiles were deleted. I would make fake profiles simply to be able to be active in my own groups. The second I would post information, Alafair would identify me and my profiles would be gone the next morning.

Steve Best had repeatedly asked me to learn how to hack so that I could get rid of both Gary Francione's and John Symons' online presences. If I had that talent, I would have used it for the animals. But in Rhonda Brabbin (aka Alafair Robicheaux), Steve Best had found not only a hacker, but one who had no compunction about damaging the animals to please her leader. And then they would all congregate on one of the bullies' profiles to laugh at me for having to make fake profiles to support myself. If only their efforts could have been directed at helping the billions of animals who died while they played.

One morning after another battle with the University of Florida to take possession of the documents of experiments to which they were subjecting puppies, I finally got an email that they conceded and would deliver the records to me out of court. That same morning my Facebook profile was gone again. I was having difficulty getting my information out to 20 people let alone 2000 at this point. Now I was about to take possession of dog records and didn't have any means of disseminating the information effectively.

I called David. I was so distraught that I didn't trust myself to drive the hour and a half to Gainesville to get the records. He helped talk me through it and gave me permission pretty much to not drive until I composed myself. But he also decided that he would be my attorney of record and try to figure out how to find out what was going on with Facebook. How were they able to stalk me and shut me down like this with impunity? There was a cyber-fingerprint somewhere of exactly who was doing what. And we were hoping we would be able to secure it and shut down my attackers. We both knew that Steve Best would run for cover the second one of his sycophants became a liability for doing his bidding.

I finally wrote Alafair in April of 2014. I told her in no uncertain terms that she was going to stop stalking me and interfering in my business or I would publish *the pictures*. Only Steve and I knew what those pictures were. I had restrained myself and withheld those pictures despite everything he had done. I had no interest in Steve Best or damaging him anymore; I simply wanted to undo the damage he'd done to me and be left alone. I was not the same person when I got off probation. I had just been through a lot and only wanted to move forward. On my terms. And with my side of the story, the truth, being told.

At least NAALPO was publishing my book and I was planning on being at the National Animal Rights Conference in July when it was published. This was a safe venue. Out in Los Angeles that year and with Steve having boycotted this event for over a decade, it was neutral territory. My colleagues out in California and I were looking forward to getting together and discussing a bi-coastal campaign against a huge vivisection business, Burnham Institute. I received a call at home one day from a number in California that I didn't recognize. On the other end was Alex Hershaft, the organizer of the National Animal Rights Conference and the founder of Farm Animal Rights Movement (FARM). I knew his name. But I knew nothing about him. Apparently, Steve Best, Jerry Friedman, and Michael Budkie wanted me banned from the conference.

I began to realize that the animal rights movement is largely regulated by a patriarchy of white men who have the power and want to enforce the rules by which activists can conduct themselves. Clearly, I had not only taken on Steve Best but an entire movement and now, as a *scorned woman*, any attempt to defend myself was being framed as me *attacking* the patriarchs. I started to remember other female activists who had come forward to accuse other high-profile male activists of physical abuse, sexual abuse, and outright rape. Those women who had no voice in this paradigm were easily dismissed as hysterical, emotional, and scorned women before they were retaliated against with defamation lawsuits. I had dismissed these women. Now I was one of them. I did not know what happened to any of them. But now it seemed to me that my fight for the animals had morphed into a fight for all female activists who dared challenge the white male power structure within our movement, a power structure that gives lip service to anti-oppression philosophy while oppressing female activists with no access to their old boy's network.

I was utterly shocked when Alex said to me that he had fixed things so that "you can attend Steve's lecture but you have to sit in the back." WTF! Steve was now going to this conference that he openly derided for years? It would be nearly impossible to remain 100 feet from him within the confined conference venue. I surmised his sole reason to attend was to enforce his Domestic Violence Restraining Order and have me arrested in California.

Why would Alex or anyone else think that I had any interest in listening to Best drone on yet again? There is nothing new that he hasn't said a billion times before. We get it: "militant direct action" [from his armchair], "every motherfucker who hurts animals is gonna feel the fear" [before he runs to the state to have activists prosecuted for doing just that], "alliance politics" [while snorting Ritalin], "total liberation" [while beating Alicia], blah, blah, blah.

Alex wanted to read a copy of my book to make sure I wasn't *attacking* other activists in it. In other words, the patriarchy seemed to have decided that if I ever told my story about the unmitigated attacks to which I'd been subjected, that I would be cast as the emotional offender attacking veteran male activists. It was a patriarchy, indeed. I didn't recognize how it would close ranks against me when I would refuse to bow down to Dr. Steve Best and go away quietly. It was becoming very clear to me, however, that I was on my own. I wasn't even sure I would attend the conference but I sent Alex a copy of the book. He said since I hadn't attacked anyone in it and that since I hadn't told my story, I could sell it at the conference. As my publisher, I wrote to NAALPO to apprise them of the situation. The person with whom I sensed friction asked me in an encrypted message "did you tell Steve that you were going to tell your story in this book?" As if I would equivocate before him or god almighty, I wrote back, "yes." Of course, I did. This was my book.

All hell broke loose. The move on the internet to get me taken off Facebook and banned from the conference went into high gear. My Facebook profile was deleted again. The conference page was polluted with slurs about me. Since my own profile was down, I was now speaking through my public fan page which was created for me while I was in jail.

In May, I was contacted on Facebook by a colleague who told me he had something I needed to see. I gave him my address and received a green thumb drive in the mail. Steve Best had made a one-hour long video, uploaded it to Google+, and was privately disseminating it in my community. My colleague downloaded it from the internet and sent it to me. In it, Steve reiterated everything he had said in court two years earlier plus a slew of lies and misinformation that I had never heard before. He went on interminably about how I stalked him. I had sent him three emails in three other people's names when I was in the middle of a full-blown breakdown in 2012. He said I stalked him by writing to UTEP. I had written to the University of Texas, El Paso in the summer of 2012 and confessed that I had graded his students' work and taken his compliance exams for him. He said that I filed a false police report and sent the police to his house in 2012. He never said that I sent them to make sure Alicia and her baby were safe because he is an abusive woman-beating bastard.

He said that I have a history of terrorizing vivisectors and that he was establishing a "pattern." He said I was a whore, a drug addict, a jail bird, a sociopath, and the dignified professor made fun of me for having a limp and being "trailer trash." But all I really focused on was his interminably long soliloquy about how I sent Donal O'Leary an email in 2010. It is true that as soon as I hit send, I called Steve and I told him I thought I had crossed some invisible line. So far, so good. Unbelievably, he was now saying that his response was "yes, that was a really stupid thing to do." Apparently, he had forgotten that his actual response to the email I had blind copied him on was to publish the Freddy Kruger letter. In fact, he wanted the world to believe that I was prosecuted for sending an email! To my knowledge, no one in the history of mankind has ever been prosecuted for sending an email. I was prosecuted for the Freddy Kruger letter which Dr. Steven Best authored and published on my website. I knew it. He knew it. My prosecutor articulated it. And the vivisectors knew it.

According to Dr. Steven Best, I had been prosecuted for the felony of posting a [public] message for sending a private email. I didn't want to take responsibility for my actions so I was trying to implicate him. This was one of the main reasons for the hatred and sabotage to which I'd been subjected for two years by then. Every article that discussed my charges quoted his words about cracked testicles, decapitation, and severed limbs. Yet Steve Best was on a mission to persuade anyone who would listen that a private email earned me a felony charge; further, afraid of prosecution, I was trying to hide behind him. Finally, I understood. The reason everyone was telling me to "take responsibility" was because, while I was being prosecuted for his actions, the magnificent coward was telling the world in a network of private messages that I wanted him to take responsibility for my actions. Again, WTF!

MCLS § 750.411s (2014)

§ 750.411s. Posting a public message through electronic medium; prohibitions; penalty; exceptions; definitions.

Sec. 411s. (1) A person shall not post a message through the use of any medium of communication, including the internet or a computer, computer program, computer system, or computer network, or other electronic medium of communication, without the victim's consent, if all of the following apply:

(a) The person knows or has reason to know that posting the message could cause 2 or more separate noncontinuous acts of unconsented contact with the victim. [the PUBLIC "Freddy Kruger" Letter]

(b) Posting the message is intended to cause conduct that would make the victim feel terrorized, frightened, intimidated, threatened, harassed, or molested.

(c) Conduct arising from posting the message would cause a reasonable person to suffer emotional distress and to feel terrorized, frightened, intimidated, threatened, harassed, or molested.

(d) Conduct arising from posting the message causes the victim to suffer emotional distress and to feel terrorized, frightened, intimidated, threatened, harassed, or molested.

His soliloquy alleged that he had never supported my student vivisection campaign, the one that he was actually using his PayPal account to fund. He contended that he never agreed with my tactics, although he was publicly quoted in the newspapers defending me. And in the same breath that he maintained he supports militant direct action against vivisectors, he shamelessly condemned my activism: "...her tactics were evil, were based upon a pattern of, of a, intimidation and threats, she would threaten vivisectors, from coast to coast, literally from coast to coast, from California to Florida." While animals were being mercilessly tortured to death, Dr. Steven Best argued that I was victimizing vivisectors.

The insidious campaign to rewrite history was well into its second year, yet I was only first beginning to understand how my former mentor's lies had gained any traction. And, clearly, he had to extinguish me in order to perpetuate his tale unchallenged. That meant he had to get me off the internet so that I could never publish the court documents where he defended vivisectors.

Once I received the video, I republished the most hypocritical and outright lies and simply mocked him without saying a word. In a three-minute clip, I had a frame of him telling activists that "every motherfucker who hurts animals is gonna feel the fear" followed by him telling the camera "she made a number of really serious threats against vivisectors... So really it was the whole pattern of harassment that she established. I mean this woman had personal protection orders or PPO's against her from researchers, if you will in quotes right, in California, in Michigan, in Florida, also from a lot of people loosely associated with them... She had established a pattern of harassment, intimidation, and abuse and threats and that was her main tactical approach. And, I started to distance myself from that."

It was all clear. The lying coward was a revisionist.

I had told Alafair that if they hacked me once more, my response would be swift. But I didn't act until after he made that video and sent it to everyone with whom I worked. He wanted to lie about me? Well I had the proof about him. I published the pictures of the "junkie professor" snorting drugs. I published the pictures of Steve Best with straws up his nose and that vacant stare of a mindless drug addict looking wide-eyed and disheveled for the camera. I published the texts where he used *the N word*, I published the emails of how he really spoke about his "bitches," and I published the emails he sent me of naked *Christian* women. I put up a post that I wouldn't be caught dead at a conference that would allow this "junkie hypocrite" a platform. I would yield the floor at the National Animal Rights Conference to the "junkie professor."

Within minutes of that post going up, Sybelle Foxcroft sent a message to my publisher that I was *attacking* Steve and the conference. Sybelle was Steve's friend had spent days interviewing and editing him in the scathing and defamatory video they produced. I promptly received an email from NAALPO that they were dropping my book. Because of a phrase that was included in that message, "and don't write to us anymore," I'm fairly confident I know who authored that email. There is only one individual associated with that office that I know to be prone to knee-jerk, emotional reactions. Nonetheless, it was received by me as just another slap in the face while I was down. As far as the press office itself, its mission is to amplify the voice of the underground and thus the enslaved animals. And while I wish I had had more support from some corner of the movement, this spectacle appeared to everyone on the outside as two crazy people engaged in he-said/she-said drama. While personally hurtful, I understand the decision to shelve my book and choose to believe it was political. Dr. Jerry Vlasak was the person I considered my senior publisher and we did exchange emails a few times after this episode; his allegiance was never to me or Steve but to the struggle alone and I have great respect for that.

Now that Steve was finally out of hiding, his frenzied posts aimed at me began, especially those labeling me a stalker which featured my extradition mugshot to embarrass me. My former friend has consistently demonstrated that he will go to extraordinary lengths to secure my silence and protect his reputation. I believe that he worked so hard to cultivate an appearance of strength and courage because behind it he was empty. When Steve Best looks at that photo, he undoubtedly sees only an unflattering image. I suspect he is incapable of understanding that behind the washed-out face and unkempt hair, I was only beginning to find a source of inner strength and courage that continues to propel me. He began frantic blogs called me a whore, a drug addict, a coward, and every other slur with which he had armed his followers since I was behind bars in August of 2012.

In mid-June, Sybelle sent me a few messages. In one she wrote that "you are a joke" and not to be surprised "if you are banned from the AR conference." She ended it with "you'll never see us coming. :)" In her next email she wrote "I will be in the US soon, would love to meet you in person." And the final email said "I am an army girl, toe to toe might not go exactly as you think." Two weeks later I was walking Brutus in the woods at 7:30 am. It was July 2. When I came out of the woods my car was on fire. I jumped in to grab my cell phone and then my only thought was to get Brutus far enough away to safety. The car exploded into flames while I was on the phone with the fire department. It never occurred to me to tell them I was being stalked and threatened. It never occurred to me to do anything but get Brutus home. It never occurred to me until it was too late.

I began getting mail sent to my home for mental health programs, bipolar support groups, drug addiction treatment centers, and free samples of adult diapers. On my birthday, July 5, I went out to eat and I was getting hundreds of notifications. I had been being spammed for days but that night while I was out eating I received over 500 spam emails. On the dark net, you can pay a small price in bitcoins and submit someone's email address to have it rendered useless by spam. I believe this comprised one facet of their attack. In addition, they must have spent days signing me up for every magazine and blog they could find. I never reacted publicly. That would have given them satisfaction. I patiently unsubscribed from as many emails as I could, but months later my email had still been rendered virtually useless and I had to close it. That same night, I got a notification on my meetup group in Orlando. *Angela Caparella* had friended me.

My middle name is Angela. My mother's name was Caparella. Only Steve knew that I had used that as an alias sometimes along with an anonymous woman's image I found online; the same image used in their Meetup profile. Now my stalkers had adopted my alias to stalk me. I went home and posted pictures of the vegan Indian food that we had on my birthday. As far as my haters would know, their punches hadn't landed.

Since I wasn't going to the conference and now NAALPO was not going to sell my book, I donated 10 books to Kevin Storm to sell at the conference to support his radio show. I so wanted to meet him and Su and spend some time with my colleagues but I also didn't want to appear in such a hostile environment. Anne and David agreed that it was entirely possible that I would be physically assaulted; we all entertained the thought that if that were to happen, people might actually begin to see what was going on. However, I had no intention of doing anything that would allow my former-friend-turned-traitor to get me arrested.

As it turned out, it was Steve Best who was almost arrested. The 6-foot-tall college professor accosted 13-year-old Kevin Storm at the conference for selling my book, angrily grabbing his arm, loudly calling him "you little shit," and threatening the boy. In the administration office, Steve Best spewed profanities at Alex Hershaft. It was reported that Alex asked Steve to sit down and talk; he refused and continued his tirade. Alex finally told Steve to leave the conference. Several activists reported that Dr. Best was pacing the hallways and they were scared. Hotel security was forced to confront him and physically escort him out of the building. Dr. Steve Best was banned from the conference. Susan Schindler called me to tell me that Steve was not allowed back and that the administration told her I was welcomed to attend the following year. I spoke to Kevin who was considerably shaken. Before I had even finished speaking with Kevin and Su, Rhonda Brabbin was on Facebook announcing that Steve was thrown out of the conference because I had victimized him yet again.

I'm Baaack!

Alafair Robicheaux
14 hours ago

#AR2014 Kevin Storm sociopathic protégé of fellow sociopath, Camille Marino, was distributing slanderous (to Dr Best) leaflets (purposely inserted inside of Camilles "book" given to Storm to distribute throughout the conference.
Steve Best went to the FARM office to voice his concern and was asked to leave the conference for referring to Storm as a "little shit" — feeling the continuous injustice of the ALM turning their backs on Dr. Best, and giving

I published an article where Kevin made a statement about his experience and how scared he was. I objectively balanced it out with quotes from Steve's spokespeople defending his actions by saying that I was a "drug addict" and "a whore" with "a fatal attraction."

Without a struggle, there can be no progress. -Frederick Douglass

Knock, Knock

David was committed to helping me find out who was stalking and sabotaging me. We all knew who it was. But proving it and making it stop so I could get back to work was another matter entirely. He sent a notarized letter to Facebook as my attorney of record in late June and we were prepared to go forward. On July 14, 2014, there was a knock on the door. It was my process server again. We greeted each other and exchanged pleasantries. It had been a few months since we'd seen one another. Who was serving me now?

Unbelievably, it was a summons to appear in court in New Mexico the following day on July 15 in the case of Steven Best, Petitioner vs. Camille Marino, Respondent. Jerry Friedman had finally passed his bar exam was acting as Steve Best's legal adviser. He apparently guided Best to file an Order to Show Cause alleging that I had violated the Domestic Violence Restraining Order by publishing information demonstrating the depth of Petitioner's lies, cowardice, and hypocrisy. Essentially, they were claiming that my posting articles about Steve being thrown out of the conference for accosting Kevin and that my posting pictures of Steve snorting drugs *in response* to his video disparaging me amounted to stalking and harassment; posting on my web

277

sites, under his outstanding restraining order, constituted an act of domestic violence. I was now being prosecuted for defending myself.

It became clear to me now. My former friend was using his restraining order like a noose around my neck to choke me from 1700 miles away. Just as he had done to Alicia, he was squeezing my throat with all of his might to shut me up. And now I understood who Jerry Friedman was and why this person to whom I never spoke was obsessed with me. He was Steve's new Camille. I was almost embarrassed for him. Yet being bashed by these two men from across the country took its toll. I had no money. I had no lawyer. I hadn't even been free for six months. And now they were trying to put me back in jail. I couldn't breathe. I wound up being hospitalized that day. After three days I was diagnosed with an anxiety disorder and prescribed Xanax again.

While I was in the hospital, Anne and David worked feverishly to try to find local counsel; they were able to get an extension so I could at least participate. The hearing would take place on August 1. I *borrowed* another $2,000 from my brother and now had to secure representation out in New Mexico. I wrote lawyers. I called lawyers. No criminal attorneys were interested in defending me on a civil violation. The one attorney I did find wanted $10,000 up front. I had no access to a public defender because, technically, this was a civil proceeding. David and Anne both made themselves available to help me with pro se filings where I would act as my own attorney in lieu of representation. Then, on Saturday night, July 26, David found a lawyer working in his office who answered his phone in Las Cruces.

John D. Watson was a warm man with a generous personality. He was a civil attorney and had over two decades of extensive experience in civil litigation. Between David and me, we explained my predicament to the best of our ability, although it was impossible to paint the layers and layers of deception and sabotage that Steve Best had created for over two years. John listened and accepted my case. I paid his retainer and he became my attorney of record across the country on July 31, 2014.

The following morning, on August 1, John Watson appeared at my hearing and requested a continuance. Steve had hired a local criminal attorney, Margaret Strickland; a paid assassin. She objected to a continuance saying that I was being cited for criminal contempt for violating the DVRO and so I should have been present that day, but John won on that issue. In the interim, Steve's video to which I had responded would be viewed by the hearing officer. The proceedings ultimately resumed on September 16 after two more continuances were filed by Best and his attorney.

On September 16, 2014, John argued vehemently that I should be allowed to appear at this proceeding by phone. We submitted documentation to the court demonstrating that I had less than $1 in my bank account. Had I purchased a plane ticket for either of two prior dates that were canceled and re-scheduled by my accuser, I'd have lost that money. Further, John argued, I was not ignoring these proceedings; I had retained him to represent me. Steve's attorney argued that I should have been there period so the court could throw me in jail. The Domestic Violence Hearing Officer (DVHO) denied our motion to allow me to appear by phone and allowed my prosecution to begin in absentia. She further barred me from participating in my own hearing. She ruled that I could listen if I wanted, but I could neither speak nor defend myself.

Dr. Steven Best took the stand and again recited his diatribe about me stalking him, having a fatal attraction, sending the police to his house in 2012, sending him emails in 2012, and, even though I had no contact with him whatsoever since November of 2012, he contended that my posts on my web pages constituted contact. And then he once again invoked his new colleagues, the vivisectors:

- He testified about my history of threatening "college professors" (he no longer used the word "vivisector") and referred to my Detroit prosecution for his Freddy Kruger letter to establish a pattern of threatening said professors.
- Referring to the Freddy Kruger letter he authored, he astonishingly testified: "She is trying to blame me for why she

went to jail for threatening a vivisector in Detroit, Michigan. She sent him a direct threat that I had nothing to do with."

- He entered into evidence an image of my arrest on the campus of Wayne State: "Yes that is a picture of Ms. Marino being arrested for civil disobedience, "stalking a researcher" out in Detroit."

He testified that I had a history of attacking prominent people in the movement. He forgot to mention that he directed every single one of those attacks. He said I started to threaten students and that's when he began to distance himself from me. He apparently forgot that we used his PayPal account to accept donations for that campaign, that he defended me publicly in the newspapers and, in fact, was responsible for amping up the rhetoric in my campaign announcements. He screenshot the lyrics from the Sick Puppies song that I published on my Facebook page and recited the lyrics

"don't cry like a bitch when you feel the pain"

and telling the court he felt *threatened* by the song. If I didn't despise the word "bitch," I'd be compelled to mock him for acting like one. He claimed that by posting the pictures of him doing drugs that I was harassing and stalking him. He claimed that by identifying him as a coward, a traitor, and a liar that I was stalking and harassing him. He testified that by publishing an article about him being thrown out of the conference for accosting 13-year old Kevin Storm that I was stalking and harassing him. He claimed that by publicly discussing the fact that he beat Alicia Rodriguez breaking three of his girlfriend's ribs, that I was in contempt for violating his Domestic Violence Restraining Order.

There was a new accusation as well. Apparently, while I was in jail in 2013, a man called his house and threatened to come kill him. He told the court, without a shred of proof, that I had orchestrated that call from behind bars. He failed to tell the court that snitches and collaborators are the lowest forms of life to activists and that he was now widely hated in my community. I had never before heard of that call. His hours-long diatribe consisted of half-truths, misrepresentations, and outright perjury. But after having repeated it over and over again for years, first in private messages to all of my colleagues, then in court under oath, and finally on his hour-long video – all venues where he was entirely unchallenged thus far – his talking points evolved with a persuasive cohesion.

John Watson was unprepared to catch Steve in his lies. How could he? This had been going on for over 2 years and without me or Anne or David or any of the people who had lived and breathed the lies and abuse every day, it was impossible to even know where to start. Without me allowed to participate, I had no defense. John argued that this was not a domestic violence case and the court had no jurisdiction. He argued that a Domestic Violence Restraining Order should never even have been issued; we were colleagues who lived on opposite sides of the country and never had anything resembling a domestic partnership. He argued to no avail. Best testified on the stand for four hours. On cross examination, John was able to get him to admit that I had not tried to phone, write, visit or contact him in anyway whatsoever since 2012. John got him to admit that I had never "hacked" his Facebook page in 2012 but that I had had the password. John was able to bring several of his obvious lies to light. But Steve refused to discuss the fact that *he* authored the *threats* against O'Leary with which he was now trying to paint me into a stalker's box. And he steadfastly maintained that he never accosted 13-year-old Kevin Storm; he swore that he was never thrown out of the conference. Where he had sworn in 2012 that he was not a drug addict, now that he had entered his own pictures into evidence he was forced to concede that he lied. Being unfamiliar with my community and the relentless cyberbullying campaign, John was unable to effectively show that every single one of my posts was in response to about 50 multi-faceted attacks orchestrated by Best from every direction.

Officially barred from defending myself, Joy Goldbaum, the Domestic Violence Hearing Officer, ruled that I had violated the Domestic Violence Restraining Order by speaking about him on my sites. John argued that this was a violation of my First

Amendment rights to no avail. She sentenced me to 179 days in jail with all but 21 days suspended provided I remove every reference to Steve Best from my sites. Steve Best, on the other hand, was deemed to be exercising his free speech in his video and his multiple attacks on me.

Steve Best had achieved that which he sought since October of 2012. He had successfully made it a criminal offense for me to use his name. The woman beater was now free to rewrite history with the full support and protection of his local Domestic Violence Court in New Mexico. My First Amendment rights had been summarily suspended. And it looked like I would be heading back to jail. Again, courtesy of my former mentor.

On September 16, 2014, I was quoted in an article entitled "UF under scrutiny for alleged unethical animal treatment since '11[55]." Michael Budkie had filed another welfare complaint and spoke about the violations he reported. Irrespective of how I feel about Budkie, this was an amazing opportunity to give depth to this welfare nonsense in the same article. While he spoke about the violations, I believe I effectively conveyed the egregious nature of the regulated torture of the animals, including monkeys and dogs, that happens every single day. No reader was allowed to walk away thinking that welfare violations were the exception. The atrocities to which animals are subjected in full compliance with the law is as heinous and unconscionable as any violation.

Then there were comments. And other activists or, by this time, unabashed collaborators, came to UF's rescue to discredit me as a terrorist, a drug addict, a prostitute, a fraud, and anything else they could type from their fake profiles. They rarely used their real names anymore. And with the hearing having concluded minutes before, the inner circle returned to the comments section of the article about animal abuse inside the University of Florida to report what had happened in court. They gloated that I was stalking Dr. Best and was going back to jail. And I was barred by

55 Chabeli Herrera, "UF under scrutiny for alleged unethical animal treatment since '11," The Independent Alligator (September 16, 2014) http://www.alligator.org/news/campus/article_7235b190-3d52-11e4-907b-2b968c487f4a.html

the court from defending myself.

So what if this was an article that gave lab animals a voice? Steve's inner circle obviously believed that his agenda is far more important than theirs. His expense-paid annual trips to Europe were funded with the blood and screams of condemned animals. Once he initiated proceedings against me and those invitations ceased, so did his presence in the movement. For the animals, indeed! It's taken me time and distance to understand that Steve Best was never an activist. He was merely a self-serving demagogue. He could hate me as much as he wanted. Destroying my work for the animals, however, was unconscionable. My former mentor was now a full-blown collaborator, acting vehemently to advance his own agenda as well as that of the vivisectors. There was no difference anymore. There hadn't been for some time.

On September 22, 2014, a bench warrant was issued for my arrest for failure to appear at the hearing.

If you tell a big enough lie and tell it frequently enough, it will be believed. -Adolf Hitler

District Court, Las Cruces

Under New Mexico law, Domestic Violence Hearing Officer Joy Goldbaum could only make recommendations that would then have to be affirmed or rejected by the District Court. She had no authority to sentence me to jail and the arrest warrant was only a technicality. It was now incumbent upon my attorney and me to challenge her recommendations and present our defense, after the fact as it were.

John knew that District Court generally affirms the lower court as matter of practice; but he also knew the reputation of our judge, Darren M. Kugler, as a no-nonsense jurist who maintains strict order in his courtroom. From all he'd heard practicing in the New Mexico court system, John believed that Judge Kugler would not allow Steve Best to hijack his courtroom with a four-hour narrative of irrelevant details and perjury. We hoped for fairness and justice, but, ultimately, prepared ourselves for a rubber-stamp decision.

Anne O'Berry, on the other hand, has a long history as a meticulous and successful appellate criminal attorney. Years before in New York and Florida, she built her career representing death row inmates on appeal as well as battered women seeking executive clemency after they were sent to prison for killing their abusers. (We would figure out one day that we worked across the street from one another on Third Avenue in Manhattan two decades earlier.) But the toll of seeing abused women who killed their attackers in self-defense being railroaded into life sentences and young men of color without the means to buy any justice falling victim to the prison industry took a tremendous toll on her. She relayed the story of one mentally-disabled young man whose attorney showed up in court drunk. He was later disbarred. But the young man was sentenced to death anyway. Anne is nothing if not fully committed to those for whom she advocates, whether her clients are human animals in a courtroom or nonhuman animals being killed in shelters and labs. About ten years earlier, she had to take a break. The weight she carried advocating for those who were destroyed under the wheels of an unjust system had become overwhelming. She needed time to re-center herself. And then I came along.

If history was any indicator, Anne was confident I would be railroaded through District Court and would have to secure justice and vindication at an appellate level. From the very beginning, while we hoped we would receive a modicum of relief in District, all we could do was to saturate the record with all of the evidence and documentation that would be necessary if we were to argue successfully on appeal. My legal team worked day and night preparing our objections to Goldbaum's recommendations, almost 100 pages of testimony and exhibits in that instrument alone, documenting Steve Best's repeated perjured testimony. We also provided our own testimony and exhibits demonstrating the siege to which he subjected me. We submitted affidavits of compliance demonstrating that I had taken every reasonable step to comply with the DVHO's unconstitutional order to remove Steve's name from my sites while knowing it was impossible to erase information from the internet once it had been published. We filed a motion to appear by phone. We filed motions asking the court to discharge the original restraining order which was secured through flagrant perjured testimony, especially the fact that I was on house arrest in Florida on the night Steve Best swore I showed up at his house in New Mexico and threatened him with weapons. We filed a motion to dismiss the DVRO because the court lacked subject matter jurisdiction. We filed a motion to remove the domestic violence hearing officer who in 2012 said "I can't tell her that she can never comment on you" and in 2014 decided that commenting on Best was a violation of the original DVRO.

We submitted nearly 200 pages of motions to Judge Kugler's court. The depth to which we needed to dig to begin to unravel all of the lies that had been contextualized on the stand was substantial and time consuming. And it was taking a toll on Anne and causing friction in her marriage. I was desperately grateful for her counsel. Had I been wealthy I could not have asked for a better advocate. But I was extremely conscious of the distress my persecution had already caused her. I saw the toll that defending me in this malicious prosecution was further taking on my friend. She was doing everything in her power to protect and help me. Everyone was.

David spent days researching case law to substantiate our arguments. I had been summarily denied due process by being banned from participating in my own hearing. And now I was stuck in this gray area of being criminally prosecuted without the basic protections afforded criminal defendants in this country. I was being criminally prosecuted for my first amendment protected speech which had been criminalized by the Domestic Violence Hearing Officer. I was being criminally prosecuted in civil court. I was being criminally prosecuted without having any access to a court-appointed criminal defense attorney.

John and I had extensive phone conversations at the rate of $300 an hour as well as spending many hours consulting online. I had no idea how I was going to pay him and, as he came to fully understand that the restraining order was being wielded like a club to bash me in Florida, he earnestly wanted to protect me. He could see the injustice in what was happening. John Watson, a virtual stranger, knew my finances were exhausted. Yet he continued to spend more and more hours working on my defense. He wanted to win me relief.

On Halloween, October 31, 2014, a status conference was held in Judge Kugler's courtroom in New Mexico. The court was to schedule a hearing in our case and John was going to argue our motion to allow me to appear telephonically. I waited by the phone for John's call to patch me in so I could address the court if necessary. Steve's lawyer argued to reject my motion to appear telephonically; Judge Kugler complied and denied my motion. He asked John if there was anything else? John asked for a court date so we could argue all of the motions we had just filed. Kugler wanted him to argue them impromptu at this status hearing. John was unprepared to do so. Strickland agreed to schedule the next hearing for December 11 and then petitioned the court to have me arrested. She told the court that I was not in court because I was partying in Orlando for Halloween. I was actually home. But Orlando is one hour away from home. She gave the court the impression that I had flown off on vacation somewhere with my friends. Steve Best had certainly found a kindred spirit in his lawyer. They both lied shamelessly and with great proficiency.

Kugler ended the proceeding:

> *"In the meantime, we're just gonna amend the warrant to reissue it. Based on representations that she's in Florida, I'm going to issue a bench warrant authorizing an extradition from anywhere within the U.S."*

I had Steve Best blocked and no longer had any interest in seeing his relentless attacks on me. My counsel forwarded to me a copy of his blog. That night his exuberance could not be contained. He and the inner circle were overjoyed at the prospect of my having to endure another extradition in the tomb enclosed in the tiny van. Steve was my best friend and confidante when my legal issues first arose. Of all the people in the universe, he knew exactly how harrowing that extradition had been.

I have never run from anyone in my life and was not about to start. A fugitive now, I went into hiding. I was spending a few days in a motel room that someone had reserved in their name. I had a few things to get in order before I turned myself in *on my terms*.

I had a big global campaign scheduled for November 15. On several continents from the Middle East to Europe to Australia to the US, from Florida to California to Georgia to Minnesota to New York, from Russia to Israel to the UK, and several undisclosed locations in between, I had rallied activists everywhere to take to the streets and go knock on vivisectors' doors. We would bring loud speakers. We would do home demos. We would talk to their neighbors. We would let them know we knew who they were and where they slept. And we were watching them. I had decided that it was time for the Animal Liberation community to declare a global siege on vivisectors.

Every day another activist would contact me for help finding researchers in their neighborhood. This is my area of expertise and I was only too happy to help. And in less than a month, we were all scheduled to take to the streets together and confront the vivisection complex en masse. Now I had to issue a statement from my undisclosed location alerting everyone that I was about to turn myself in, but that the action needed to go on whether I was in custody or not. I begged and encouraged my colleagues to not let the animals down. Many re-doubled their efforts and were now declaring war on vivisectors in my name.

I never mentioned Steve Best's name. It would have been another criminal offense if I had. But the war was well-known and well documented by now and everyone knew who was putting me back in jail. *Snitch* posts popped up across Facebook, from continent to continent, and one by one, more and more activists were expressing solidarity with me and denouncing him as a traitor and a snitch. The inner circle went into high gear again sending out their private messages to everyone who expressed support for me pushing their same old tired talking points. But very few were listening anymore. It seemed they were now doing more damage to their own cause than I ever had.

The inner circle failing, Jerry Friedman ran to his toy chest and pulled out his Cracker-Jack-prize JD to save the day. He sent a Cease and Desist order to everyone across the globe who was accurately calling Best a snitch. Identical notices were forwarded to me from activists in Israel, France, the UK, and several of the states. They all found this threat in their inbox:

> *"CEASE AND DESIST*
>
> *MICHAEL CRANDALL, CAMILLE A. MARINO and all people reading this, you are hereby given notice to cease and desist any contact of Dr. Steve Best, his employer and coworkers, and members of his family and household; any publication of his name and/or contact information or any of his personal information; any publication of his likeness; any accounts made in his name; in all media including social media (Facebook, Twitter, etc.) and print; in any manner that may violate the laws or Personal Protection Order ("PPO") listed below.*
>
> *You are in violation of 18 USC § 875 federal anti-stalking law, NM Statute § 30-3A-2 harassment, NM Statute § 30-16-9 extortion, and the PPO restraining CAMILLE A. MARINO issued from the New Mexico Court, Third District.*
>
> ****Any person who contacts Dr. Best, his employer or coworkers, members of his family or household, may be guilty of violating the aforementioned laws and/or aiding and abetting.****
>
> *The Court ordered CAMILLE A. MARINO, identified as a stalker:*
>
> *1. To be restrained from committing further acts of abuse of threats of abuse.*
>
> *2. To be restrained from any contact with the protected party.*

3. CAMILLE A. MARINO shall not abuse Dr. Best or members of Dr. Best's household. "Abuse" means any incident by one party against the other party or another household member resulting in (1) physical harm; (2) severe emotional distress; (3) bodily injury or assault; (4) threat by CAMILLE A. MARINO causing imminent fear of bodily injury to Dr. Best or any household member; (5) criminal trespass; (6) criminal damage to property; (7) repeatedly driving by Dr. Best's or a household member's residence or workplace; (8) telephone harassment; (9) stalking; (10) harassment; or (11) harm or threatened harm to children in any manner set forth above.

4. CAMILLE A. MARINO shall not ask or cause other persons to abuse Dr. Best or any other household members.

5. CAMILLE A. MARINO shall not telephone, talk to, visit or contact Dr. Best in any way including social media.

Violation of the terms of the PPO may result in you being charged with a misdemeanor, which is punishable by imprisonment of up to three hundred sixty-four (364) days and a fine of up to one thousand ($1,000) dollars or both. You may also be found in contempt of court.

*The Court found that **an act of domestic abuse** was committed by CAMILLE A. MARINO that necessitates an order of protection. For the PPO to be effective until October 26, 2026. You are ordered not to post or share any private information regarding Dr. Best whether in textual, visual, audio, or any other format. You are ordered to stop stalking and harassing Dr. Best. You are ordered to remove all references, images, and accounts you've published that directly or indirectly identify Dr. Best.*

Any violation of this Cease and Desist Order will make

you liable for fines, civil penalties, attorney's fees, and applicable criminal laws. CAMILLE A. MARINO must not contact my law office. Instead, contact your attorney. Any person other than CAMILLE A. MARINO may contact my law office with questions.

Signed,

Jerold D. Friedman Attorney for Dr. Steve Best lawoffice.jdf@gmail.com"

Seeing it in their own inboxes brought the campaign to intimidate activists into silence into focus for many. We deal with these kinds of assaults from industrial abusers as a matter of course. Activists in France and Israel reposted Jerry Friedman's threats to prosecute them for mentioning Steve Best's name. Many shared it in disbelief that this man was suggesting that they too might be prosecuted for "stalking" or "domestic abuse" for publicly identifying a snitch. Were they "aiding and abetting" me by supporting me?

Understanding the influence and manipulation Steve Best enjoys over those close to him, I am proud that I stopped attacking people on his behalf early in our friendship. I would still vehemently defend him throughout our association when he deemed it necessary, but I took a giant step back and refused to feed into his obsessions. When I removed myself from the Gary Francione drama, Steve never let it go. I would counsel him repeatedly that as long as he focused his energy on Gary, he was giving away his power. Now I watched Jerry Friedman doing to me what I once did to Francione, except amplified by 1000. I don't know Gary Francione. Jerry Friedman doesn't know me. There's only one common denominator in this equation. But where I was once embarrassed for him because his actions paralleled my own, now I just looked at him like a fool; a mindless marionette. And it occurred to me that if he really was a friend rather than a puppet, he would not have been exacerbating Steve's obsession with me. But it was as if he was equally as frantic as his master now. Several messages I began to receive, however, indicated that others in the inner circle were growing tired with Steve's obsession with me.

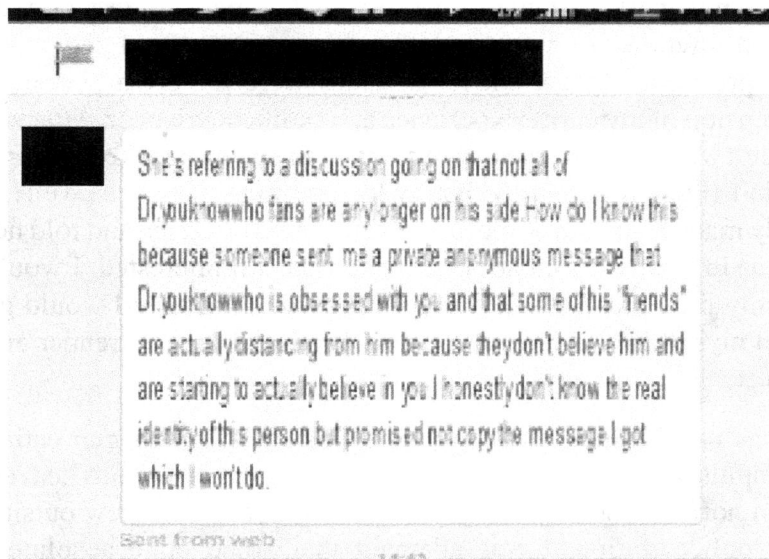

She's referring to a discussion going on that not all of Dr.youknowwho fans are any longer on his side. How do I know this because someone sent me a private anonymous message that Dr.youknowwho is obsessed with you and that some of his "friends" are actually distancing from him because they don't believe him and are starting to actually believe in you. I honestly don't know the real identity of this person but promised not copy the message I got which I won't do.

Sent from web

14:43

I cut my hair off. I was not going back to jail with a head full of long thick bleached hair. In Detroit, commissary accommodated a largely black population. Other than shampoo and watery gel, the only other hair care products were grease and picks. My friends braided my hair frequently, but it was ultimately damaged beyond repair by the time I was released. I didn't want to be bothered this time around.

During the summer I had been contacted by Jessica Vale, a film producer and owner of Vale Productions. She was doing a documentary about controversial and high-profile female activists and had been profiling Judy Clark, a revolutionary with the Weather Underground in the 1970s. Later, working with both the Black Panthers and the Black Liberation Army, they repatriated $1.6 million in a Brinks robbery in 1981 in which two police officers were killed. The funds were to go to the people to finance the revolution. Captured soon after, Judith Alice Clark remained unapologetic and unrepentant in court. She was sentenced to 75 years to life and is currently serving her sentence at Bedford Hills Correctional Facility in New York.

With my work in tatters once again, I initially didn't believe I had anything of value to offer this project. But I rethought my position. My current legal issues were merely a perverted extension of my entire experience as a political prisoner. After all, hadn't Malcolm X's mentor turned out to be a hypocrite too? And didn't Elijah Muhammad betray his one-time mentee as well? It only made Malcolm X more iconic. I emailed Jessica and told her I was in hiding. I told her that if she was still interested, I would do my first interview on film as a fugitive. And then I would go turn myself in and offered to allow her to film my surrender and arrest.

I was not drinking at all anymore. Instead, I had begun eating compulsively. On Saturday, November 8, I was 40 pounds heavier than normal when I did my interview with the film crew outside the police station. I was adamant that I had done absolutely nothing wrong and was running from no one. I welcomed my day in court to face my abuser and if this is how he wanted to do it, then I was prepared to see it through. I also offered a few observations about the coward hiding behind his DVRO.

In the police station, I identified myself and told them I was surrendering on a bench warrant out of New Mexico. The sergeant came out and didn't look very pleased with the cameras. But he explained on film that the warrant was issued *in state* which meant that it would only be enforced inside of New Mexico. They refused to arrest me. This was great news. I went back home, no longer in hiding. I celebrated my freedom on Facebook openly. I hugged my dogs that I had painfully said my goodbyes to hours earlier. And the *Vivisector Next Door* action was now on track with my full participation.

The next week I bought a plane ticket to fly out to New Mexico to appear in court on December 11.

May all that have life be delivered from suffering. -Buddha

Global Action for Animals

November 15, 2014 was a great success. Activists across the globe went out into their communities to visit their local vivisectors. A colleague in Russia created the graphics that we used to promote the event all month long, images of vivisectors peering through their doors with incriminating blood spilling out from under it, ominous images of staircases with blood dripping down them from the vivisector's door, images of vivisectors inside their homes hiding behind their windows. We had some great energy and enthusiasm.

It carried over into that Saturday's actions. I went to Tampa with a small group of activists to visit Kendall Morris who experiments on cats at the University of Central Florida. Although I had announced an action in Gainesville, I never had any intention of being there. It was simply an opportunity to keep UF's vivisectors on edge and under police protection while I turned my attention elsewhere. Morris rightly deserved some exposure of his own. He and UF Vivisector Paul Davenport share a collaborative taxpayer-funded grant awarding each of them over $733,000 annually to sew cats' mouth shut, put cement in their noses, and induce strokes in them.[56] Science indeed! We found Morris'

56 NIH Project No. 5R01HL109025-03 awarded $733,292 annually, Protocol 201107179,

son-in-law, Chad, and had some very informative door-to-door discussions with his neighbors.

Actions were staged in over a dozen announced locations and three that still remain anonymous. But among the highlighted actions, between 70 and 80 activists with The Monkey Struggle in Israel staged a demo for the Mazor Farms monkeys. In Russia, Irina Kondratieva of the Moscow State University was visited at home. For 30 years, she has maimed and murdered thousands of animals from rats to rabbits, and many other species. My colleagues showed up at her door and a loud confrontation ensued. In Minnesota, activists with Progress for Science showed up at wife/husband vivisector duo Marilyn Carroll and Peter Santi's home chanting "1, 2, 3, 4! A vivisector lives next door! 5, 6, 7, 8, hide your dogs and lock your gates!" Following the trend among abusers, Carroll and Santi have taken out injunctions against these activists, including Dr. Kim Socha and Dr. Carol Glasser. But these activists didn't let the court orders or the snow deter them. All of these actions were filmed and footage sent to Jessica Vale. I wanted the animals and the vivisectors to get as much exposure as possible in the continuing documentary.

Jessica was able to film the demonstration in New York at Rockefeller University in person. This event was staged by Kate Riviello, founder of the New York Animal Rights Alliance. We've long discussed how to merge Kate's extensive work with rescues and no-kill shelters with my area of expertise, vivisection. And we are both clear that Class B dealers are the link to bring our groups together. As previously discussed, Donal O'Leary had secured Queenie through a Class B dealer and this industry remains pervasive yet unnoticed. Families have no idea that when they surrender their pets, their family members, to a shelter or place them through Craig's List, there is a high probability those animals will end up being tortured in a lab for profit. Kate and I both wanted this action to be the beginning of a more effective working alliance between us, finally focusing our resources and bringing some much-needed attention to Class B dealers. But it was not to be.

At 10 pm on Friday, December 5, I was walking Max and Jazz. I noticed two police cruisers go around the block. They came back. They stopped in front of a neighbor's house, turned their lights off and watched me for a few minutes. I knew exactly what was happening although I wasn't quite sure how. I had turned myself in. They wouldn't arrest me. I was supposed to be on a plane after the weekend to be in court in New Mexico two days later. And now they were showing up to arrest me?

The cops turned their lights on and pulled up the street to surround me. They got out. "What's your name?" "You know who I am. Can I please put my dogs in the house before you arrest me?" They conceded. I called Mike to let him know I was off to jail again and let him know he had to finish walking the dogs. They cuffed me tightly and put me in the cruiser. One of my neighbors ran over and started yelling at them to leave me alone. She had read one of the now-out-of-print copies of *Danger to Society* and was incensed that I was being arrested again. Her husband had to come and get her or she was about to be arrested with me. I would get booked into Sumter County Jail somewhere around midnight.

One of the male cops who was in the station sarcastically said, "frequent flyer?" I was in no mood. "Do you even know what I'm here for?" "For breaking the law." "If you ever decide to actually stand up for justice in your lifetime instead of hiding behind your badge, then you can talk to me." We exchanged some loud angry words for a couple of minutes. And then he actually apologized.

A woman who behaves like a full human being should be warned that the armies of the status quo will treat her as something of a dirty joke. -Gloria Steinem

Banned from the Internet... AGAIN!

This was a nightmare. Now I was not only being bullied and stalked online, but Dr. Best was manipulating the court system to jump in the bashing with this malicious prosecution. How could this be happening? Anne, David, and John worked on an emergency motion to get me released from jail in Florida so that I could fly out to New Mexico on Tuesday. On the following Monday morning, December 8, John argued the emergency motion before Judge Kugler. Much to all of our surprise, however, he signed an order releasing me that night. The following afternoon I boarded my plane as scheduled.

Jessica Vale flew out to New Mexico to document the proceedings. We discussed my case, met with John Watson, and took the opportunity to film local dairy farms. From our vantage point, we looked down and could see what looked like a concentration camp straight out of Nazi Germany. Later on in court, after noting that Dr. Best and I had "already made a lot of national news," Kugler granted her permission to film in the courtroom at the December 11 proceeding.

Although it was difficult to believe that I was just jailed and dragged across the country to answer for my part in a Facebook war, I was relieved that I would finally – after three years – have an opportunity to speak in my own defense. First things first. Kugler denied all of our motions without ever allowing John to argue their merits. When John raised the issue of the hearing officer's recommendations being unconstitutional, Kugler simply dispensed with the Constitution of the United States:

> *"...you're absolutely right that we've infringed on her constitutional rights because that's what's required under federal law. And the court may continue to do that, because I may put additional prohibitions on her ability to exercise her first amendment free speech rights if it's going to affect Dr. Best... And I'm trying to specifically address that by saying that you bet we've eliminated her first amendment rights and I may continue to do so. I may prohibit her from access to the internet at all. You're welcome to challenge that in a higher court..."*

Then Steve Best was put on the stand and sworn in. He spent another four hours reciting his well-rehearsed diatribe. If we thought Kugler was going to maintain any kind of order or decorum, we were sadly mistaken. He laid out his case for my *fatal attraction* emails from the summer of 2012 and, of course, discussed my charges for *his* Freddy Kruger letter and his new colleague, vivisector Donal O'Leary:

> *"her arrest in Detroit [was] for sending a death threat to a vivisector... he was a university professor."*

He would claim that he had nothing to do with my Facebook pages being hacked:

> *"I was off Facebook."*

It is clear to me that if Rhonda Brabbin is ever held accountable for her part in hacking and cyberstalking me, in his words, *that is a road she is going to walk alone.* Later, on cross examination, John would get Steve Best to admit that

> *"she has me blocked on Facebook."*

Did he forget that he just swore he was not on Facebook? The only profiles I had blocked, aside from his known cultists, were the malicious Tyler Newman and Susan Oleson profiles that were obsessed with destroying me. He appears to have admitted on the stand that he was either Tyler Newman, Susan Oleson, or both. He complained to the court that I referred to him as "a sexist, racist, woman beater... a coward, a hypocrite... a junkie professor."

Then the real reason why we were all there, Margaret Strickland asked Steve Best about my book:

> *Strickland: Does Miss Marino threaten to publish a book documenting the depth and scope of Steve Best's cowardice and treason?*
>
> *Best: Yes*

I sat next to John scribbling notes and getting very anxious that he was not objecting. He was allowing Best to spew his nonsense again, uninterrupted. I was fighting with myself. I wanted to stand up and ask the court to allow me to represent myself. But I didn't. I sat there and let the train roll over me. I really liked John. He is a very nice man. But we both knew that my civil proceeding had turned in to an all-out criminal lynching. John is skilled and competent in his civil practice. But this was like taking an accomplished speaker and expecting that person to be able to get up on stage and perform an aria. John was not a criminal attorney and I was not entitled to a public defender. But he stuck with me through the entire ordeal, taking many of his own lumps from the gratuitously-abusive little man in a black robe. The only issue on which Kugler seemed at all concerned was how to admonish John for being unfamiliar with making appropriate criminal objections.

Banned from the Internet... AGAIN!

At the end of the day I just wanted to go back to my hotel. I still had not had an opportunity to utter a single word. I still had not had an opportunity to enter a shred of evidence in my defense. I hoped I would get my turn the next day. Imagine my surprise when Kugler decided to throw me in jail for the hell of it, with no findings, no trial, nothing:

> *"The court is very concerned for the safety and welfare of Dr. Best. The court finds that Miss Marino presents a clear and present danger of harm to herself and others. I'm going to take her into custody at this time. She'll be detained until the hearing resumes. Certainly, she'll get credit for any time served, but at a minimum, the court's going to be imposing the 21 days... We'll have Miss Marino transported. We're adjourned. "*

The Baker Act allows for the involuntary commitment of someone deemed to have a mental illness who presents a danger to themselves or others. Was I just Baker Acted? Before I ever even uttered a single word, the Honorable Judge Darren Kugler had already decided that I was going to be serving time, that he was going to find me guilty, and, so, he dispensed with the formalities of entertaining a defense. Why bother? I had stopped asking the rhetorical question "who else could join in?" Apparently, the courts were not only being manipulated and process being abused, but the campaign of harassment and bullying appears to have provided sport for many including this tyrant.

Thankfully, Jessica was able to give my luggage to John Watson to hold for me while I was in jail. Steve Best declined to take part in the documentary. But after I was arrested yet again, Jerry Friedman contacted Jessica to try to persuade her to rethink documenting my story.

Court was reconvened on December 17, 2014. Mike's father had had a heart attack the day before and it was a really bad time to have to be in New Mexico, let alone in jail. On that morning, I was brought into court in handcuffs, shackles, and wearing a waist chain that attaches to the two sets of restraints. I was wearing my giant red Teletubby jumpsuit that is the women's uniform in the Dona Ana County Detention Center and my jailhouse slippers that were falling off my feet. This is how the state saw fit to have me face my abuser. Steve Best could hardly contain his glee. I simply held my head high, laughing and joking with the bailiff and my attorney.

John put me on the stand and I was sworn in. He walked me through our exhibits to get them on the record. We submitted documentation that demonstrated I was on house arrest in Florida in 2012 when Steve swore I showed up at his house with weapons. John then tried to establish that I was about to go to trial in Detroit for the threats that Steve authored; the sole reason Dr. Steven Best betrayed me. Kugler did not allow me to testify about this saying he already heard about our relationship. WTF! We presented trial transcripts from 2012 demonstrating that I was tried for Steve Best's words; we entered Sybelle Foxcroft's threats followed by pictures of my car exploding two weeks later; we entered into evidence the proof that Steve was feeding my emails to Ann Parkes and Susan Duke. We attempted to get our evidence on the record that demonstrated that I was under a third-party siege orchestrated by Steve Best that began in August of 2012 while I was still in jail. And then Kugler got tired of listening to us go through our exhibits. He called a bench conference and the court was in recess.

Two months earlier, on October 12, 2014, Alicia Rodriguez reached out to me and sent me an email:

> *"Isn't it ironic that Steve left me bruised, battered and with 3 broken ribs because I refused to contribute to your legal fund? I just explained some of the ironies of life to Steve, and told him maybe I would finally come around and contribute to your current NM legal fund. He didn't like that very much, but, hey, sometimes people get what they wish for right?"*

John tried to enter it into evidence to demonstrate that Alicia was not at all in fear of me. The content confirmed everything

I'd been saying for three years. I had never threatened her with weapons as Steve contended to secure his restraining order. I have never threatened Dr. Best's girlfriend in anyway whatsoever. But Kugler refused to admit the email into evidence or even consider it. He had zero interest in facts.

Demonstrating that he had heard all he needed to from Steve Best and that he had no interest in my version of what transpired, Judge Kugler ruled:

> *"I'm trying to make it clear for the record that I do understand that history. The record establishes that."*

And so our history as narrated by my abuser was all the judge needed. He had already convicted me before I had ever even arrived in New Mexico. The hearings would all prove to be perfunctory exercises to give the illusion of judiciousness. And then he said he would release me on a $100,000 unsecured bond, meaning I didn't have to put down the standard 10%, until the next hearing with the condition that I was banned from the internet:

> *"She's not to use any social media or the internet in any way, shape or form. There will be the standard conditions associated with the order of protection – no contact with Dr. Best, no harassment, etc. She is to remain in the state of Florida, not to leave the State of Florida, until she returns to New Mexico. She's not authorized to use any social media, that being Facebook, My space, Pinterest, Twitter. She's not to access the internet; no viewing of the internet, no posting on the internet, directly or indirectly."*

I barely got my efforts for the animals off the ground and now here I was being shut down again. If my father-in-law had not had a heart attack the day before, I would never have agreed to go home under these conditions.

On January 12, 2015, we appeared in court again. This time Kugler was citing Steve Best for contempt for violating his own restraining order by contacting me. Kugler opened the proceeding:

"Dr. Best, before we begin, let me admonish you of one issue. You signed a sworn statement in your petition that the allegations that you are a drug abuser are a lie, and last time you were in court you admitted to snorting Ritalin. I'm warning you now. Take that oath seriously. I'm not referring this case to the D.A. if you commit perjury in here. I'm going to enforce this court's authority by citing you for contempt. I expect you to tell the truth, and only the truth."

Jerry Friedman was smiling smugly at me in the courtroom with the exact same arrogant leer as Donal O'Leary, had in Detroit as his client was sworn in. Best was granted permission to make an opening statement which Kugler promptly interrupted:

"Dr. Best, stop speaking. Stop speaking! Stop waxing indignant in my court. You're becoming a bore. Do you understand what that term means?

Returning to one of Steve's contacts with me in violation of his own restraining order, the judge focused his questioning:

"Do you admit, deny or take no position on the court's belief that you had taunted the respondent?"

Petitioner denied ever taunting me and followed up by returning to his well-rehearsed diatribe, by now regurgitating it verbatim. Kugler simply cut him off again and wrapped it up:

"...you seem to believe that you can turn off and turn on the provisions of a court order. If that's your choosing, you are sadly mistaken. Court's finding you in violation, citing you for contempt, ordering 30 days incarceration. I'm going to suspend that, as long as you don't commit any more violations. Dr. Best, this is your one and only warning. You've invoked the powers of the court. You no longer have the choice of when to enforce those versus when you decide to ignore those."

Petitioner walked away with a contempt conviction and a slap on the wrist, despite Kugler's mantra repeated throughout all the proceedings. "If I have to alternate holding them in contempt for the next 14 years, six months at a time, I will do so."

Between his hearing, however, and our next scheduled appearance in early February, Steve Best filed a motion to have my bond revoked. I had appeared on the Kevin Storm show. He swore in this document that my bond should be revoked for discussing civil disobedience and referring to a malicious prosecution:

> *Host: Question for Camille. What good does it do for animals and the movement for activists to get arrested and incarcerated?*
>
> *Marino: It does absolutely no good – OK, wait, let me rephrase that. I've no problem getting arrested for my views and for my dedication. And if the law is wrong, I will break it. And I will not complain or apologize for doing so.*
>
> *Host: So what has NIO accomplished in 2014 and what do they plan on accomplishing in 2015?*
>
> *Marino: Thank you for asking that. Actually in 2014, you know, all of us on this show know about the litigation I'm involved in. Very malicious prosecution. So it really served to disrupt our work.*
>
> *Host: So what is your film going to be about?*
>
> *Marino: It's a rewrite of "Danger to Society" and it's about a lot of distractions in my life right now.*

The man who swears in court that I have a fatal attraction has documented his obsession with me on public court records repeatedly. I could no longer utter a word, whether about him or not, without Dr. Steven Best running to the state to punish me. And the only way in which anyone would know every move I made and every word I uttered was if they were monitoring me obsessively (i.e. *stalking me*).

As we moved into wrapping up this side show, several people

submitted sworn declarations to the court to testify to my character as well as speak to the siege under which I had been living since 2012. One of those people was *Green Consciousness* whose identity was still closely guarded at this time. Virginia Ray was instrumental in getting the original stalking laws on the books 30 years ago to protect abused women. For her efforts, she still lives with threats of violence. She knew of Steve's abusive nature first hand and was one of the few people who encouraged me to stand up to him. Having been financially ruined and battered by her abuser, she lost in the lower court and always regretted not having been able to appeal. The domestic violence advocate was very saddened that the laws she worked so hard to get on the books were now being perverted and used by an abuser to silence his victim. She came out of hiding to put her real name on a sworn statement and her voice was critical. Dr. Barry Friedman and several others submitted sworn statements as well.

On December 17, John Watson presented the Declarations filed in my support to the court, gave Kugler a copy and asked him to consider them as mitigating factors. Kugler replied "certainly." Not remembering, or simply not caring, what he said from one hearing to the next, on February 3, John asked him whether he had read the Declarations. Kugler admonished John Watson: "Are you proposing we're gonna do a trial by affidavit? I'm not even going to need an objection on that. I'm not gonna allow any questions based on an affidavit. You have anything else, Mr. Watson?" I suspect he read the affidavits and needed to squash them.

And to drive home the point that Steven Best, Donal O'Leary, and David Jentsch were now and forever colleagues, his lawyer cross-examined me on this subject:

> *Strickland: You haven't been charged - just charged - with stalking and harassing anybody?*
>
> *Marino: Aggravated stalking for a civil disobedience.*
>
> *Strickland: And that was also against university professors, correct?*

Banned from the Internet... AGAIN!

*Marino: **He was a vivisector!** [I was incredulous.]*

Strickland: And that person was a professor at a university, correct?

Marino: Yes.

Then we finished up the pretense of my hearing. On February 3, 2015, Kugler found me guilty of indirect criminal contempt and sentenced me to 179 days in jail with no good time; my internet ban became permanent. I would serve a full six months. After the bailiffs took me from the court, we were in the back room where they took possession of my purse and personal effects. As I was sitting there handcuffed in a chair, Kugler walked in to throw some paperwork on their desk. The stellar jurist sneered at me as if he had just flexed his muscles against an innocent woman and was quite pleased with himself.

Jessica had once again documented everything on film.

That afternoon when I got booked into jail, I called Anne O'Berry. She already knew what had happened. For the very first time out of all of my arrests and incarcerations, I broke down on the phone as we spoke. How could my fight for the animals overcome this? Everything for which I had fought so vehemently was just taken from me... was just taken from the monkeys. They would never be released now. My voice was once again taken from me. My name was once again taken from me. I was just exiled from my own community. I reasoned that I fought against the world for my right to express myself, I'd stood up to unimaginable obstacles being thrown at me from every direction, I'd stood up to slander, stalking, harassment, a viral hate campaign, and a malignant former friend, and now a malicious prosecution and corrupt judge. I fought with everything I had for what I believed was right. And I lost.

Although I didn't know how I would live with this decision, my work for the animals now utterly destroyed, I was more concerned about the toll it would take on Anne if we went forward with an appeal. I knew I needed to appeal. I wanted to fight this. Inasmuch as this was a really bad situation, I held onto my discussions with my friend, the domestic abuse advocate. She had lost to her abuser and her encouragement to stand up against mine grounded me. I knew I had to take this to a higher court. On some level, I knew I was where I needed to be to see this through to its conclusion. I knew I was where I needed to be if I was ever to be vindicated and restored to wholeness.

But I also knew the bulk of the weight of my appeal would fall onto Anne. I didn't want to drag her, her marriage, or anyone else down with me.

There is no better than adversity. Every defeat, every heartbreak, every loss, contains its own seed, its own lesson on how to improve your performance the next time.
-Malcolm X

Dona Ana County Detention Center (DACDC)

The DACDC was unlike any jail I had experienced. When I was booked in and saw the nurse, I was taken aback by how polite, courteous, and respectful she was. At first, I didn't trust her demeanor. Eventually I thought to myself how fortunate I was to be sitting with this woman. But she was not an aberration. Everyone in this facility was courteous and respectful. Huh! This threw me off balance a little. I was comfortable with the *us-and-them* mentality behind bars. Inmates against oppressors. And even where I'd formed alliances within the system, I never lost sight of the fact that these were my captors. In this facility, we only addressed one another by last names.

Lieutenant Alatorre is a devout Christian woman. I would come to enjoy talking to her privately from time to time. We discussed my work, my book, her life, our beliefs. And she was very clear that but for the choices we make, she understood that we could easily be sitting on different sides of the desk. I was a vegan atheist and she was a conservative religious woman, but there was not a hint of hypocrisy in either of us. I respected her for that. We believed differently, but we lived our beliefs. Alatorre demanded that her correctional officers treat the inmates with respect. I was amazed one day when I actually saw her reprimand a guard for being gratuitously rude to a prisoner. And the jail was an extension of this lieutenant.

My vegan trays were amazing. The commissary was extensive. I was even able to buy white sneakers and get rid those horrible jail slippers. The facility was clean. They steam-washed the showers every two weeks. The medical staff, Corizon, was an outside contractor and treated us with respect. I fully understand that these corporations are profit centers of the prison industrial complex and provide only minimal care, but the alternative was far worse in my experience.

In Dickerson, a woman had fallen off the sink in her cell trying to cover up a light that relentlessly shone in her eyes. It took two weeks before they took her to a hospital with a broken ankle. I had slipped in the showers one day and gashed open my chin. They gave me a Band-Aid to cover the open wound and then the guard screamed at me to go clean up my blood. A woman there had a seizure; she lay in the middle of the dayroom contorting for about 20 minutes before she was still. The Dickerson medical staff wandered in laughing sometime thereafter to check on the unconscious woman.

In DACDC, if we had a medical issue, we put a request in the kiosk and would be called out the same day. If someone had a seizure or other emergency, the guards would lock everyone down and the medical staff would rush into the unit in probably under a minute. They also had a psychiatrist, and counselors available. There were AA classes, parenting classes, a priest would come in to allow the Catholics to go to confession, pastors would come in several times a week to do bible study with the inmates, and there were GED

309

classes. Our uniforms, towels and bedding were changed twice a week. Aramark did our laundry, ran commissary, and prepared our food trays. If there was an issue with my vegan food, I could complain straight to them. Obviously profit-motivated, Aramark would offer the inmates *hot meals* three times a week. This was outside food that the prisoners could buy through Aramark and have delivered. I found this interesting. While, of course, I had no interest in this amenity on a personal level, it did provide me some insight. Aramark not only contracts with penal institutions. They also contract with factory farms, providing uniforms and infrastructure services. It was clear to me how the factory farm excesses were being funneled into jails via Aramark to insulate the abusers' profits. And whether human inmates or nonhuman slaves, we were all a headcount in this complex.

I was placed in general population. It was a large unit with two tiers and between 40 and 60 women on any given day. The ten cells accommodated four women each, so there was always a shortage of beds. I was given a *boat*, a hard-plastic, canoe-shaped platform in which you lay your mat. You live and sleep there. My boat was on the upper tier outside the showers.

I was out in the open and didn't have to lock down at ten with everyone else. I had a *balcony* to look over in the morning when I drank my coffee. And when everyone else was locked in their cells, I had a private bathroom and shower all to myself. Additionally, there were pod workers that would sweep, mop, and clean up 3 times a day. So, I had *maid* service as well. After about three weeks, I was moved into a cell. *Giron* is a legend at DACDC. She's been there about 30 years and is extremely rigid about the rules. I came to understand that she simply will not tolerate anyone trying to make a fool out of her. But Giron knew I loved my boat. And she was really good about moving everyone else into cells first and letting me stay out on the floor as long as possible.

I initially could not stand Giron because of the rules she enforced. But I grew to respect her. And I think we developed something that would have been a friendship outside of DACDC. On the day I was released, she called me over to the guards' booth and made the sign of the cross over me. It brought tears to my eyes. I knew I did not belong in jail. But I was okay here. I came to understand that it was not a function of where I was. My ability to come through everything I had already endured and still be standing tall was a function of who I am.

And the vicious campaign to eradicate my presence outside continued. On December 17, 2014, Judge Kugler said to Steve Best:

> *"The war ends today. I am serious, as I advised your counsel, if the only way I can end this war is to alternate incarceration of both of you, six months at a time in the Dona Ana County Detention Center, I will do that. Do you understand me, Dr. Best?"*

Steve replied, "yes." Yet, after I was in jail, taken off the internet, and silenced, they still couldn't leave me alone. Gary Yourofsky had put up a support post for me and another long-time political prisoner, Marius Mason. He never mentioned Steve Best. He only encouraged his followers to support me:

> *"Camille Marino of Negotiation Is Over/Eleventh Hour was sentenced to 6 months in prison earlier this week. She has been endlessly harassed by our government (and others) for her unwavering activism."*

But Steve Best couldn't leave me alone. He had his lawyer, Jerry Friedman, and the rest of his cult descend on that post. Jerry wrote:

> *"Marino is in jail for violating a restraining order against Dr. Steven Best. Marino tried to use a 'free speech' defense for her threats against and harassment of Dr. Best but that defense was rejected."*

Then Alafair, Ann Parkes, and the rest of the inner circle jumped on to bash me. Natalie Beach, Karen Kline, my friend in the UK, Aran Mattai, and others jumped on to defend me and called out Steve Best as a snitch and collaborator. They were eloquent that

311

Dona Ana County Detention Center (DACDC)

Steve Best was only hurting the animals by having me jailed and that Jerry Friedman should be proud of himself for advancing the vivisectors' agenda. The war raged on for days until Gary finally had to delete the post. If anyone supported me publicly, Steve would have his lawyer and other followers descend upon them.

So what if Kugler said "the war ends today?" I had no access to that court, no access to the Internet, and no access to anything resembling justice at that point. I wrote to Gary profusely apologizing for my stalkers' behavior. I didn't know how to stop them. I also knew that Gary Yourofsky hated all of the self-promotion and nonsense that is Facebook. He had only just created his page days before and the post to support me was one of the first things on his page. He wrote me back and told me I had nothing for which to apologize. And he was never going to stop speaking out for Animal Liberation.

Then I had to remove myself. I knew the war being waged against me would never end. I didn't know how to stop Steve who now had the full authority of the court helping him destroy me. But I did know that the only person over whom I had control was me. I would have to find a way to go on. I had no way of knowing it at this point, but DACDC would be the place in which I would go through a profound personal transformation that would change my life.

March 17, 2015

Almost every day, I've been wanting to record my experiences in the Dona Ana County Detention Center, but I just haven't. I guess I'll try to catch up on the last five or six weeks since I was thrown back in jail on February 3. The jail itself is run like clockwork and very professionally. Compared to Detroit, the guards are courteous, helpful, and respectful. I never lose sight of the fact that they are cops, but they function more like guardians. Except for some Michigan COs who went out of their way to get me online, encourage me, or secure vegan food occasionally, Detroit guards were abusive and gratuitously condescending.

I froze and had goosebumps every single day of my incarceration in Wayne County Jail. In Dickerson I would freeze and shiver all night long. We all would. And it was painful to wake up. I never bought thermals or long johns. I had no desire to wash clothes by hand and make myself at home. I guess I learned to be a minimalist, one pair of underwear that I wore when I walked in the door; I would wash them in the shower and alternate days wearing them. I got by.

I prefer the one-person cells there though. I have three cellmates here, sometimes four. The temperature is comfortable. I have two very thick mats which make a comfortable mattress. There is no black mold on the walls and bedding is changed weekly. My tray is supposed to be 100% vegan but I still see eggs and milk on occasion. And phone calls are reasonable, less than $2 a call. I bought plenty of changes of socks and granny panties this time around. My laundry is done for me twice a week. And I bought a pair of white sneakers from commissary so I don't have to wear those ridiculous shower slippers all day.

On the whole, I am having way too much fun for being in jail. I have a couple of really good friends with whom I know I'll stay in touch as well as several associates with whom I play spades. My group is comprised mainly of women who know how to do their time and stay under the radar. Some of them are long-time convicts or gang-affiliated. Many have associates in a men's prison gang called the *Cruces Boys*. One of my good friends in

313

here is called Loca. I was a little intimidated by her at first. She was itching to fight with someone. Anyone. I've seen her step in the middle of two raging fights to protect our friends. Tiffiny (spelled correctly) looks like the person you have nightmares about coming into jail. She is Big Bertha! Fortunately, she's also my friend.

There are six of us who consider each other family. And in our pod, it's a matter of survival. Since I've been here, there have been three serious attacks. We were raided once by SERT (the Special Emergency Response Team), a bunch of scattered outbursts, and we just had to clean up a lot of blood in our cell yesterday morning. I'll tell you that story in a little bit.

March 21, 2015

I stopped writing the other day because a girl jumped from the second tier and landed on a table unconscious. She is a black girl named Stephanie who identifies as a *boy-girl*, a term that appears to be unique to this region. The vernacular with which I am familiar is *stud*, a term used to describe masculine lesbians. They put a collar on Stephanie and wheeled her out on a stretcher. She was thought to have broken her back but our guard told us that she didn't. All I know about the situation is that she's in here for trying to kill her parents, has been very depressed, and she shaved her head bald on Wednesday.

It's now Saturday morning, about 6:30 am. An interesting side note is that my hair is now GI Jane short. If I had known they had a salon in this jail, I many not have cut my hair off. But as long as it's here, I started clipping my hair very close to my head every few weeks. It is so liberating. I didn't have the time or patience to deal with hair in here again anyway. And now when new inmates first come in, I am regularly mistaken for a boy-girl. I get a lot of attention and it's flattering. A couple of women have serious crushes on me. But everyone knows I'm straight. It was a little uncomfortable at first. Now we laugh about it.

March 24, 2015

Let's talk about the distinguished Judge Darren Kugler. There was a woman in here who he had arrested in courtroom. She and her boyfriend held mutual restraining orders against one another; she had custody of their children. He showed up drunk at her door one night threatening her. She texted him that if he didn't leave her alone she was going to call the cops. Eventually the police had to intervene and the case came before Kugler. He admonished the boyfriend and sent the woman here for violating her restraining order by *threatening* him! Imagine that, Kugler protecting an abuser and throwing the victim in jail. We talked at length about our parallel situations. Because of her children, this woman was being forced to do something that I've had the luxury of not having to consider: grovel before this megalomaniacal jurist. He wanted her to apologize for *disrespecting his authority.* Initially she refused and here we were; however, she has kids at home. She finally conceded and went home in a little over a week.

Las Cruces is small and everyone here seems to know everyone else. I've been privy to a lot of unconfirmed gossip. One girl went to school with Kugler's daughter. She is said to have run away in high school to escape her father's abuse. And Kugler's wife left him a year ago because she could no longer endure his emotional and mental abuse. Having seen the manner in which he conducts his courtroom, I have no difficulty believing any of this.

Judge Kugler's father was a drill sergeant and disciplinarian. It is widely believed from those who have worked with him in his courtroom that he was an abused child who uses his authority to mete out to others that which he endured as a young, helpless victim. I've been reprimanded several times for *disrespecting* his courtroom: once or twice I was not sitting straight in my chair, once he didn't like my facial expression, and another time I had my reading glasses on my head. Eventually I tuned him out; he clearly had his own agenda and telling him to fuck himself would have only allowed him to heap more gratuitous abuse on me.

His abuse is not only reserved for litigants; he is notorious for

denigrating and insulting the lawyers who practice before him.
I've seen this repeatedly with my own eyes.

March 28, 2015

It's Saturday and Tiffiny (Koby) Lomax, Sara (Badass) Contreras, me (New York), and another girl in here have been on 23-hour lockdown since Wednesday. There was a fifth girl in here, four of us who knew how to play spades, so that made the time go by. But she left on Friday. It was also more stressful and claustrophobic with five of us.

Anyway, the guard just buzzed the intercom in our room and said something we didn't understand. Sara and I looked at each other with our jailhouse facials (toothpaste and sugar) as if to ask the other what she said. Koby buzzed back to the guards' bubble and said "we can't understand you." Alvarez buzzed back. She said "Bravo." We all started cracking up.

Tiff is a celebrity in this pod (E6) and all the guards have been congratulating her ever since about 10 days ago when there was the incident in our cell. Tiff (aka Koby aka Chocolate Thunder) has been on disciplinary lockdown ever since. The rest of the pod only joined her a few days ago. And 23-hour lockdown is definitely hard time. The fact that I'm so comfortable with the violence and repercussions speaks to how much jail has changed me. But here's what really happened...

On March 16, Miller was moved into our cell with Lomax, Cabreras and me. Our fourth cellmate is in her bunk sleeping off her depression. She's basically invisible which is good because when she speaks I find her infinitely annoying; I call her *The Princess*. Miller was a problem from the minute she came into the pod. When they put her on the bunk above Tiffiny, she threw a perpetual tantrum – cursing out the guards, provoking everyone; she got locked down the first day she was here. That's really a pain for the rest of us because anytime we need to come in or out of our cell, we need to get a guard to buzz the door to unlock it. We were essentially stuck in here babysitting this woman.

The first night she was here, I had to ask her to control herself because the rest of us did not appreciate her behavior. We had a brief verbal exchange, she apologized and went to sleep. Before I continue, I think it's important to have a mental image of Tiffiny. She is a large black woman with the most innocent smile I've ever seen and a huge sense of humor... until she gets angry. She is 5'8" and about 280 pounds of solid muscle. Contreras is about 5'3" and 160 pounds of solid muscle. She works as a mechanic and roofer and can definitely hold her own. I'm 5'6", about 175 right now and have never been in a fight in my life.

The morning after Miller arrived, we all woke up as usual. Sara and Tiff went downstairs to eat breakfast. I finished working out on the stairs for an hour, took my shower, and came back to my room to finish getting dressed. Miller's insanity escalated from the night before. I'm patting powder on myself and watching her on the bunk across from me start banging on the windows and screaming, calling the guards bitches and spewing a string of profanity. Then she jumped off the bunk and started pounding on the intercom a good 30 times screaming into the guards' bubble, "whore" "cunt" "you ugly bitch" "I want to see your sergeant now." We're both locked in the room together and she was very annoying; maybe a little bit entertaining as well. I expected SERT to storm my room any second.

Dow, the guard in the bubble, buzzed back and said "ma'am, I have to let you know that I'm writing you up again and now you're on *predis* (pre-disciplinary lockdown)." Miller jumped back on her bunk, pounding on the window. Half of the inmates were still asleep; the other half were downstairs eating breakfast. She yells out "fuck you" at no one and everyone. The guards weren't responding. Tiffiny had Dow buzz our room open and she and Sara came back upstairs, in part to make sure I was okay, and then to get the situation under control. The door slammed locked shut behind them. No one could get in or out.

Tiffiny went over to Miller's bunk and with a very pleasant smile asked "what's wrong? Can we talk about it?" Miller screamed something unintelligible in response. Tiff said "look, it's early. Even the girls downstairs are telling you to shut up." Valentina said "fuck them" and continued pounding on the window yelling at everyone to "go fuck yourselves."

Dona Ana County Detention Center (DACDC)

In a split second, I saw the whites of Tiffiny's eyes turn red. I had never seen that before. I stepped in between Tiffiny and Valentina to try to defuse the situation but it was too late. Tiffiny never even looked at me. Her eyes were fixed on Miller. With her right hand, she gently moved me out of the way. She reached up and grabbed Miller by the back of her uniform and said "you don't have to worry about them. You have to worry about me. This is *my* house!"

As if she was pulling the arm on a slot machine, Lomax took Miller from the top bunk to the cement floor in one smooth motion. It happened really fast from there. Tiff took her head and dribbled it across the room; one correctional officer would give her the name *Koby* after learning the details. She bounced the girl's face off the floor, the desk, the toilet, and over to the other side of the room where Sara's mat was on the floor. Lomax pummeled her while the blood ran all over Sara's bed. Sara and I looked at each other. We were suddenly afraid that Tiffiny was going to kill her, but neither of us was even remotely capable of stopping the assault.

Two doors down, Loca jumped out of bed and tried to run to our room with her uniform half on and half off. She didn't know who was getting beaten but, if we needed help, she was going to jump in. All the guards, sergeants, and other uniforms stormed our pod. By the time they got up the stairs and opened the door, Tiffiny had stepped away from the bloodied girl. Her eyes were now white again and she was her usual calm self. Everyone stood around with our eyes glued on Miller as she got to her feet. She brushed her bloody hair out of her face and, to her credit, said to the guards, "everything's alright." They were both taken away in handcuffs.

Later when Tiff was returned to the pod, she got a standing ovation – guards and inmates all standing and applauding her. Unless you are a part of jail culture, it is probably difficult to understand the response. But disrespect is not tolerated on any level behind bars. Tiffiny has been on lockdown and lost two months of good time.

And for a few more days, we're all *caged animals*. Whenever I hear that expression it allows me to connect the dots. I'll get out shortly for my hour to exercise, use the phones, shower, and decompress. Barry Friedman has written me three times a week since I've been in here. He's also put up a support page for me on his site at the University of North Georgia. I talk to Anne and Mike almost every day. I speak to David too, but he's a little uncomfortable on jail phones. And I have colleagues trying to keep Eleventh Hour for Animals alive. But without me being active, my initiatives for the animals are on life support. With the time constraints this week, I can only call one person a day and I need to call Barry. He's been amazing through this whole thing. Everyone has. I am so fortunate to have such amazing people in my life. No one wants my friendship right now because they're getting something out of it. It would be a lot easier and less stressful to just walk away from me. I'm beginning to understand that if some I once called friends had not abandoned and betrayed me, I might never have known the value of having real friends. That's a silver lining; a priceless gift that can't be bought.

I was up the other night while everyone slept, crying inconsolably by myself. I was told that they started blinding monkeys and dogs inside UF. Steve Best has me sealed up in here to silence me. And those individuals will never know that I care. They will probably never know that anyone cares. I must keep my sanity. We will go through with an appeal. I will get through this and I'll come out even stronger. I hope the monkeys can hold on too. As soon as fate allows, I need to document it and tell the world what they are doing.

March 29, 2015

Sunday is always slow and seems to last forever in county. Compound that with being locked in a cell with three other women for 23 hours and I've been dreading today all week. Now I'm almost reveling in it... almost... My cellmates are still asleep. It's probably about 7; the pod is still asleep and you could hear a pin drop. I am embracing my solitude with a cup of black coffee and I so love being able to refocus and catch up.

I am loving myself more and more every day. Despite everything that's transpired over the last three years, when I look in the mirror, I like who I see. I love who I see. I'm proud of the way in which I continue to handle everything that's been thrown at me. I never compromised my beliefs or the mission. I never lied and, contrary to having anything to hide, I look forward to the final publication of this book. I have nothing to hide from anyone. I own my entire journey. And that is liberating.

My story is important on so many levels. I am sitting in jail in the United States of America for doing nothing more than telling the truth, prosecuted under domestic violence laws invoked by a domestic abuser. At the same time, billions of individuals are also on lockdown in their cages, enduring unfathomable forms of torture, being driven insane, their cries and screams silenced behind the concrete walls of their windowless bunkers. We share a journey now; mine, however, is far more benign. We've all been silenced. At least for now. But my voice will rise from these ashes. It will resound for them, for all of us.

I am not having nearly as much success veganizing anyone in here as I did in Detroit jails. When I first got here, two of my old cellmates went vegetarian. They're gone now. And I had a very difficult time with everyone in my cell clinging to their carnism. It's tough. My family and lifelong friends remain flesh eaters. I no longer associate with many. I don't have that option here. I need to deal with my disgust. Tiff and The Princess try to respect me by not talking about meat in front of me. But that's mainly because I had a war with an insipid inmate named Sheila who was in here for a few weeks. If you drink milk or salivate over carcasses in my room, I have an obligation to educate. Uncomfortable as it is sometimes, I take that duty very seriously. It was very heated and contentious in here for a while and now she's gone. I'm pretty sure I'm going to get my ass kicked eventually. I'm not a fighter. But that's okay. Better bruised than coward.

Outside my cell, a woman named Robin woke up one morning, shoved her cup in the toilet downstairs and flooded the bathroom. Then she went over to one of the phones in the dayroom and smashed it against the wall until the receiver shattered. When the guards came in, she charged the first one and hit her once before she was restrained. One of my favorite guards, Rentaria, fell wrong as she took Robin down. She broke her wrist. There was a trail of blood out the door when they took Robin away.

A few days later, our unit was raided by SOG (the Special Operations Group). They stormed our pod and before anyone could move, they were in our cells with guns that cast little red dots of light where they were trained on us. They were dressed in full riot gear and screamed all of their orders. Within seconds, we were all on the floor on our stomachs facing the wall. One by one, we were taken out to go through a portable metal detector that they brought in, we were strip searched by female guards, then taken out to the yard to wait. Incidentally, I've never had to do a squat-and-cough here. Once we were all in the yard, our cells were ransacked. We all knew there was a snitch in the pod. They were looking for a shank. But they found nothing except some pills that one girl had cheeked (hid between her gum and cheek when the nurse administered medication) to sell.

The next day, my friend Val was attacked in her cell two doors down from me. A mother and daughter pair of inmates came in a few days earlier. The mother was a lowlife piece of trash looking for a fight. The daughter was a boy-girl who wanted to be called *Brady* and wanted people to use the pronouns *he* and *him*. They were both here waiting to be extradited back to California. Val had a minor exchange with the mother over a mop that Val carried to go clean her room. Brady ran up the stairs and jumped her in her cell from behind. He beat Val until she was on the floor and then he kicked her over and over again in the head and body. Loca was at our table downstairs. She got up to that room in a matter of seconds. When Brady saw Loca about to take him down, he stepped back from Val. The guards got there and took him and his mother to seg.

One day they put the sister of a snitch in the room next door with one of the federal inmates on whom her sister snitched. They *kited her out* of room 218. Kiting out means you remove yourself or you get your head broken in the shower. The next day we confirmed who the snitch was. Another boy-girl, he was actually caught telling the guards that someone had sharpened an object to deal with matters in 218. Angel (Alatorre's niece) was put on predis and is now awaiting disciplinary action. Now the individual who was giving the guards information about the pod was identified and confirmed; they kited him out of 219, Loca's room. Loca would have killed him.

Since then they put the whole pod on 23-hour lockdown. They found the weapon but they never found the heroin, Xanax, or hooch (fermented orange juice) they were looking for. I had been making hooch in my room too when we were put on lockdown; several of us were. We were planning to have a party. I flushed mine. My cell will remain clean until after we're off lockdown and we get our next shakedown.

Contreras and I are up to doing 100 knee bends and 100 sit-ups every day. Want to get that done now so I can get at least 30 minutes to exercise on the stairs when I get my hour out of my cell today. After a good workout to de-stress and a long shower to revive, I feel brand new.

March 30, 2015

I no longer view this chapter of my life as a distraction from my work, but rather an opportunity to lend a depth and context to the struggle; a perspective that I've earned. In the universe of Animal Liberation, welfare generally refers to a school of thought that advocates for better conditions for the enslaved (e.g., larger cages, anesthetics for gruesome experiments, less pain). Never mistake *welfare* as being analogous to *comfort*. It is largely a form of marketing propaganda. And I summarily reject this approach. But I do so with some personal discomfort; I cannot discuss this subject in the abstract. I am living it. I fight for, and would give my life for, Animal Liberation. That is, I don't believe in humane torture or a kind and gentle holocaust. The cages and chains that bind the slaves need to be opened and destroyed. Freedom from human domination is the sole objective.

Having said that, compared to Wayne County jails, the only thing missing in Dona Ana County is a mint on my pillow when I go to sleep... and the pillow itself is missing as well. The reason is Aramark. They run everything from laundry to commissary to cleaning to maintenance. In fact, not more than 20 minutes ago, one of the employees wearing a uniform with the Aramark logo handed me a fresh, clean uniform. Trustees also work in commissary, laundry, in the kitchen and in maintenance. Each worker spends 20 to 40 hours a week at their jobs and is paid a grand total of $15 for their labor. This is slave labor.

Two of my friends work in commissary. A nameless inmate always packs my order and takes care of me with extra free items in my bag. She also went to the head of the kitchen to make sure my trays are vegan instead of vegetarian. Aramark was insisting on giving me eggs and cheese no matter how much I argued with them. My interest in Aramark has little to do with the manner in which they profit from my incarceration. I'm far more interested in understanding and observing close up how a huge piece of the holocaust infrastructure functions, weaving together human and nonhuman slavery inside the agri-prison/industrial prison complex.

325

Dona Ana County Detention Center (DACDC)

I guess my point is that I enjoy the welfare accommodations afforded me at this facility but never lose sight of the fact that we are all slaves and captives serving to perpetuate profits for the oppressors. And I know that animals will never be afforded anything nearly resembling comfort where their welfare standards are concerned. I don't want them to suffer. But it is very difficult for me to enjoy my own welfare improvements while dismissing welfare improvements for them. Further, I know that activists working toward improving the conditions in which animals are confined are dedicated and genuine. I also draw a line between those selfless advocates and welfare orgs that simply profit from manipulating welfare regulations for their own benefit. If I thought it would help alleviate their suffering, maybe I would change my own course. I don't know. I do know that many who argue against welfare do it from a place of ideological sanctimony, never even considering the consequences of their words. I am no longer afforded this luxury. I carry the weight of understanding this issue on a level most will never know.

April 12, 2015

Something has taken hold and it is entirely new me. It's been growing inside me since my first extradition three years ago, but it's now consumed me. I absolutely love myself. When I look in the mirror every day, I like and respect the person I see looking back and I can't help but tell everyone about this new awareness of being. I know I'm repeating myself. But I can't help it. I've never known such empowerment and I can't keep it to myself. Perhaps out of necessity, perhaps as a function of personal growth, those who slandered, bullied, maligned, and jailed me are so pathetic that, barring having to contend with this situation, they have all become largely irrelevant and wholly insignificant. The only person whose opinion matters to me is my own.

It's like I had some hole inside me that I was always looking for others to fill; I needed validation. I needed others to tell me I was okay. And, suddenly, that hole inside of me was ripped wide open. What I found inside was me. I don't need to see myself through others' eyes anymore. I see myself clearly through my own. And my path is illuminated before me. Everything in the world is possible for me.

We're going forward with our appeal and now I am entitled to an appellate public defender. On Thursday, April 9, we went to court because Steve is opposing me having competent representation. Again, they brought me into court in handcuffs, shackles, a waist chain, and my bright red Teletubby suit. And I smiled. They cannot penetrate my self-esteem. I won't let them. It took me a day or two to bounce back though after having to see my abuser again. I wish he would just go away. I know of no other word than *pathetic*. How pathetic does one have to be to sink to such extreme and dirty tactics solely to silence another? He wanted to drag me across the country and take me to court. Now he wants me to stand in court without a lawyer. In my world, I wake up in sunlight. They can lie about me, put me behind bars, and they have, in fact, taken every dirty shot to break me. But they haven't.

As long as I continue to act with integrity and honor today, I'll never have to be concerned about what anyone has to say tomorrow.

As expected, Judge Kugler refused to appoint me counsel citing some alleged procedural issue. No matter. We officially filed our Notice of Appeal the following day as planned. Anne has been in constant contact with the New Mexico Public Defender's office. I am entitled to representation and they are going to represent me despite Kugler. And when we go back in front of him, if history is any indicator, he will undoubtedly not have a clue what he said last week. He will likely reverse himself again. He seems to rule with little attention to the law as a preponderance of the evidence is not determinative in his court.

We're in the next phase and I can't wait until my appeal is finally filed. I have so much going on when I get home and I'm determined to walk out of here the way I walked into jail for the first time three years ago, happy and healthy. As of last week, I lost 8 pounds and I'm looking toward losing another 26 over the next three months. I'm leaving at 140 and a size 7. If we can set up shop in August in Gainesville, I need to be physically whole and engaged. I'm not sure how to do any effective anti-vivisection activism with this internet ban, but I'll figure it out.

I haven't been writing nearly as much as I think I should, mostly because I'm just having too much fun. Sometimes I laugh so hard that I'm actually crying. We had a lot of April Fool's pranks in here – both the inmates and the guards. We got the night guard to call a Code Mary (medical emergency). One of the inmates who's like a son to me, Little G, laid down at the foot of the stairs and feigned unconsciousness. The guards thought he fell down the stairs. Before our prank, one of the corporals came in and called out 10 women for B&B, (bed and baggage) meaning to pack it up because they're leaving. In this case, B&B was called to roll out to prison. One of the names called was Tiffiny's. All of the inmates were stunned. Why were they taking these women away? And why was Koby being sent back to prison? Then the corporal started laughing, said "April Fool's," and gave everyone a bag of potato chips.

There are also more drugs in here than I've seen since I left New York. Out here they use tar heroin. I'd never even seen it before. Someone showed me how to melt it down and snort it in the bathroom. I hadn't tasted heroin in over a decade. It no longer held any fascination for me. The high was marginal. There's so much meth in here it's unbelievable. Some of the women get arrested just to bring in drugs. I've never done meth and have no desire to try it. But when everyone in the pod is up before me in the morning exercising, you know they're all on meth. There's also a lot of Xanax and Suboxone. I have no comment on how they get into the jail.

April 18, 2015

I pretty much decided that NIO has exhausted its useful life. I'm looking toward a new, fresh start, greater reach, and less liability. I envision a tight-knit global network of activists. And all of my work thus far will serve as the stepping stone upon which the future is built.

April 21, 2015
Without question, the most difficult part of being locked up is knowing that everything you've done for Animal Liberation is dead and, while I'm in here, the animals keep dying. And it's largely impossible to write with the inescapable idiocy all around me in here. Three more months and I'm done.

Dona Ana County Detention Center (DACDC)

April 22, 2015

My friends here stormed a snitch's cell last night. Everyone involved went to seg or is on lockdown. My tattoo artist was taken away. I guess it'll be a little while before I get my first tat. Lost two more pounds as of Monday, way less than I expected, but I'm happy to be 10 pounds lighter.

My appellate public defender was finally appointed. Her name is Theodosia Johnson. So now Anne can finally officially come in as co-counsel. Almost the entire weight of my case has been on her shoulders. And while I'm grateful and indebted for everything she continues to do, I am more than a little relieved that the bulk of the burden will hopefully shift back where it belongs. I will be elated about this as soon as I sort out some very disturbing news I just received: Budkie is back in Gainesville and did his annual welfare protest 2 weeks ago. Not thrilled with the thought of another collaborator re-emerging while I'm in here. But that's the whole point of trying so hard to eradicate me, isn't it? Back to business as usual and making sure no one disturbs the status quo.

Vivisectors keep killing.

Welfarists keep telling the public they're making sure the animals are protected in the labs.

And everyone gets rich on their blood and pain.

April 28, 2015

Yesterday I received documents from Steve's lawyer contesting my appointment of an appellate public defender. Even though I'm penniless and I'm in jail, he claims I should be denied representation because I paid my lawyer $5000 in 2014. This individual pays more attention to my affairs than I do. Just his latest effort to use the legal system as a bat with which to keep bashing me. We'll see what happens. But there's some really good news here. This man who has made himself a cancer, who has relentlessly stalked me and done everything in his power to cause me harm, no longer has any power over me. I feel sorry for him. What a sad existence it must be when your sole purpose in life – your fatal obsession – is trying to keep another person silent. My words, my truth, my entire being is too much of a threat to this man to co-exist in the same universe. He keeps swatting at me. Yes, it is unpleasant. But I really feel sorry for him today.

The show *Criminal Minds* is about FBI profilers who work to stop serial killers. On one episode, the subject was a malignant narcissist. It struck a chord with me when one of the profilers advised a peripheral character to not challenge the killer. When the malignant narcissist's ego is damaged, said the profiler, they become very dangerous; obsessed with destroying the person who dared to unmask them. When the facade slips away, there's nothing left for them. Could this be what I'm dealing with?

Jail is very transitory and people are always coming and going. One woman named Audrey Keding came in. She's in Loca's room. The first thing she bought from commissary was a deck of cards, just like me. Audrey and I are both up early in the morning, we have our coffee, we laugh and get a lot of dirty looks while others are sleeping, and we're spades partners now. I am an excellent player, a skill that is very useful in jail. Audrey is an excellent player also. And I think we have never won a single game. We're always laughing too much. She walks up behind people and starts humping them in the dayroom. And we give people jolly ranchers if they'll take our dares.

A woman named Amanda Vargas was assigned to my cell. She's

in jail for parking tickets! Two months. But I'm so glad she's in my room. We can actually have an intelligent conversation. She's been in a really bad place because the man with whom she lives betrayed her while she's in here. I know she has to go through it in her own time, but I also know that once she gets over Daniel, she will be free to go forward and find someone worthy of her.

Amanda is in here for tickets. I'm in here for having a Facebook war. How would we even begin to explain? When people ask us what we did, sometimes we tell them we went to Seaman's and tore all the tags off the mattresses. It's a felony. The looks of disbelief we get are hysterical. Other times we tell people we did a drive-by. Is it really any dumber than our real charges? Once I was playing cards with a woman I call *Abuella* (grandma). She is about 20 years younger than I, she's not a grandmother, but I just like the way the word sounds. So she became Abuella. A new girl came in and sat with us. She asked why we were there. I said I sold Abuella my children to use in child pornography. And Abuella didn't miss a beat. She said, yeah, when the cops raided her house, they found all the videos. The girl started to cry. She had been abused as a child. We felt kind of bad. Then we went to my room and laughed. Jail has changed me; I'm a little appalled at my own reaction.

I've been seeing a counselor every two weeks since I got here and I'm grateful for the opportunity. I've wanted to talk to someone for a while but haven't been able to afford it. I'm working on forgiving Steve and it has nothing to do with him. I simply want to go forward uncontaminated by him and I need to let go of any anger that keeps me connected to him. He's making it very difficult. In an ideal world, I would finish this book, finish telling my story – hopefully give a voice to the enslaved animals in the process – and go forward. I'd like to close this chapter of my life. It's doubtful that he will ever move on though so I need to come to a place within myself where I'm okay, despite having him constantly grabbing for my ankles trying to drag me back. I see my counselor again on Monday night and in 6 days I'll also find out how much more weight I lost. My homework was to write a letter forgiving Steve Best. After our session, I'll flush it. But I think I'll write it this weekend after I process all of my feelings.

Meanwhile, the utter idiocy and inanity in here was starting to get to me. I couldn't even think, let alone write. Amanda and I are each other's refuge. We can talk. Go to our room and shut the door to keep the morons out. Or just sit together and read. There's always methamphetamine in the pod. I'll direct some of the traffic between people I trust to keep my cellmates out of the line of snitches or other prying eyes, but I have no desire to try it myself. I don't even know what it looks like. Suboxone strips are in here pretty frequently as well. It is unreal how many drugs and how much alcohol are in this unit every week. `

I finally decided to do a Suboxone strip last Thursday. As soon as it kicked it, I got called out of my pod to go see the psychiatrist. I meet with him once a month while I'm in counseling and didn't realize that was my day. Normally, we discuss everything from living in New York to my politics to why he rejects veganism. It's refreshing to have an intelligent conversation occasionally. When I sat down in his office that Thursday, my only concern was to stay focused and not nod off. I told him I just finished exercising and was really tired; that he just caught me at a bad moment. He knows about my rigid exercise routine so it was plausible. I'm really not sure whether he knew I was high or not, but he let me go back to my pod without staying the full hour. That was pretty intense. Anyway, Loca and I were out of our minds for two days. I had a blast. I needed it. But by Saturday I was straight and feeling like me again. Our tier was making hooch all week for Saturday night. By the time it was ready, I didn't even want any. While I was exercising Sunday morning, I was amused that the whole upper tier was unconscious and hungover from the night before. Amanda doesn't get high. And Audrey is staying sober. Being in this unit is a tremendous test for anyone struggling with an active addiction.

Got a letter from my friends in Israel. One of them is in the states and will visit me. Even though my stalkers forced Gary to take down his support post, I have had two people visit me here simply because he asked his followers to reach out to me. I must have gotten 50 letters because of Gary's support alone. And Natalie and Ziv are finally getting married now that the Mazor monkeys are free. I love Natalie and am honored to call her a friend. She is an amazing person. And even though we live on different continents, we have developed a deep and sincere friendship talking to one another on Skype. I'm told that the Israelis broke into an egg factory and liberated the chickens. They also shut down the shredder that the live male chicks are thrown into to dispose of them. This is standard practice on egg farms across the globe. Male chicks cannot produce eggs so they are thrown away like trash and endure excruciating deaths being shredded to death.

April 29, 2015

I am allowing myself time to heal and am really trying to take care of myself. I fully understand that I can do nothing for the animals unless I am whole. Nonetheless, the guilt of taking this time from them is burdensome.

I spoke to Anne this morning and our docketing statement will be filed by next Friday, May 8. I know nothing about the appeals process but am learning as we go along. In New Mexico, the trial lawyer, John Watson, is required to submit a docketing statement to the trial court outlining the issues going up for appeal. Anne will write it. John will file it. The Appeals Court will then be alerted and decide whether the case will be expedited or given a full appeal. We want the later and hope to make good law, although a full appeal means this can easily stretch out a full two years. The issues in this case are complex and deal with fundamental Constitutional rights that, in my case, are rescinded at the moment. Anne is brilliant and I don't know what I would do without her. She relayed a message for me to call David tonight. I don't know how I got so lucky to be surrounded by such amazing friends. But I am feeling incredibly fortunate and grateful. And Mike sent me an *ICare* package with Maxwell House as a present because I am now officially conserving money. He said I needed something to enjoy while I'm here.

April 30, 2015

I had a sobering discussion with Anne this morning. Now that we're moving into the appeals phase, I could not understand how the appellate court could rule against me. But the reality is not what has been presented in court for three years. When Steve Best betrayed me in 2012, I had a total emotional breakdown. He not only left me hanging to take a felony for his essay, but ran to my colleagues to begin to rewrite history. And he ran to the state with the same lies. All that remains on the record is *evidence* of my *stalking* him; my defense was never entered. And it may never be.

The starting point for the appeals court is that I'm an unbalanced individual who stalks college professors, Steven Best and his vivisector friends. Under this restraining order, I cannot do anything to cause my *victim* emotional distress. Were it not for this fact, nothing I have said or done would be even remotely actionable. In 2012, Joy Goldbaum said she could protect his physical safety, not his reputation. Somewhere along the line, Steve Best's reputation became synonymous with his physical safety. Steven Best, PhD fears truth. And this is why I'm here. The First Amendment issues in this case are extremely complex. And I'm still getting a grasp on this. I maintain that I did nothing wrong; that I acted with honor. Unfortunately, the courts don't seem to care.

May 1, 2015
Brutus is hopefully getting a new puppy today. Some woman who lives across from my father-in-law bought a pit bull puppy for $200 rather than adopt one from a shelter. And now, the 7-week old puppy is too "yappy." He has too much energy so she doesn't want him anymore. So typical. And so sad. Mike should be bringing Brutus over there right now to see if they get along. Max has Jazz. Brutus needs a friend too. I'm so excited.

May 2, 2015

Very difficult to write today. So maybe that's why I probably should.

This appeal is a complete uphill battle and the reality is setting in. John is a really nice guy and I am indebted to him for standing by me. But this case was so far outside of his area of competence that I basically had no representation in the courtroom. Best recited his hours-long diatribe over and over and over again without objection and little to no challenge on cross. And where we did try to enter evidence, Steve's lawyer and the judge shut us down at every turn. My story was never told. Our evidence was never admitted. His lies comprise the record. The truth is lost to posterity.

I understand my case is on a new frontier as far as the Internet goes and we might eventually have to go to the Supreme Court. David says to let him and Anne do this appeal and to just stay strong. Anne has done the bulk of this since day one at great personal cost. David has probably invested hundreds of hours as well. I could not ask for better friends or legal counsel. Nonetheless, I am fighting off tears all day. I need relief. I want to be the fuck out of here already. I want my life back. And just for today, I'm allowing myself a little empathy for myself. This is all so unfair. Isn't that odd? I'm so removed from my own emotions that I need to empathize with myself. I'm supposed to be writing a letter to forgive Steve this weekend. But I think this is something I need to discuss with my counselor on Monday. I just want to cry. But I can't.

Brutus jumped up on the bed with his tail between his legs when Mike brought the puppy home. Then he warmed up and they played for 1 ½ hours last night. That made me smile. Max and Jazz are pretty disinterested with the new arrival. I'll be happier about all this tomorrow.

May 3, 2015

Spent a lot of time thinking and feeling sorry for myself yesterday. And I had to take myself out of my own skin and think about this as if I were giving advice to a third party. If a woman were being battered and abused on an ongoing basis, it would be foolish to expect her to forgive her abuser and go on with her life as if she weren't being battered. The correct course of action would be to extricate herself from the situation, neutralize the threat to the best of her ability, and *then* forgive him and let it go.

I may well lose my appeal. I may win and gain some relief. Either way, the situation cannot get worse than what it is now. Steve Best insists upon keeping us attached at the hip courtesy of the legal system. I am not forgiving him today. I'm considering going to the Florida police when I get home and opening a formal investigation into the relentless stalking and hacking to which I've been subjected. This is a malicious prosecution. He is abusing process. And that may be my only recourse to make them all leave me alone once and for all.

Today I am back to my old self. I am whole and healthy. Brutus loves his puppy who will probably be named Petey. Max and Jazz not so much. But the puppy jumps all over the Brut's blockhead and Brutus just rolls over and plays with him. This morning they went to the field and he ran all over trying to catch Petey. But the puppy was too fast.

Life is good. And I can't wait to be home.

May 6, 2015

Big news is that I lost another 4 pounds; that makes 14 pounds total. I now weigh 160, exactly what I weighed when I did my CD at Wayne State in May of 2012. I've turned the clock back exactly 3 years and shed all the weight, trauma, and toxicity I'd taken on. About another 10 or 20 pounds to go; and along with renewed energy and spirit, I'll be just about in the shape I was before I was ever arrested. I feel good.

Just got off the phone with Anne and she is absolutely brilliant. The docketing statement is taking shape and we're arguing several issues and/or errors of the lower court. I'll be able to discuss it more accurately after it is filed and I have a hard copy. My colleague is researching the new experiments at UF and locating the animals that are being blinded in their labs. Is it any wonder they're making noise about handing over the records and pictures again? If we have to sue a fourth time, so be it! I'm sure the vivisectors thought they were off the hook with me in here, courtesy of their fellow college professor. It's so much easier being here knowing someone is at least *trying* to help them outside.

Had a very productive session with a new counselor. I was using the word *forgiveness* as the elusive goal I was looking toward. But she observed more accurately that what I was really describing was wanting to reach the point of complete *indifference* on the subject of Steve Best. I want no connection whatsoever.

May 15, 2015

It's been a fairly somber day; not sad, just pensive and introspective I guess. Today I learned that the entire NM judicial system is a rubber stamp operation and our chances of winning on appeal are roughly 10% - 20%. But I have to believe that we will fall through that window. My appeal will be one that merits close judicial review and reversal. I am going to win my appeal. Period.

If I had paid $100,000 to an attorney, no one could have done a more thorough and effective job of stating a more compelling case in such minute and meticulous detail than Anne and David. She spent at least an entire weekend transcribing hours of every single hearing in this case, from 2012 through 2015, analyzed 100s of exhibits, found inconsistencies and arguments of which I was unaware, and prepared a docketing statement quoting major and significant portions of the proceedings and rulings.

The Issues Outlined in Our Docketing Statement:

1. Whether or not Judge Kugler erred in ruling that my intent was irrelevant when deciding that I stalked and harassed Best. I spoke truthful words. If he felt harassed by the truth, that is not a burden I should have had to bear. And by law, I would have had to have intended to stalk and harass him;
2. Whether the district court violated my first amendment rights and deprived me of a defense by not allowing me to present and testify about our evidence;
3. Whether the district court violated my constitutional rights by banning me from the Internet without any compelling state interest whatsoever;
4. Whether I was denied my freedom of speech and right to due process by the Court's failure to make clear that my speech would be interpreted as a violation of the domestic violence protection order;
5. Whether the district court erred in determining that I had forfeited my first amendment rights by sending angry emails in 2012.

If anyone ever had a chance to prevail on appeal, I do. Yet I

343

can't shake the reality of the system in which I am ensnared. I remember talking about my UF appeal in 2012 and saying that I needed a win. The animals needed a win. Well those sentiments were never truer than they are tonight.

I've not had much success here imparting any substantial or significant enlightenment. But I am now navigating two avenues that may allow me to transcend this resistant population. First, I'm beginning a GED prep course on Sunday at 6. I have 10 women signed up to start with. And to teach them reading comprehension and writing skills, as well as grammar, I am deviating from the standardized material. I'm preparing reading and discussion exercises that will touch upon animal slavery and the barbarity of the conventional food system. But I will not proselytize. They will simply read the material and summarize it in writing. Of course, I can only assess their work for grammar, sentence structure, and spelling. But this will also allow me to make greater inroads with three younger women that I am mentoring in here.

Next, Alatorre essentially runs the women's jail, reporting only to the captain. All the sergeants, corporals, and guards report to her. She's a very devout Christian for whom I have a lot of respect. One morning when I was waiting to get my hair clipped, she and I began talking. She went to Amazon to see my book on there, of course she couldn't order one as it's out of print, but from there we developed a friendly rapport. I was in her office this morning and we were talking about all kinds of things, our lives, our work, my mission. And inevitably the subject of her faith came up. I told her I was an atheist. We had a very intense discussion. She asked me if I would be willing to speak to a friend of hers with whom I share a very similar abusive childhood; this woman was also an atheist at some point and is now one of her religious advisers of sorts. Her name is Veronica.

Alatorre told Veronica that she was going to write a book about her experiences in this jail. The lieutenant asked me to come up with a title for her book. The first thing that came to mind that seemed to describe what she had related to me was *The Spirit Behind Bars*. I will read it when it's published. And given the communication between us, I am anxious for the opportunity to meet Veronica. I want to challenge the deeply-ingrained tenet that humans have some celestially-ordained duty to consume other beings. Maybe nothing will come of it. Maybe something will. Alatorre is a woman of conviction. I have no desire to debate the bible or the human-crafted concept of dominion. My goal is to educate these women about the horrors of the holocaust and then challenge them to reconcile for me how a loving creator would condone the abject torture to which we subject his creations. My dream is that this would become the first vegan jail. But that's just a fantasy. I guess it remains to be seen whether I can influence some kind of change here.

May 20, 2015

Haven't seen the lieutenant yet or followed up. GED classes start tonight. Lost 18 pounds so far but had to cut my exercise short yesterday. I'm blowing out my knees climbing stairs roughly 60 to 90 minutes a day. Very painful. Needed to take 24 hours to recuperate. Will resume tonight. Also allowing myself 24 hours to eat an extra chili Ramen, beans, or granola bars for comfort. It's okay. No guilt. I'm now 156, roughly at my pre-arrest weight. Proud of myself. And feeling good.

I heard over the weekend that I'm "bad as fuck," a high honor in here. I think I'm arguably *dumb as fuck*. Some woman named Herrera was sent down from prison to go to trial on a new charge. And she's typical of countless emotionally-stunted individuals I've seen erupt in here; grown women prone to tantrums and angry, volatile outbursts just itching for a fight. She was here about three weeks and the tension was palpable. They finally took her out yesterday. Amanda and I were shocked one day when we were talking and Herrera turned around and said "I don't want to brag, but my son's been in prison since he was 14." I thought to myself, "Well, you must be very proud!" I need not say any more about this woman's mentality. That statement says it all. And the fact that Amanda and I are among the few who find that statement disturbing says even more about incarceration culture.

About the third day she was here I was watching CNN and she yelled out in the middle of the dayroom "these bitches got no respect. Why's the tv on so loud?" I looked her straight in the eyes and said "because I'm watching it and I'd appreciate it if you could keep your voice down." I never raise my voice and I never equivocate. She didn't beat me up. She actually shut up and treated me with respect thereafter.

Over the weekend, two 20-year-olds were put in the cell with Amanda and me. Tiff finally left a few weeks ago. And these girls weigh about 100 pounds soaking wet. Apparently, Herrera went after them for walking up the stairs too loudly. I was in my cell so didn't see anything. But when they came in to our room, they were afraid to go back out. I probably would have left it alone but she was downstairs in the dayroom still yelling, cursing, and pointing to my room. Everyone is quiet and watching. I was about to go down the stairs to talk to her when the guard in the bubble, Sanchez, buzzed the intercom to call me back to my room. Sanchez says "don't go down. She'll punch you in the face." I said, "yeah, maybe" and went down.

I had a tissue in my hand. I walked right over to the table where she was yelling and screaming, sat down, and started folding up my tissue to put in my pocket. I said "what's the problem, Jennifer?" She said something like "they weren't little girls when they came in here and now they want to run to their room. This is some baby shit. They're running on the stairs while I'm sleeping." "They *are* little girls, the stairs are here for us to go up and down, and it's 2 o'clock in the afternoon. If there's another problem, let's sit down and discuss it like women." "This isn't your business, New York." "Those girls are in my room and I just made it my business." You could have heard a pin drop. All eyes in the pod are on us. My voice stayed soft and controlled. She was getting louder. Out of the corner of my eye, I saw three guards inside the bubble watching. We were all sure I was dead. But I needed to make my point and be understood. I cringed internally at the next words that escaped from my mouth, "Look, I'm not a fighter and I'm not even gonna front. If you wanna swing on me like a fucking lunatic, then you do what you have to do. But don't ever think you're gonna intimidate me or bully anyone in my room." Silence. "The stairs are here to walk on. I will make sure they're respectful in the mornings when the pod is quiet. Okay?" We shook hands and smiled. The next morning I heard the *bad as fuck* comments. Herrera was ultimately sent to seg after she swung on a guard.

Making a lot of progress with my counselor. A lot more I want to write but it's about 4:30 am. I want to have some black coffee and enjoy some me time before everyone wakes up. In an hour, they'll buzz my door so I can come out and exercise while everyone sleeps. I really appreciate the guards here. They try to make this as bearable as possible for all of us.

Dona Ana County Detention Center (DACDC)

May 24, 2015

When I saw my counselor last, I mentioned Gabby and was shocked at how choked up I got. I was surprised to even hear her name try to escape my lips. I couldn't speak. To my utter surprise, I was fighting back tears and had no idea why. My counselor suggested I write Gabby a letter to process my feelings. It wound up being cathartic:

Dear Gabby,

While I'm in jail this time, I view it as something like being inside my own cocoon. By the time I emerge on July 20, my metamorphosis will be complete. Physically, I lost 18 pounds at last weigh-in so far with a goal of losing another 11 – 16 pounds more. Aside from being healthier and more comfortable with myself, to me it represents turning back the calendar about 3 ½ or 4 years, to before all the arrests, betrayals, attacks, and stress that took its toll on me. It's about releasing all the toxicity I allowed into my life and that I absorbed into my being.

I'm very fortunate to be working with an amazing counselor that is helping me heal. And no one was more surprised than I that tears began to fill my eyes when your name came up last week, much like they are again now. But I think these are cleansing tears.

A lot of people I thought were friends have betrayed me and turned on me over the past 3+ years. I really couldn't care less about the whole lot of them. You're different. We called ourselves sisters and I loved you like one. I still do. You are a tremendous activist. I celebrate anyone's success fighting for the animals, more so with you. And I was always proud to have you as a friend.

After my first arrests in 2012, I was arguably the most celebrated activist – definitely one of the highest profile people – in our movement. Several animals were liberated in Spain and in the UK and named after me.

There were several solidarity demos across Europe and in the states. I never asked for the accolades, but the global support was overwhelming. Everyone wanted to be my friend. You really were.

Six months later when Steve betrayed me and the vicious hate campaign started, my community imploded. It was no longer popular to support me. The hangers on fell away and moved on to the next big thing. Facing prison and under unprecedented attacks, I had a complete nervous breakdown. I know it was difficult to be around me at that time, but I won't apologize for my behavior anymore. It was my breakdown and I had to go through it in my own time. You disappeared from my life. Never once wrote me in jail. Never inquired of anyone to find out if I was okay. You forgot about me.

When I was free again and wrote you in 2014, we spoke about all of this and I was genuinely happy that we had mended our friendship. I think you were too. I loved re-posting all of our pics together on Facebook. And it was so good to see you this year on the weekend before I came back to jail. But I've been in here 4 months and, to the best of my knowledge, you've not even put up my support page on your profile nor have I heard from you a single time. I know you're busy and writing letters sucks. But that's not an excuse. I deserve more. People I don't even know personally have spent time and energy to seek me out and offer encouragement. And the people who remain in my life now are those I know I can truly count on. I am very fortunate.

I came to the table with a lot of baggage. My father abandoned me before I was born. My mother never wanted me. I was a burden. I've carried that throughout my life. I always felt like I was in the way, worthless, and certainly didn't deserve to ask for anything from anyone. This is something I'm leaving here in my cocoon when I emerge. Irrespective of what anyone thinks, says, how

Dona Ana County Detention Center (DACDC)

they act, or how circumstances around me may change, I finally know my own value. I love myself. I respect myself. I am proud of myself. And I will accept nothing less from those in my life. Because I deserve it. And I deserved more from you.

When I get home, we will continue shooting the documentary and I expect to be in South Florida. If we see each other, it will make me happy. And if not, that will be okay too. But we'll never be friends again. At least not without a sincere apology and acknowledgement of all that's transpired. I hold no grudges and I was never angry. But now that I've finished writing, I'm not even hurt. I still love you. That hasn't changed. The only thing that has changed is what I'm willing to accept from others.

June 7, 2015

I wrote my letter about two weeks ago. And I feel like my story – the person I've become – is now complete. A free speech case before the Supreme Court, *Elonis v. the United States*, was decided last week. Anthony Elonis' conviction for posting threatening material on his Facebook page was overturned. Since one of the issues we're appealing is specific intent, this is very good news for us. Elonis was expressing himself, just like me. He did not intend to threaten anyone, just like me. And the Supreme Court ruled in his favor. Pretty good authority. But we're in New Mexico, so who knows.

My appeal can take between 3 months and 2 years. Irrespective of my appeal, Petitioner in this case is determined to keep us joined at the hip with his domestic violence restraining order. He will be obsessed with me for the rest of his life. I, however, am free and I am vindicated within myself. My path is not determined by nor contingent upon the actions of my abuser. I have risen above all of this. I am happy.

When I began writing this book, I was filled with hubris... "look at me" ... "I'm the warrior princess" ... My sincere and genuine goal was to free the slaves. It still is. But I had so much baggage that I've carried through life weighing me down. It's very chaotic to go through life judging yourself and getting your validation according to others' yardsticks. I no longer suffer from this condition. And it's taken me getting to this point to understand that it was solely my own responsibility for allowing myself to be manipulated by my former mentor. I don't fault him. He is who he is and has to take his journey alone, as do we all. But now I know my own worth.

I love myself. I follow my own drummer. And even though I'll be 51 in a month, this is the first time in my life that I really know who I am. Whether others love me or hate me, approve or disapprove, is inconsequential to me. Some will follow. Some will turn away. Some will applaud. Some will hiss. And the animals will keep dying. I hope the entirety of my experience, this book, will provide the vehicle that will allow me to enlighten others about the animals' plight.

I've always had an equal need to expose Steve as much as to tell my own story. I no longer do. I have no anger, no hostility, no hatred. In fact, today I can forgive Steve Best. This is my story. It's about what I've learned. And he was only incidental to my journey.

As of last week, I weighed 151 and lost a total of 23 pounds so far. I'm certain I've broken 150 by now. Can't wait to get home and back into my size 7s. I have nothing more to say.

Until the animals are free...

*If you know the enemy and know
yourself you need not fear the
results of a hundred battles.*
-Sun Tzu

Conclusion

Two weeks before I was released from jail on July 20, 2015, I was moved to a semi-segregation unit. After Tiffiny, Loca, Amanda, Audrey, and a few others were gone, a big woman named Crystal Baca decided she wanted control of my room. Having already clashed repeatedly over the vegan issue, she became overtly hostile. One night, she began waving her hands in my face as I tried to sleep, taunting me with "meat, meat, meat... I love meat." I sat up and said "go fuck yourself, Baca." Her two friends left our room slamming the door shut behind them. Crystal refused to throw the first punch, choosing instead to tell me how much she enjoyed eating dead animals. I calmly responded that "you wear your acne well" and "enjoy your obesity." If she was intent upon provoking a physical confrontation and knowing I would take a serious beating, I suggested we go to the showers where there are no cameras. Typical of the procession of cowards with whom I had dealt over the past several years, *she* chose to run to the guards instead.

When Alatorre moved me out of my room the next day, she told me "they're all uncomfortable eating meat in front of you." I was quite proud of myself. Flesh-eaters need to be relegated to dark alleys like smokers. I was moved into a private cell in E5 where they house problem inmates. Baca was moved into a boat in the middle of the E6 dayroom floor where the guards could watch her. There is absolutely no worse place in this jail than on a boat in front of the guards' bubble in the middle of the dayroom; it's loud, inmates walk over and around you all day; there is no privacy at all, and I think I would find it maddening. I laughed with Alatorre a few days later that "I heard Baca got what she wanted; she's now the captain of her boat." I lost 35 pounds by the time I walked out of jail, transformed both physically and mentally.

Days before I was released, I was served with papers from Dr. Steven Best who had chosen to initiate civil proceedings. The scribbled documents seemed to reflect a frantic state of mind. It was unclear about exactly for what he was seeking remedy – defamation? stalking? It was abundantly clear, however, that in the court system he had found a vehicle to perpetuate his obsession, maintain a hold on me, and continue his abusive campaign. Jerry Friedman is not only enabling Best's behavior but is, in fact, now representing him. David Tenenbaum is my attorney of record and has already appeared in court telephonically in New Mexico several times. I have not. Just as I tried to run interference between the animals and their tormentors, David is now running interference to keep Best and Friedman away from me.

For four individuals who only know one another because we are vegan and allege to fight for Animal Liberation, one must note that neither Best nor Friedman have ever devoted a fraction of the energy they direct at me to stopping any single animal abuser. David and I, on the other hand, have watched in horror and sadness as they've repeatedly betrayed everything in which we believe.

David successfully had that first civil assault thrown out of magistrate court without my ever having to engage. Jerry Friedman then chose to reinforce Best's efforts by refiling as his attorney of record in District Court. Those proceedings are on hold pending the outcome of my appeal.

It has become clear to me that I challenged the patriarchy and now I stand virtually alone against its wrath. My challenge is to remain focused on myself, trusting that my inner strength will keep me grounded irrespective of the chaos this man continues to create around me. I have considered simply defaulting on the civil suits. I do not wish to be on call for my abuser's whims.

To put everything in perspective, when I was freed from probation in January of 2014 and began to refocus on shutting down the University of Florida's monkey labs, the records I secured indicated that every single monkey experiment was to end by October 2016. Raymond Bergeron was retiring and his victims would likely go to a sanctuary. But it was critical to make sure that the balance of monkeys not become the subject of new experiments and that no new monkeys were brought into the labs. I firmly believe it had simply become too much of a liability to continue; they demonstrated this premise to be true by the time, energy, and money they devoted to stopping me. That was a victory I wanted to declare more than anything. I wanted to celebrate the day those labs shut down.

With my voice and my campaign having been all but eradicated by the combined efforts of the vivisectors and Dr. Steven Best, those monkeys are currently involved in new experiments for at least the next 5 years, being poisoned, maimed, and now, blinded. Steven Best could not have accomplished this without the dedication and commitment of Jerry Friedman. And the vivisectors should forever remain grateful to their new comrades.

Since learning about the new experiments, my colleagues have filed numerous records requests. And since the University of Florida now provides these documents online, I can neither submit the requests nor obtain the documents without violating Kugler's order. William Hauswirth is blinding dogs and may or may not be blinding monkeys as of this date. We have no way of knowing since the court deemed his experiments *proprietary information*, thus, upholding UF's decision to withhold that documentation from Eleventh Hour. They're also withholding records documenting the *Column E* (intentional pain) experiments to which they are subjecting horses. My very first arrest was UF's response to my penetrating their labs and publishing their secrets. This entire exercise has been about silencing me so that others could keep their secrets as well. Ironically, Dr. Steven Best is the only person who stands between the vivisectors and me today. The real tragedy is that the animals are paying the ultimate price with their blood.

I wake up some mornings feeling the extraordinary weight of everything to which I've been subjected, my work destroyed, my reputation decimated, nothing but lies having been disseminated by Steve Best and his camp to discredit me, his talking points still available all over the internet, my presence extinguished, having been jailed for telling the truth, having been jailed for defending myself, having been muzzled upon penalty of further incarceration if I merely try to set history straight.

In the middle of the night when it's only me and my thoughts, I know the animals are dying and I failed them. But I would do nothing differently, with the exception of employing some wisdom over poor judgment. While the full wrath of the state, the patriarchy, the bullies, and the inner circle were sabotaging my work, hacking my sites, and destroying my credibility, I was told by a colleague to "go take a walk and meditate because you're not helping the animals right now." All those who sat back and watched it happen, who stayed silent or looked away, share the responsibility of having allowed a cancer to flourish. In hindsight, we can see clearly that the tormented animals have been the true beneficiaries of everyone's actions as well as inaction. Martin Luther King, Jr. said that it's not the attacks of our enemies that we will remember, but the silence of our friends. And the silence of my *friends* is memorialized in Gabby's words to me, indelibly etched in my brain: "I am a very well-respected activist..." and can't get involved.

I live in exile from my community, not even speaking to another person for days sometimes. Entering the third year of this crushing isolation inside my virtual prison is brutal. In the morning when I open my eyes, I am usually first aware of the constant headache with which I live, the physical manifestation of all of the stress. Sometimes I need to close my eyes and go back to sleep for an hour until I can shift my thinking and wake up in the right state of mind. I must wake up grateful for my strength and integrity and happy to be alive. I must wake up knowing that even if the whole world is attacking me, I have to hide from no one. That is an extraordinary freedom for which I've paid a very high price. I am grateful for my home, my freedom, my dogs, and the friends I have upon whom I know I can count. I'm grateful for the people in my life that believe in me and give me strength. This is priceless.

Then I walk from my bedroom to the couch where I turn on the TV and wait for another day to expire, endless hours punctuated only by walking my dogs. Each day takes me one day closer to resolution and my challenge is to use this downtime to prepare myself for the day when I will emerge rather than let it destroy me. Now more than ever, I need to take care of myself lest I fall back into destructive habits, thus accomplishing my enemies' agenda for them. I put myself together and head to the gym to work off the stress, go swimming to enjoy the fresh air and sunshine, and appreciate my health and freedom. I know I'm stronger than this circumstance and simply need to see it through. And after months of filling up my days however I may, I return to my routine of dragging myself out of bed and into the living room to stare vacantly at a TV.

A few days ago, Camille Perry said to me that when this is over, my story will inspire others who are facing overwhelming challenges to stand their ground. That meant a lot to me. I also touched base with Jessica Vale who said "the icing on the cake will be to see you back involved and active." On the days when I might allow myself to weaken momentarily, these simple words from others empower me and allow me to keep my perspective.

After I was home for a few weeks, Jerry Friedman wrote to David in August of 2015 demanding that information about his client that remained online for over 2 years be removed from Twitter and NIO or he would drag me back across the country. Even though Judge Kugler banned me from the Internet, even though if I even touched my own websites I would be put back in jail for violating the court order, Best and Friedman were threatening to put me back in jail if I didn't violate it. I ultimately had someone take down my NIO website and my Twitter account. I decided that the sites were not helping the animals at this point and I had long ago decided that NIO had run its useful course. I just want these men to leave me alone. NIO is still actually fully intact. I may or may not put it back up in the future.

In September of 2015, Jerry Friedman wrote to David Tenenbaum to *negotiate*. Steve Best would stop litigating against me if I promised to never write my book or tell my story. In the alternative, they would continue to extort my silence, promising that they intended to "harm her credit and any other financial ambitions" with civil suits. Essentially, he suggested that, after having taken a felony conviction over Steve Best's graphic essay, having been betrayed by him, having my campaign, websites, and work sabotaged and shut down, having been subjected to a comprehensive campaign of bullying, harassment, character assassination, stalking, incarcerations, and, now, repeated malicious prosecutions, that if I promise never to tell my story they will leave me alone. My one-time friend has repeatedly gone into court invoking the names of David Jentsch and Donal O'Leary, aligning himself over and over again with his fellow "college professors." It's very sad that every time Dr. Steven Best opens his mouth, it gives him even more reason to need to silence me.

I do not wish to be a free speech martyr. However, I will never be able to fight for the animals again with any shred of authenticity until I successfully win the battle to make myself whole – my reputation, my truth, and my voice intact. This is non-negotiable. The actions out of New Mexico are not even remotely about justice or fairness; these are measures being implemented by men whose sole purpose is to silence me or, in the alternative, punish me for refusing to acquiesce. Clearly, when this manuscript is published, I may well find myself back in the courtroom. But if I am successful at gaining a platform and exposure with this book, I think it will become increasingly difficult for them to keep abusing process to batter me.

I have transcended the point in my life where Steve Best has any relevance; he now exists only as a cancer from which I must shield myself. The one time I struggled mightily with violating the court order was in November of 2015. James David Jentsch moved across the country and is now mutilating animals in Binghamton, New York. I was in the gym one morning and couldn't fight back the tears. Someone said "good morning," we exchanged pleasantries, and I choked on tears trying to get the words "I'm okay" out of my mouth with a smile. I called David. I didn't think I could restrain myself. I needed to get online and make one final stand for the animals. He talked to me for a long time and I didn't violate my ban. I understand the information about Jentsch's new mansion went out before Christmas. I am told that without me online to promote it through NIO, it was like publishing in a vacuum. Again, Steven Best is the only person standing in front of me protecting the vivisectors, his *fellow college professor*s.

Judge Kugler's order allows me to use the internet to communicate with my lawyers. On May 16, 2016, I woke up to a set of emails from my legal team. Jerry Friedman filed some motion for Steve Best on May 11 asking the New Mexico Court of Appeals to squash my appeal and award him attorney's fees. I read this thread at about 5 am after I walked my dogs and sent Anne back a private email copying no one saying "wtf are they doing now?!" How much time to these men really spend thinking about me? The courts have literally restrained me so that my abusers are free to keep taking shot after shot after shot at me. My public defender, Theodosia Johnson, filed my appeal on May 19, 2016 and she did an outstanding job. I think Anne, David, and I agree that it served us well to have a neutral set of eyes working on the final product. She wasn't bogged down in all the minutia that those of us living through this ordeal are. In the end, all of us had meaningful input on the final arguments which are currently before the Court of Appeals of the State of New Mexico:

Conclusion

1. Protection Orders issued under the Family Violence Protection Act protect people from harm, but cannot be used to protect reputations from tarnish; the order was improperly issued and should be vacated;
2. I was not on notice that postings on my own Facebook page or my own website or a third party's Facebook page would constitute contact with Petitioner and violate the terms of the protection order; the trial court did not even have a consistent definition as Kugler ruled my posts about Best were interpreted to be contact yet Best's posts about me were deemed protected free speech;
3. The district court cannot ban me from speaking about Dr. Best; it can only ban me from speaking to him. Relabeling my speech as conduct, such as harassment, does not remove it from the protections of the First Amendment; my criminal contempt conviction must be vacated;
4. The court's order that I cannot use the internet is overbroad and violates the First Amendment; it must be vacated.

The New Mexico Court of Appeals accepted our motion and denied the pre-emptory one filed by Best. In the response that Theodosia was obligated to file, she was clear that Jerry Friedman himself had never complied with New Mexico law to be admitted as out-of-state counsel for his friend. Additionally, since we are appealing my criminal conviction for indirect contempt of court, the state is the other party in this appeal. An individual cannot bring a criminal action against another; only the state may prosecute criminally. Steve Best is not even a party to our current case. He's only arguing to uphold my indirect criminal contempt conviction because the state of New Mexico refused to do so. I took a step back. These two men who once caused me so much pain now took on the countenance of Alfalfa and Spanky. I envisioned them with their trusty slingshots standing behind their wall 1700 miles away trying frantically to launch their rocks at me.

We've already enjoyed our first small victory. In New Mexico, only 10% to 20% of appellants are granted a full appeal, as opposed to an expedited summary judgment. As I predicted from my jail cell in Las Cruces, we did, indeed, fall into that narrow window. While it can take a full two years for the court to issue its opinion, the issues in my case are finally getting the judicial review they merit. This is where we will make good law.

Even though he does not have standing to do so, Steve Best filed an opposition brief in the appeals court which was 40 pages of re-entering into the record the emails I wrote in the fall of 2012, repeatedly alleging that I am obsessed with "college professors," alleging that I am a stalker, a criminal, and that the court must protect my "future victims" (i.e., vivisectors) by upholding my Internet ban. He repeatedly refers to my "campaign to destroy Dr. Best" because it seems that if he says it enough, it becomes truth. Most astounding of all is their insistence upon referring to the "graphic blog posts" about Donal O'Leary, the ones authored by Steven Best for which I was prosecuted, to demonstrate that I am a "dangerous" individual.

In this brief Jerry Friedman repeatedly refers to my speaking or writing words as "stalking" and argues that because Steve Best feels harassed by my thoughts, I should continue to forfeit my First Amendment rights. This from a man who is building a reputation in my community as a "social justice lawyer." It is incredible that these men have been able to turn the truth upside down and are using the system to continue to batter, bash, and abuse me while arguing that I am the party from whom they need protection. I am thankful that my legal team insulates me from having to absorb any more than is necessary. I couldn't bring myself to read their last 40-page document; it affects me too deeply. Anne and David told me what I needed to know and I read only enough to summarize it here. Even Theodosia Johnson, my appellate attorney, advised me not to read the malicious tome for my own "well-being." Having to relive the last several years to write this book and having to re-read the court filings has taken its toll. But it was necessary for me to tell my story so that I can let it go and move forward. On September 26, 2016, we filed our response to their opposition and now I am simply waiting for the appellate court's decision.

Conclusion

I learned recently that during the *Vivisector Next Door* global action in November of 2014 that my colleagues with Progress for Science were approached by another activist who was concerned that I support fascism. I reflexively assumed that it was another sabotage attempt emanating from the inner circle. In this case, however, the concern was genuine so I want to address it here. I unequivocally condemn fascism as well as any repressive ideology. In fact, when a white supremacist showed up at one of my protests in Gainesville, he eventually threw down his sign and left yelling at me that "you're part of the problem." However, I also do not approach the subject of Animal Liberation with a moral checklist. If Adolf Hitler rose from the grave and began exterminating vivisectors and torching labs, it is wholly consistent for me to celebrate the action yet condemn the man.

A close colleague in the U.K. came under fire in recent years for allowing someone alleged to be a white national to protest with him. I know nothing about the individual in question and have no use for gossip. I have complete confidence that my colleague is not a fascist and is equally as dedicated to liberating animals as I. I support him completely. On a personal level, though, I struggle a little bit with this issue. My former mentor has repeatedly demonstrated that he is a hypocrite who sold out the movement and the animals. Yet, I'm not sure that matters if his oratory alone can inspire activists to militant action for the animals. I am comfortable that the animals wouldn't care who breaks their chains and frees them from bondage. So that must be my mandate as well; and I'd be lying if I said it wasn't a struggle to reach my final thinking on the subject -- I would never want to watch one of Best's militant oratories knowing the person behind the words. But I would never attack his work itself if it serves to inspire a new activist. The man, however, needs to be condemned in the most vehement of terms to preserve the integrity of the movement, especially the integrity of front line activists. My treatment of fascists is consistent.

Mike and I finally separated in March of this year and are real friends again. He has Brutus and Petey. I see them every day. I live with Max and Jazz. I haven't had a car since mine blew up two years ago and, ironically, after having been bashed and slandered online when his father bought him a little red sports car, I'm now driving it exclusively.

In December of 2015, I flew to New York to film for Jessica's documentary. I finally met Elizabeth Tobier in person and it was wonderful to give her a hug. Jessica and I went back to Brooklyn where I grew up and she met my family. We went to the cemetery too where my mother, grandmother, Uncle Sonny and Uncle Mickey are buried. I remember way back when I used to fantasize about someone taking Dr. Best on a tour of Fountain Ave where many snitches were buried in the trunks of their cars. Not anymore. I'd have to care to feel that way. And I just don't. I have finally achieved complete indifference, an emotional state of disinterest even though his outstanding legal instruments preclude absolute detachment.

Before I went back to jail in Cruces, we filmed at Anne O'Berry's home and got some footage in South Florida as well as New Mexico. I'm not sure what it will be yet, but to finish this documentary I want to do something big to give the animals a real voice and proclaim to the world that I survived. I think Jessica agrees. I finally met David when he flew in and spent some time with Anne and me earlier this year. It was like being with old friends I've known my whole life. I enjoy getting together with Anne from time to time and greatly value our friendship. I wish David was closer too. I am considering selling my house and moving, but I won't make any changes that may be precipitated more by my trying to run away from this condition than joyfully moving toward the next chapter in my life.

When I was in jail in New Mexico, a lot of women would get arrested and their dogs would be stranded alone. I was constantly on the phone with Anne who worked to network out in Las Cruces. We successfully rescued some of these animals. Some we couldn't help. But Anne is now heavily involved in rescuing animals, mainly dogs and cats, from shelters in South Florida, one of which she privately calls *Auschwitz*. I have lost track of how many lives she has personally saved. But I continue to stand

363

back and watch this woman in awe. Her energy and dedication are unparalleled.

Disenchanted with the egos, infighting, and politics inherent in our movement, Ron Roberts has moved away from the protest cliques and is focused more on rescue work as well these days. Anne and Ron have been in touch recently and are working together to try to help save many animals. It seems to me that those who focus their energies on shelters and rescues are the most selfless and genuine actors of us all. I'm not sure how those people handle seeing all of the heartbreak and horror up close and personal every day.

David continues to represent activists and those who fight for Animal Liberation. Officially representing me is a full-time job in itself. Yet he is also working with his local shelters and both he and Anne have had great success exposing the issues that are endemic in kill shelters across the country. It is a business like any other and the animals merely represent a dollar sign to their captors. David is also looking into founding a not-for-profit legal network to represent activists and is heavily involved in several campaigns out in California where he's licensed.

Susan Schindler and Kevin (Storm) Klopfer came down from New Jersey to visit in July. Kevin is a young man. He's 15-years old, 6-feet tall, has a deep voice, and is an exceptionally handsome kid with a lot of edge. He is working at becoming a hardcore metal vocalist and I envision him opening up vital and militant avenues for the cause through his music. He's also got his first three tattoos toward the sleeves on which he's working. In fact, the three of us got tattoos to commemorate finally getting together. My first one says "vegan." and is on my back-left shoulder. I think my next one will be on my forearm in December when they come back for the holidays.

Natalie and Ziv were married while I was in jail. They are a wonderful couple and such genuine and sincere people. I still write Walter Bond almost every month. The Bureau of Prisons has not given him permission to write back but I understand he is doing well. I talk to Barry Friedman frequently and plan to guest lecture in his classes in the future. Joshua Durden and I have been in touch by text, but I have not seen him in several years. I will never forget his honesty and fierce loyalty; I am proud to call him a friend and look forward to seeing him in the near future. I've been working with my colleagues in Gainesville behind the scenes, but it's very frustrating to not be able to do what needs to be done. As soon as this Internet ban is lifted, I hope to return to the struggle for Animal Liberation.

And as far as the women I met behind bars, I could never have imagined that they would become my sisters.

Tiffiny and I lost contact. I speak to Loca occasionally and we will definitely get together if I ever have to go back out to New Mexico. I know that one of our friends just went back to jail; she was picked up on a fugitive warrant. And another woman with whom we were incarcerated was just given life.

Audrey Keding has been sober over a year. She is happy, healthy, positive and just met a wonderful man. I know that if I ever need someone with whom to talk, she will always be there. She already has been more than once. And I love her for that.

Amanda Vargas got over Daniel. She is now with a wonderful man named Albert and they've been together for over a year. They knew each other as kids and it is like it was meant to be. He treats her like a queen. Amanda is my *prima* – a term we picked up at DACDC; it means cousin in Spanish. And after everything we lived through together, it is wonderful to see her living such a charmed life. I told her that when they get married, they need to take their honeymoon in Florida. I love this woman and so value our friendship.

Camille Perry will be my sister forever. Camille graduated Magna Cum Laude with a major in social work and a minor in psychology from Wayne State Community College and is now working toward her Bachelor's Degree. She is considering moving here to finish her studies. She is grateful that she got time to spend with her mom before she passed away but, sadly,

Conclusion

her mother didn't live to see her graduate. Yesterday, Camille was finally released from probation and is completely free of all restraints. We both know we've gained a lot of strength over the past few years, but my sister has a profound store of wisdom that fascinates me. She understands people and life; I'm fortunate to have her counsel. I walked my dogs at midnight last night and was filled with joy. I could not be happier for her than I will be when my own issues are finally resolved.

And Ebony Malcom is maybe the most kindred spirit I met behind bars. She is still incarcerated at the Huron Valley Women's prison but has never been broken and has never stopped fighting. One of her last letters had me laughing out loud. She was teaching classes in prison and in one of the rooms, there was debris falling from the ceiling. The institution ignored it until she initiated proceedings to sue the prison for hazardous working conditions. While they were scattering to remedy the situation, Ebony discreetly took some of the debris and sent it to her colleague to have it tested. She's awaiting the results. She since resigned from her position and is challenging her conviction and other violations of her rights in five different courts at the moment. While separate and distinct, we have both lived very parallel existences the past few years fighting for our rights from inside a corrupt system. I am glad that Ebony's husband, sons, and family still rally around her.

As for me, I miss my community. When I do go back online, I'm not sure if my first post will be "OMG, I've missed all of you so much" or "Fuck You, I'm Back!" It will ultimately depend on my mood. But with my community stripped away from me, I've clung to my vegan identity even more. This has more to do with me than the animals. I don't think anyone is entirely altruistic. I fight for the animals because I can't live with the knowledge otherwise. Every morning I make a decision to take care of myself and prepare for the day I emerge victorious. I am wholly vindicated within myself. I am simply waiting for the courts to catch up with me.

Camille A. Marino
October 29, 2016

The cyclone derives its power from
a calm center. So does a person.
-Norman Vincent Peale

Epilogue

The monkey labs inside the University of Florida were permanently shut down, on schedule, in the winter of 2016. As I was preparing to file yet another suit to obtain current lab records, I received Freedom of Information Act (FOIA) documents from the USDA demonstrating that as of July 2017, there was not a single monkey left in their dungeon. Despite information I received in jail suggesting new experiments had begun, it was based upon sloppy and unconfirmed research. Subsequent discussions with a colleague confirmed that our efforts had created too great of a liability by 2013 – both personally for the vivisectors and in terms of UF's reputation in the community -- for this extraordinarily lucrative business to remain viable. Further, a new administration is less than enthusiastic about their university remaining complicit in the archaic practice of animal experimentation; so once this lab was shut, it was shut for good. This victory in and of itself makes everything that transpired in this book more than worth it.

Thanks to the combined efforts of industrial abusers & the state, Steven Best, Jerry Friedman, Michael Budkie and their hoards of obstructionists, my ability to launch another effort to shut down the dog labs has been destroyed. I no longer enjoy the following I once did. I always intended to take the industry apart piece by piece and that's exactly what we would have done. This is a difficult pill to swallow. However, I've been invited to speak to students inside the University of Florida in November of 2018. I am choosing to take this opportunity to hand to mantle to them, give them the exact nature of the horrors to which these dogs are being subjected as well as the dollar signs attached to their suffering. With a new administration in place, pressure from a well-informed student body could potentially create more real change than I ever would. My tactics worked for me. The students would not need to be nearly as confrontational as I. And irrespective of the tactics we choose to employ, our only concern must be realizing the ultimate objective of ending vivisection for good.

On December 19, 2016, Dr. Steven Best was finally arrested for beating his girlfriend, Alicia Rodriguez. His intake file at the Dona Ana County Detention Center (DACDC) reads "Assault Against a Household Member."[57]

On January 3, 2017, Judge Darren M. Kugler was forced off the bench. He agreed to officially step down effective January 31 to

57 Dona Ana County Detention Center, Booking Details (https://donaanacounty.org/inmates/viewprofile_archived/1600011879)

avoid further disciplinary action.[58] In a child custody case, he decided to have a mother and father alternate custody of their child each week, with the parents alternating weeks of incarceration as well. In the case of the father, he jailed him for 179 days for indirect criminal contempt and, when he was released, jailed him again on the same charge without provocation. I had put my home up for sale in 2016 because I had no doubt that if the appellate court remanded my case back down to Kugler, he would throw me in jail again for indirect criminal contempt -- without provocation -- and even though I had already served every hour of my sentence. The Supreme Court of New Mexico stripped Kugler of all of his authority; he may not even officiate at a wedding, nor may he ever seek public office again.

On June 29, 2017, the Appellate Court of the State of New Mexico issued its opinion. It upheld my conviction as well as all of Kugler's judicial errors. They did, however, overturn the Internet ban finding it too broad and unconstitutional. The appellate ruling holds that I cannot cause Steve Best "severe emotional distress." They fail to understand that the fact that I'm breathing causes him severe emotional distress. On July 31, 2017, Theodosia Johnson filed certiorari in our appeal to the Supreme Court of New Mexico. One month later, on August 31, the court denied our request and refused to hear my case.

All appeals are exhausted and I am bound by Steven Best's domestic violence restraining order until October 26, 2026. Yet Dr. Best remains obsessed and unsatisfied. On the day before Thanksgiving, I found a registered letter on my doorstep from another of Petitioner's attorneys, Jill V. Johnson Vigil. Her letter dated November 17, 2017 threatened to prosecute me for:

1. "your continuous attempts to contact Dr. Best, his girlfriend, and other members of his household via text messages and telephone;"
2. "your continuous and ongoing blogging defamatory remarks

58 Carlos Andres Lopez, "Las Cruces district judge permanently resigns from bench," Las Cruces Sun News (February 14, 2017) http://www.lcsun-news.com/story/news/local/courts/2017/02/14/las-cruces-district-judge-permanently-resigns-bench/97920890/

about Dr. Best on the internet;"
3. "your attempts to publish two books;"
4. "your efforts to produce a documentary regarding your legal battle with Dr. Best have become unbearable."

I think even Jerry Freidman stood back and questioned whether he wanted to put his name on such rubbish. I've not had even a passing thought about contacting this man since November of 2012 -- over five years -- nor do I wish to pollute my sites by invoking his name. The books to which he refers are *Danger to Society: jailhouse diary of a political prisoner* which I published on March 1, 2018 and this memoir, *#uncensored: inside the animal liberation movement*, scheduled to go to print on April 1, 2018. My story is about me and my work; it is about animal slavery and my struggle for Animal Liberation. It's unfortunate that by incessantly insinuating himself into my life, Dr. Best has made himself an inextricable part of my story and evolution; both pivotal and incidental to my journey. *My* evolution. *My* journey.

In truth, on the final edit of this manuscript, I considered using a pseudonym for my abuser simply because I don't want to ever see his name again. Legally, however, it would be a null issue as my community knows full well about the public feud and would clearly understand about whom I was speaking. Logistically, it would be difficult to cite public records, news articles, and court cases. It was more important to me that my memoir be factual and authentic rather than blur into the margins of fiction.

I filed a motion for an order to show cause with the District Court in New Mexico for repeatedly using lawyers to contact and intimidate me, as well as to hold him accountable for all of his lies and threats in his Thanksgiving letter. That motion was denied, the court determining it was "legally insufficient."

David Tenenbaum is the only attorney on record in the past five years to have gained any traction or claim any victories in New Mexico. If Best insists upon going after me civilly there, I finally decided I would default in New Mexico and have to file civil suit against him here for intentional infliction of emotional distress as well as a host of other torts. In addition to successfully having Best's civil suit thrown out of court in its first incarnation three years ago, David successfully convinced Friedman to advise his client to withdraw his current civil suit or we would retaliate in Florida. In January of 2018, Steven Best withdrew his own civil suit with prejudice, meaning he can never refile.

I have no desire to engage Best in civil court, to exact my pound of flesh or retaliate for his courtroom terrorism, and simply want to be left alone. And since David gave Jerry his word, I am bound to respect David. I sincerely hoped that we could move past this issue once and for all. But that was not to be.

I've been back online now for 9 months. It was incredible to come out of exile and reconnect with my peers. But it was very difficult to have to admit to myself that the networks I built were destroyed. Raymond Bergeron retired in 2016 and his 7 primates were released to a sanctuary. Michael Budkie does his annual welfare protests and everything is back to normal. It's clear to me that both the state and welfare organizations share a symbiotic relationship, both sides working to protect animal slavery and, indeed, profit from it.

#uncensored goes to print on April 1 and this is the end of the road. I lived through it all and that gives me a tremendous sense of power that cannot be taken from me. I am already living under siege as Dr. Best works furiously to stop publication. I do not want to go back to jail; but if I am incarcerated for publishing my memoir, I can only hope that those who would never have had any interest in my story will suddenly become curious about what I have to say.

My official book launch was to take place in Manhattan at a bookstore/activist center called *Bluestockings*. I promoted this event publicly. As soon as my confirmed event was cancelled, I understood that I was being stalked again. *Bluestockings* confirmed that Steven Best contacted them; he "colored you in a certain way" and it was "alarming." I have other promotional events ahead but can neither discuss them here nor enjoy my success publicly as my abuser is always lurking in the shadows waiting to pounce. This is a condition from which I will need to legally seek relief when time affords it.

On March 14, Dr. Best published his first blog in several years. Entitled *The Tortured and Terrible Lies of My Stalker,*[59] it was forwarded to me by a concerned colleague. Dr. Best expresses his anguish over *my* continued obsession with *him*; that it is in its "sixth year" and I make his life unbearable. His writing tends to confirm that the simple fact that I am breathing is what haunts him. Other than to pen my memoir, I've not given this individual a second thought in years. He writes that he is authoring a book about me. Should I be flattered? He also indicates that Jerry Friedman will likely try to have my memoir criminalized so that Best's manuscript will record history according to my oppressor. They've also begun to post character assassinations as *reviews* on Amazon's page for *Danger to Society.*

Dr. Steven Best has left me no alternative but to seek relief from the courts. I filed a motion with the New Mexico courts, asking them to find the philosophy professor in violation of his own restraining order by stalking me and contacting my agent. It was found to be "legally insufficient" to proceed. I also sought relief in Florida but was denied an order of protection citing "no credible threat of imminent violence." I spent March 21, 2018 distraught; it seemed Dr. Best could harass me to his heart's content and no one would protect me.

The following day, I received an "Affidavit of Violation" that Best had filed with the courts on the same day my motion was filed. He hired yet another lawyer, Larissa Duran, to swear that I am unrepentant and continue to cause my stalker severe emotional distress by harassing and defaming him. She goes on to site several of my Facebook comments to demonstrate said *harassment and defamation*:

> "Criminal charges filed against Michael 'lock her up'

---

59 Dr. Steven Best, "The Tortured and Terrible Lies of My Stalker," March 14, 2018 (https://drstevebest.wordpress.com/2018/03/14/the-tortured-and-terrible-lies-of-my-stalker/)

Flynn this morning. lol I hope that everyone who enjoys gratuitously putting someone else behind bars enjoys it as much when their time comes."

And

"It saddens me when other women feel overshadowed by me and resent me. I only want to empower others. But make no mistake, I explain myself to no one. And I have so much on my plate that I don't have time to watch what anyone else does. My advice to anyone who wants to criticize or chip away at me is to strengthen yourself; try to focus on the animals. Because unless you've been in a coma for the last 5 years, it should be obvious by now that I don't bow and I don't break."

And, of course, several posts identifying his real motivation for trying to have me jailed:

"Trump served a porn star with a restraining order to silence her, criminalize her telling the truth. Where have I heard that before? lol I hope she writes a book."

"Sorry guys, I thought my post was obvious. Couldn't really care less about Trump or Stormy. But I've been served with 3 restraining orders to shut me up. These are insidious instruments. And my next book deals thoroughly with how this works. I hope everyone who's served with one of these writes a book."

There were several more of my commentaries about Trump as well as pages of calls to Alicia's phone from unknown numbers in New Mexico, Chicago, and other places. Dr. Best swore that I was engaged in a "sustained" campaign of harassment. How I wish I had the power to subpoena those numbers. He is obviously trying to create some kind of record with which he can have me arrested. And even though every one of my comments expressed my opinions on various subjects, my heart sunk. Here I was with no Court granting me a modicum of relief and now I was going to be locked up again because my existence causes my abuser emotional distress. How could this be happening again?

Then I learned that Best's affidavit was also dismissed, finding it "legally insufficient." My relief was palpable. In 2013, I said publicly that no judge in their right mind would imprison me for expressing an opinion -- offensive or otherwise. I completely forgot that Judge Kugler was not in his right mind. I should never have been jailed in the first place over a Facebook war and I want to believe that if the current judge was on the bench, s/he would not have entertained all of the he said/she said idiocy in a domestic violence court in the first place. At least that appears to be where we are today.

I have not violated Steven Best's domestic violence restraining order in any way, shape, or form, nor will I ever seek to contact him in the future. I want to believe that this is all I have to do to stay out of jail. Only time will tell if I am correct.

I've been advised by legal counsel here to seek a civil restraining order for his interference with my work and sabotage. I hope this is the last sentence I ever need to write about Dr. Steven Best in this lifetime.

I can see from the inside out how truth is lost when the oppressors themselves write our history books; how nonhuman animals, women, and every other oppressed group have been marginalized and dismissed because they had no access to record their truth for posterity.

I am proud of myself for seeing everything through to its conclusion. Had I acquiesced along the way, trading my own rights to secure relief, I'd have forfeited who I am and who I have become through adversity. That was never going to happen. I took everything they threw at me and am standing more confidently today than I ever have. It is my sincere hope that my perserverance will inspire others because my struggle is the same one faced by every woman who has ever confronted an old-boy network as well as every activist whose voice has been robbed through restraining orders.

I want my errors in judgment to prevent other activists from being blinded by cults of personality that are prevalent in every social justice movement; to not lose their sense of right and wrong in service of demagoguery. Drama and trashing others can be alluring and, wherever humans come together, will always happen. Once we've found that store of confidence and peace within ourselves, the opinions, taunts, and attacks of our critics cease being of any relevance. I want the takeaway from my experience to be genuine empowerment. Every diversion from the struggle only strengthens industrial abusers and the corporate state. We must never lose sight of the fact that we are only messengers and it is the voice of the enslaved animals that needs to be paramount -- the struggle to dismantle oppressive constructs and abolish slavery taking precedence over egos, reputations, hubris, and self-interest.

I try to act with integrity and honor every day, because every decision made today will comprise who I am tomorrow. The only person to whom I hold myself accountable is the one in my mirror. Billions of animals living in agony have succumbed to excruciating deaths while the events in this book transpired. And now I need to turn my attention back to how I can most effectively be of service to them.

Camille A. Marino (March 25, 2018)

"You may write me down in history With your bitter
twisted lies
You may trod me in the very dirt
But still like dust, I RISE

Does my sassiness upset you?
Why are you beset with gloom?
Just because I walk as if I have oil wells
Pumping in my living room.

Just like suns and like moons
With the certainty of tides
Just like hope springing high
Still I RISE

Did you want to see me broken?
Bowed head and lowered eyes?
Shoulders falling down like teardrops?
Weakened by my soulful cries?

Does my sassiness upset you? haha
Don't take it so hard
Just because I laugh
As if I have goldmines
Digging in my own backyard

You can shoot me with your words
You can cut me with your lies
You can kill me with your hatefulness.
But just like life, I RISE"

Excerpt from Maya Angelou's
STILL I RISE

Dear Reader,

Thank you for taking the time to read this memoir.

I didn't know if anyone would be interested in my story, but I wanted to be transparent and maybe introduce you to a world that remains largely hidden. It remained invisible to me for 43 years.

If you enjoyed the book or have anything you might want to discuss, I'd welcome your thoughts. You may reach me at camilleamarino@gmail.com.

I'd also like to ask you to please consider leaving a review on Amazon and sharing your thoughts there.

Again, thank you for your time and attention.

All my love,

Camille

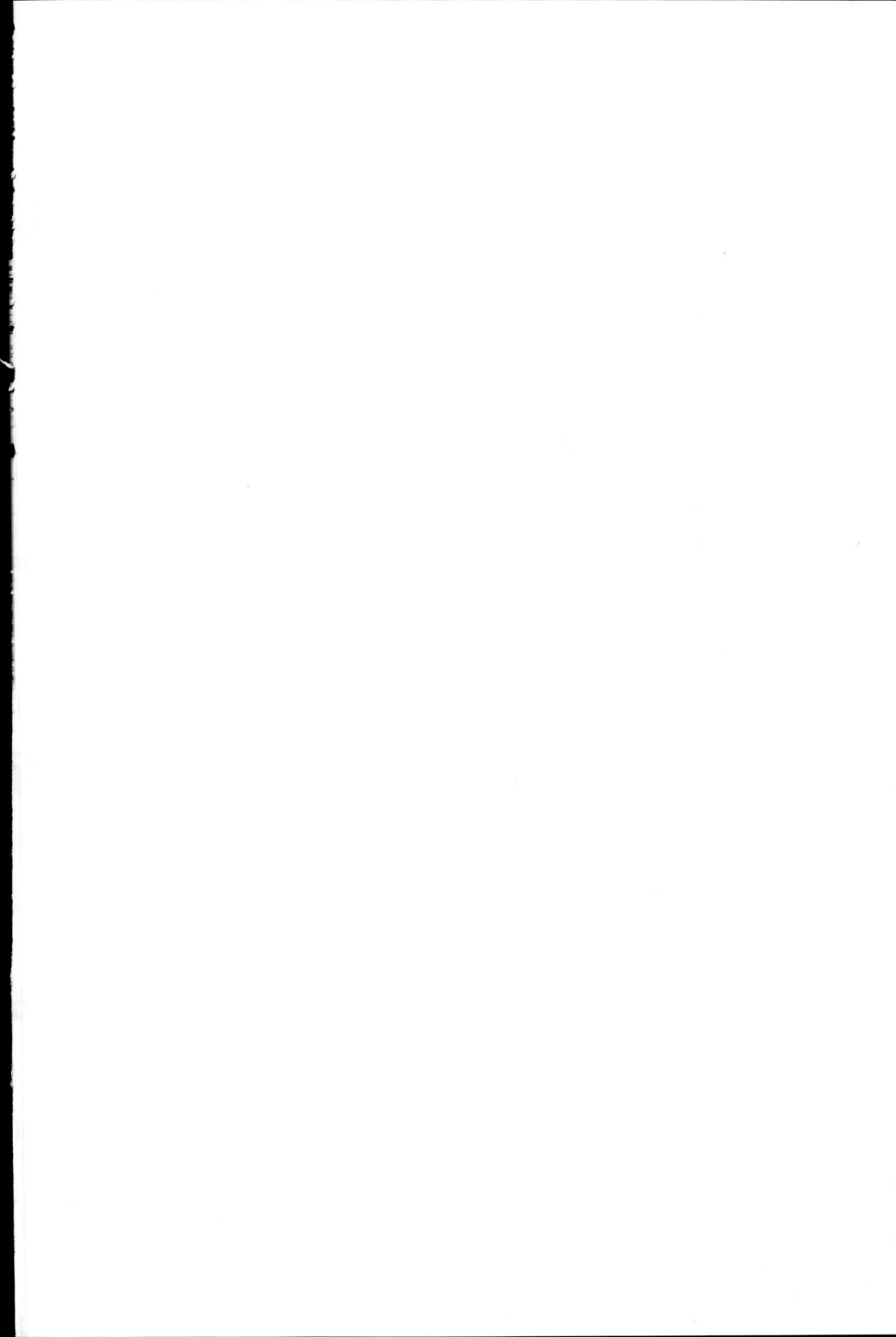

www.ingramcontent.com/pod-product-compliance
Lightning Source LLC
Chambersburg PA
CBHW060614290326
41930CB00051B/1523